Transactions with Literature

Louise M. Rosenblatt

Transactions with Literature

A Fifty-Year Perspective

For Louise M. Rosenblatt

Edited by

Edmund J. Farrell
University of Texas at Austin

James R. Squire
Silver Burdett & Ginn

National Council of Teachers of English
1111 Kenyon Road, Urbana, Illinois 61801

Grateful acknowledgment is made for permission to reprint the following material: "January Chance" from Collected and New Poems, 1924–1963 by Mark Van Doren. Copyright © 1963 by Mark Van Doren. Reprinted by permission of Hill and Wang, a division of Farrar, Straus and Giroux, Inc. Robert Clairmont for "When Did the World Begin" from FOREVER X, copyright 1951 by Robert Clairmont, published by Contemporary Poetry, Baltimore, Maryland.

Staff Editor: Mary Daniels

Cover Design: Mary Daniels and Michael J. Getz

Interior Book Design: Tom Kovacs for TGK Design

NCTE Stock Number 5510-3

It is the policy of NCTE in its journals and other publications to provide a forum for the open discussion of ideas concerning the content and the teaching of English and the language arts. Publicity accorded to any particular point of view does not imply endorsement by the Executive Committee, the Board of Directors, or the membership at large, except in announcements of policy, where such endorsement is clearly specified.

Library of Congress Cataloging-in-Publication Data

Transactions with literature : a fifty-year perspective : for Louise M. Rosenblatt
/ edited by Edmund J. Farrell, James R. Squire.
     p.   cm.
    "Symposium of articles for the 1988 Convention of the National Council of Teachers of English, held in St. Louis"—Pref.
    Includes bibliographical references.
    ISBN 0-8141-5510-3
    1. English literature—Study and teaching—Congresses.
2. American literature—Study and teaching—Congresses.
3. Rosenblatt, Louise M. (Louise Michelle). I. Rosenblatt, Louise M. (Louise Michelle) II. Farrell, Edmund J. III. Squire, James R. IV. National Council of Teachers of English. V. National Council of Teachers of English. Convention (1988 : Saint Louis, Mo.)
PR37.T7   1990
820'.7—dc20
                                           90-5670
                                             CIP

Contents

Preface

Fifty years is a remarkable life for a work on the learning and teaching of literature. Yet *Literature as Exploration* by Louise M. Rosenblatt is now in its fourth edition, published by The Modern Language Association (1983), and its influence has never been greater. What other book on teaching written fifty years ago is even read today?

To recognize, on the occasion of the fiftieth anniversary of its publication, the impact that *Literature as Exploration* has had, friends and admirers of Professor Rosenblatt's work prepared the following symposium of articles for the 1988 Convention of the National Council of Teachers of English, held in St. Louis. The Center for the Learning and Teaching of Literature contributed the annotated bibliographies of materials and approaches to literature instruction and of studies on reader-response.

The symposium demonstrates the extraordinary influence of Rosenblatt's work on the teaching of literature, on literary theory, and on educational research in all English-speaking countries. Further, it evinces the power of a point of view that embraces both the reader and the literary work while focusing on the transaction between the two.

Indeed, the widespread influence of Louise Rosenblatt's book accounts for much of the diversity of articles in this monograph. Concern with the responses to literature written expressly for children and young people has led, during the past fifty years, to an awakening of interest in such literature, to the establishment of critical standards by which it might be judged, and to its increased use in our classrooms. Concern with the transaction between book and reader had led to a reappraisal of how literature is most effectively taught and to the development of strategies to enhance the transaction. And concern with reader-response has broadened research to include attention to the nature and process of the literary transaction and to the ensuing literary experience. Thus, at least three dimensions of our knowledge about literature and its teaching have been permanently transformed and illuminated by Louise M. Rosenblatt's work, and all three are represented by articles in the separate sections of this monograph. The celebration of the influence of *Literature as Exploration* then concludes with a gracious, eloquent, and important statement by Louise Rosenblatt herself, as she reflects on how her magnum opus happened to be published and how it was initially received.

Diverse points of view exist, of course, on a subject as rich as the teaching of literature. But the commemoration of *Literature as Exploration* seems not an appropriate occasion for partisan debate. Rather, the articles in this collection document the powerful ideas unleashed by a single book five decades ago, and trace some of the ways in which these ideas have enriched our profession and our teaching. No one who has really read *Literature as Exploration* has ever been able to think about literature and its teaching in quite the same way as before.

E.J.F. and J.R.S.
Summer 1989

Introduction:
Fifty Years of *Literature as Exploration*

Edmund J. Farrell
University of Texas at Austin

Since its initial publication in 1938, Louise M. Rosenblatt's *Literature as Exploration*, now in its fourth edition, has furnished the theoretical basis for research in the teaching and study of literature and has influenced how literature is taught in classrooms both here and abroad. The contribution of *Literature as Exploration* to research has been documented in such works as *Literature and the Reader: Research in Response to Literature, Reading Interests, and the Teaching of Literature* by Alan Purves and Richard Beach (1972) and *Researching Response to Literature and the Teaching of Literature: Points of Departure*, edited by Charles R. Cooper (1985). Its continuing contributions to research have been further documented in "Research on Response to Literature," a bibliography included in this monograph that was sponsored by the Center for the Learning and Teaching of Literature, and prepared by Richard Beach and Susan Hynds specifically for the fiftieth anniversary of Rosenblatt's text. The influence of *Literature as Exploration* upon pedagogy is apparent in such recent textbooks as *Readers, Texts, Teachers*, edited by Bill Corcoran and Emrys Evans (1987), *Response and Analysis* by Robert Probst (1988), and *Close Imagining: An Introduction to Literature* by Benjamin De Mott (1988).

Now regarded as the first book in this country to advance a reader-response theory of literature, one that denies the existence of either generic text or generic reader, *Literature as Exploration* insists that

> there are in reality only the potential millions of individual readers of the potential millions of individual literary works. . . . The reading of any work of literature is, of necessity, an individual and unique occurrence, involving the mind and emotions of some particular reader. (32)[1]

At the same time, though honored as the initial work in reader-response criticism, *Literature as Exploration* makes evident why Rosenblatt has voiced discomfort in recent years with being classified as a reader-response theoretician. She views the initial response to a work of literature as being just that—a beginning—an essential first step that must be followed by the reader's judicious reflection and judgment:

Though a free, uninhibited emotional reaction to a work of art or
literature is an absolutely *necessary* condition of sound literary
judgment, it is not . . . a *sufficient* condition. . . . [The student] can
begin to achieve a sound approach to literature only when he
reflects upon his response to it, when he attempts to understand
what in the work and in himself produced that reaction and when
he goes on thoughtfully to modify, reject, or accept it. (88–89)

Just as one cannot read a work of literature for another person, a
writer cannot paraphrase or summarize *Literature as Exploration* without
doing an injustice to its artistic integrity. Yet I feel the need to mention
what are, for me, five of the salient points and arguments that
Rosenblatt advances, ones that have guided my teaching of literature
to high school and college students for close to four decades:

1. Though students should be allowed to express freely their
   reactions to a selection in both writing and class discussions,
   a process that will help them clarify their responses, the text
   must remain a constraint against total relativism or subjectivi-
   ty. Nowhere does Rosenblatt suggest that all interpretations
   of literature are equally cogent. The dialectic of class discussion offers a means of modifying or correcting interpretations
   for which there is inadequate textual support.

2. Literature has social and aesthetic elements, substance and
   form, that are inextricably interrelated, though theoretically
   distinguishable. Emphasis upon only one value—social or
   aesthetic—diminishes the work of art.

3. The essence of literature is the rejection of stereotyped
   reactions. To be a catalyst for students' investigations and to
   help them avoid stereotypic and prejudicial thinking, teachers
   need to be at least conversant with the processes and basic
   concepts of the social sciences. Characteristic to those is the
   scientific method, which fosters inquiry and an attitude of
   tentativeness, a method complementary, not antithetical, to
   the artistic spirit and to the exploration of literature. Through
   specific lived-through human situations, students can discover in literature roots to the generalizations and abstrac-
   tions of the social sciences.

4. The task of education is to provide students with the
   knowledge, mental habits, and motivation that will enable
   them to solve their own problems independently, to formulate
   with increasing maturity their own systems of value and
   philosophy. Literature can abet that task, for it helps accultur-

ate individuals, frees them from provincialism, makes them aware of alternative forms of thought and behavior, assists them in resolving personal problems and in making sound choices, and redirects their potentially antisocial behavior. It can help individuals develop the kind of imagination critical to the well-being of a democracy.

5. To liberate imaginations, teachers need to provide students with a broad range of literature, including works, both present and past, that reflect cultures quite different from the students' own. Teachers should not, however, force young people to confront "classics" in which archaic language or ways of life confound their understanding. Such works can await students' greater maturity. The test is whether the child or adolescent is intellectually and emotionally ready for what the book has to offer.

But enough of paraphrasing. What follows is a pocketful of quotations from the first edition of *Literature as Exploration,* quotations meant both to introduce the wisdom of the text to those who have not yet read it and to reacquaint those who have. Both kinds of readers are likely to find the statements as timely today as they were to 1938, for in them one sees foreshadowed a number of matters now current to the teaching of literature: how the personal schema that one brings to his or her reading influences interpretation; why a text read in varied circumstances is unstable; whether it is wise to try to transmit to immature readers a canon of literary classics; what influence authorial intent should exercise upon the reader; how diverse modes of criticism relate to personal response, reflection, and judgment.

> The reader brings to the work personality traits, memories of past events, present needs and preoccupations, a particular mood of the moment, and a particular physical condition. . . . These, and many other elements, interacting with the peculiar contribution of the work of art, produce a unique experience. (37)

> Sound literary insight and esthetic judgment will never be taught by imposing from above our ideas about what a work should mean. (41)

> We all know that the same book will have a very different meaning and value to us at different times in our lives or under different circumstances. Some pleasant or unpleasant state of mind, some worry, some temperamental bias, or some contemporary social crisis may make us either especially receptive or especially impervious to what the work offers. (43)

[A]ll the student's knowledge about literary history, about authors and periods and literary types, will be so much useless baggage if the student has not been led primarily to seek from literature a vital personal experience. (72)

The student needs to be given the opportunity and the courage to approach literature personally, to let it mean something to him directly. . . . He should be made to feel that his own response to books, even though it may not seem to resemble the standard critical comments, is worth expressing. (81)

Fundamentally, the process of understanding a work implies a recreation of it, an attempt to grasp completely all of the sensations and concepts through which the author seeks to convey the quality of his sense of life. Each of us must make a new synthesis of these elements with his own nature, but it is essential that he assimilate those elements of experience which the author has actually presented. (133, italics in original)

There is not necessarily only one "correct" interpretation of the significance of a given work. Not even the author's possible statement of his aims can be considered definitive, since the drama or poem or novel exists as a separate entity and can possess for us more values than he foresaw. The work must carry its own message to us. (134–35)

When the student is challenged to examine the \   _   f his particular understanding of the work and his judgm_ .t on it, he will be stimulated, on the one hand, to study the work itself more closely, and on the other hand, to examine whether his own personal experience and basic assumptions provide a valid foundation for his interpretation. He will attempt to discover whether he has been aware of all that the literary work itself offers. This will lead him not only to seek further knowledge of literary forms and technique; it will also provide the impetus toward acquiring the various types of information—literary history, social history, biography, psychology—that may document his understanding of the work or that may help him evaluate his own standards. (146)

Those who cram the classics down students' throats long before they are ready are careless of the fate of the great works of the past. . . . Our aim should be to develop people so much interested in what literature offers that they will read later for themselves. Thus, they will come to the classics at that point in their mental and emotional development when particular works will have particular significance for them. (257–58)

One could quote from virtually every page, for *Literature as Exploration* is a brilliant book, sensitive and humane in its attitude toward readers; perspicacious in its analysis of the processes by which each of us responds to, interprets, and evaluates literary works; sweeping in its intellectual command of both literature and the social sciences;

sanguine in its belief that the teaching and reading of literature can fortify a democratic society. Hailed by James R. Squire in the preface to the second edition (1968) as a work that "stands preeminent in its field" and by Alan Purves in the preface to the third edition (1976) as a "classic" akin in its importance to Milton's *Areopagitica* and Shelley's *Defense of Poetry, Literature as Exploration* will continue to live well beyond the interval of its golden anniversary.

Note

1. All page references are to the first edition of *Literature as Exploration,* New York: D. Appleton-Century Company, 1938.

References

Cooper, Charles R., ed. 1985. *Researching Response to Literature and the Teaching of Literature: Points of Departure.* Norwood, N.J.: Ablex.

Corcoran, Bill, and Emrys Evans, eds. 1987. *Readers, Texts, Teachers.* Upper Montclair, N.J.: Boynton/Cook.

De Mott, Benjamin. 1988. *Close Imagining: An Introduction to Literature.* New York: St. Martin's Press.

Probst, Robert. 1988. *Response and Analysis.* Upper Montclair, N.J.: Boynton/ Cook.

Purves, Alan, and Richard Beach. 1972. *Literature and the Reader: Research in Response to Literature, Reading Interests, and the Teaching of Literature.* Urbana, Ill.: National Council of Teachers of English.

Rosenblatt, Louise M. 1938. *Literature as Exploration.* New York: D. Appleton-Century.

A. *Literature as Exploration* and Books for Young People

Perhaps more than any other single factor, exploration of the literary experience stimulated by *Literature as Exploration* has led teachers to a reappraisal of the place of books written especially for children or for junior readers. When such selections really work with young readers, they have all the aesthetic power that adults experience with mature literary fare. Rudine Sims Bishop and Kenneth Donelson discuss important choices in the books written for young people during the past fifty years. Then John Dixon, a brilliant teacher who has taught teachers in most of the English-speaking countries of the world how to teach literature, demonstrates that the exploration of literary response is not only a national phenomenon but one that has enhanced classrooms internationally.

1. Fifty Years of Exploring Children's Books

Rudine Sims Bishop
Ohio State University

To revisit *Literature as Exploration* is to marvel once more at the breadth of Louise Rosenblatt's knowledge and the depth of her wisdom. I marvel, too, at the re-realization that her book is a daring one, rejecting then-current and widely accepted critical theories that focused solely on the text, and pedagogy that focused mainly on literary history. Throughout my rereading of the book, I was also struck by its undiminished relevance after fifty years in print. Little wonder then that *Literature as Exploration*, a pioneering examination of reading process and pedagogy, is a classic.

Children's literature, like all literature, is influenced by the social, philosophical, and economic environments in which it is produced. Therefore, to explore the past fifty years of children's books is to walk through the corridor of the most recent fifty years of our history—from Franklin Delano Roosevelt to George Bush, from the Second World War to "Star Wars." Throughout those fifty years, as in years past, children's books have been one of the primary ways we have attempted to relay our values to our young people. We have believed in the power of the written word, when engaged by the imagination of a reader, to promote positive attitudes and to develop insight and understanding of what it means to be an honorable, respectable human being in this society.

The United States, as we were reminded by the recent presidential election, is a democracy, governed by the people through their elected representatives. If this government is to function for the common good, then it needs an educated, thinking citizenry that will be unswayed by tawdry, mean-spirited election campaigns characterized by half-truths and appeals to fear fed by bigotry, prejudice, and racism. Louise Rosenblatt told us fifty years ago that the education of the citizens of a democracy must include attention to the heart as well as

1

the head, the soul as well as the mind. In the summary of the third edition of *Literature as Exploration* (1976) she writes:

> This book has attempted to reveal how much the experience and study of literature have to offer that is relevant to the crucial needs of personalities involved in the conflicts and stresses of life in our changing society. Indeed, literary experiences might be made the very core of the kind of educational process needed in a democracy.
>
> If we only do justice to the potentialities inherent in literature itself, we can make a vital social contribution. As the student vicariously shares through literature the emotions and aspirations of other human beings, he can gain heightened sensitivity to the needs and problems of others remote from him in temperament, in space, or in social environment; he can develop a greater imaginative capacity to grasp the meaning of abstract laws or political and social theories for actual human lives. Such sensitivity and imagination are part of the indispensable equipment of the citizen of a democracy. (274)

If, over the past five decades, literary experience had been at the core of our educational system, what sorts of vicarious experiences might elementary students have had? The obvious answer is that they might have had a great variety of experiences, since many thousands of children's books of all sorts have been published since 1938. However, it is safe to assume that only a few "landmark" books would have made their way into the school curriculum. I want to call your attention to one or two such books published in each of those decades, and examine some of "the potentialities inherent" in them.

Johnny Tremain

Arguably the major landmark novel of the 1940s was Esther Forbes's *Johnny Tremain* (1943), a book still read in many upper-elementary and middle-school classrooms. Published in the midst of World War II, its unabashedly patriotic portrayal of the American Revolution as a just and righteous war was bound to have wide appeal. The book world was also trying to do its share in the war effort.

In discussing children's book publishing in the 1940s, Dora V. Smith (1963), citing Agnes De Lima, wrote: "Books were to keep our established values before us—the good old books as well as the new ones that spoke of the dignity of the individual, regard for the human spirit, the necessity for individual freedom" (49). *Johnny Tremain* clearly speaks to those values.

Johnny Tremain, you no doubt remember, is the story of a young apprentice silversmith living in Boston at the time of the outbreak of the Revolutionary War. When, as a result of an accident that maims his hand he can no longer work with silver, he becomes involved with the rebel leaders of Boston, delivering messages and gathering intelligence from the British stationed in the city. He meets Sam Adams, John Hancock, Paul Revere, James Otis, John Adams, and others. While Johnny does not actually fight in the war, his friend Rab is killed in the very first battle.

It is James Otis, teetering, it was thought, on the edge of insanity, who provides the great theme of the book:

> [We will fight] for men and women and children all over the world.
> . . . there shall be no more tyranny. A handful of men cannot seize
> power over thousands. The peasants of France, the serfs of Russia.
> . . . they shall see freedom like a new sun rising in the west. . . . We
> give all we have, lives, property, safety, skills . . . we fight, we die,
> for a simple thing. Only that a man can stand up. (Forbes 179–80)

Johnny Tremain, through its incorporation of historical events and its abundant details of life in Boston in 1773, offers young people a chance to ponder on a personal level the meanings of some of those abstract-sounding phrases from the Declaration of Independence—for instance, that we are endowed with "certain inalienable rights" such as "life, liberty and the pursuit of happiness." *Johnny Tremain* is also a "growing up" book, and as such offers an opportunity to live through, with Johnny, his bitterness about his accident and his maturation from a cocky and proud teenager, to what Huck, Hepler, and Hickman call a "man of fortitude and courage, a new man of a new nation" (1987, 546).

Charlotte's Web

The 1950s postwar years have been described by Ann Durrell (1982a) as "the Indian summer of the Eisenhower years," during which "society was dominated by a sort of mid-Atlantic bourgeoisie that felt it had saved the world for democracy and had thus earned the right to perpetuate forever the sociological and cultural values of Edwardian England" (25). In the children's book-publishing world, everything English was considered good. Many of the English books *were* good, of course, and classics like C. S. Lewis's *Narnia* series, for example, remain from that period. But possibly the most popular and best-loved children's book of the 1950s came not from England, but from Maine and the pen (or most likely the typewriter) of E. B. White.

Charlotte's Web (1952) is an American classic. Its heroine is the spider Charlotte A. Cavatica who, through the clever weaving of words of praise into her web, saves the life of Wilbur, the runty pig who had been fattened up for slaughter. It is a story about friendship and loyalty and the cycle of life. The animals are, of course, really people in pigskin and fur, and we can see ourselves and one another in fat and lonely Wilbur, in greedy and selfish Templeton, and in Charlotte, who was "brilliant, beautiful, and loyal to the end" (White, 182). We can see ourselves, too, in Fern, who inevitably must grow up and away from childhood and her childlike concern with the barn animals and their world. Charlotte, as you know, dies, but her spirit lives on through her children and grandchildren. As for Wilbur, he spends his latter days in what may seem, with a few minor alterations, the ideal retirement:

> Mr. Zuckerman took fine care of Wilbur all the rest of his days, and the pig was often visited by friends and admirers. . . . Life in the barn was very good—night and day, winter and summer, spring and fall, dull days and bright days. It was the best place to be, thought Wilbur, this warm delicious cellar, with the garrulous geese, the changing seasons, the heat of the sun, the passage of swallows, the nearness of rats, the sameness of sheep, the love of spiders, the smell of manure, and the glory of everything. (White, 183)

There is humor as well as wisdom in *Charlotte's Web*, but most of all there is the potential to share the emotions and aspirations of the characters and to ponder the meaning of life and death.

A Wrinkle in Time

The 1960s were turbulent years, the time of Camelot and assassinations, of peaceful marches and burning cities, of The Great Society and the Vietnam War. Yet, Ann Durrell (1982a) tells us, surprisingly few children's books reflected that turbulence. With few exceptions, children's books continued to reflect traditional styles and conventions and traditional values.

One of the landmark books that followed that trend was Madeleine L'Engle's combination science fiction/high fantasy, *A Wrinkle in Time* (1968). It is a space/time fantasy in which Meg Murray, her friend Calvin, and her younger (and very precocious) brother Charles Wallace, set off to rescue their scientist-father who is being held on the planet Camazotz by the evil, all-consuming disembodied brain, IT. Aided by three angel-like women with supernatural powers, the children manage to rescue their father, but Charles Wallace falls under the spell of IT. Finally, Meg realizes she is the only one who can save him, and she is able to do so by confronting IT with the only force it does not have and cannot comprehend—love.

In *A Wrinkle in Time,* L'Engle equates evil with the loss of individuality and individual freedom, and vividly shows the kind of frighteningly conformist, stultifying world that might result from such loss. She also makes a clear and forceful statement about the power of love to overcome evil. The book thus serves one of the major functions of high fantasy—to present for readers' consideration the virtues, values, and emotions that we believe are the lasting ones.

Stevie

Literature, according to Louise Rosenblatt, also enables readers to share in the "emotions and aspirations of other human beings . . . remote from them in temperament, space, or social environment" (274). *Stevie* (1969), written and illustrated by a black teenager named John Steptoe, became a landmark book, at least in part because it opened a window on a world unfamiliar to many readers, and yet easily accessible to them. Written in an informal black vernacular, *Stevie* tells the gentle story of Robert, who is remembering Stevie, the little boy who used to stay with Robert and his mother while his own mother worked. Robert had been annoyed at all the disruptions Stevie caused in his life—the broken toys, the dirty footprints on his bed, the teasing of his friends. But when Stevie and his parents move away, Robert misses him. "He was kinda like a little brother."

Robert and Stevie are remote from the social milieu of many middle-class, suburban white children, but they permit many urban black children to see their own lives reflected in a book. Both groups can share in the sense of loss that comes from the realization that we have failed to appreciate something valuable until it is no longer a part of our lives. *Stevie* is a slim but powerful book, one that provides for young children the same kind of satisfying literary experience that older children may have in reading a novel.

Stevie was a forerunner of the 1970s, when attitudes in the book world towards women, blacks, and other so-called minorities were changing, and many traditional taboos in children's books were being broken. It was the era of the "new realism"; of books that dealt with homosexuality, drugs, alcohol, suicide, death, unwed mothers, sex, alienation, and other topics formerly thought unsuitable for childrens' books.

Roll of Thunder, Hear My Cry

In the seventies, two books by black authors were awarded the Newbery Medal—*M. C. Higgins, the Great* (1974) by Virginia Hamilton, and *Roll of Thunder, Hear My Cry* (1976) by Mildred D. Taylor. Both are landmark books, not only because they were the first books by black authors to receive children's literature's highest national honor, but because the quality of the writing in each of them is superb.

Both books deserve examination, but I want to focus here on *Roll of Thunder*, the story of the Logan family, proud black landowners in the Mississippi of the 1930s. It is narrated by nine-year-old Cassie Logan, who, in the year the story takes place, learns some hard lessons about the extremes to which people, driven by racism, will go in order to maintain their own sense of superiority and power. Cassie's mother is fired from her teaching job, Cassie is humiliated by a white girl, she sees her grandmother powerless before the unwritten rules governing interactions between blacks and whites, night riders terrorize the black community, and her father sacrifices some of his land to save a black boy from a lynch mob. Through it all, the family remains proud and strong and sure of their own sense of who they are, determined to challenge injustice at whatever cost.

Roll of Thunder is a book that offers the potential for young readers to see the pernicious effects of bigotry and racism on the everyday lives of some very real, three-dimensional characters. Taylor said, in accepting the Newbery Medal, "If they [children of today and of the future] can identify with the Logans, who are representative not only of my family, but of the many Black families who faced adversity and survived, and understand the principles by which they lived, then perhaps they can better understand and respect themselves and others" (1977, 407–08). That statement, it seems to me, speaks directly to Rosenblatt's claim that experience with literature can help to "liberate the student from anachronistic emotional attitudes," and even perhaps to "nourish the impetus toward more fruitful modes of behavior" (Rosenblatt, 275).

Bridge to Terabithia

Louise Rosenblatt wrote of developing both sensitivity and imagination. Katherine Paterson, in her landmark book *Bridge to Terabithia* (1977), also reminds us of the power of imagination to open and enrich our lives. The story tells of the friendship between Jesse Aarons and Leslie Burke, two lonely children who create an imaginary land called

Terabithia, a wooded area that can be reached only by crossing a creek. When Leslie accidentally falls into the creek and drowns, Jesse must find a way to cope with her death and continue to grow.

Most readers are deeply moved by *Bridge to Terabithia,* partly because death is universal, and at some point we must all learn to cope with its reality. Katherine Paterson (1978b), in her Newbery acceptance speech, speaks of that ending, which is difficult for some children to accept. Jesse builds a plank bridge and invites his adoring little sister Maybelle into the magic land of Terabithia.

> Perhaps someday they will understand Jesse's bridge as an act of grace which he built . . . because of who he had become crossing the gully into Terabithia. I allowed him to build the bridge because I dare to believe with the prophet Hosea that the very valley where evil and despair defeat us can become a gate of hope—if there is a bridge. (367)

And there, in the author's own words, is one example of what Rosenblatt called the "potentiality inherent in literature itself" (274).

Anthony Burns

The 1980s book I want to discuss is the winner in the nonfiction category of the 1988 Boston Globe–Horn Book Award, Virginia Hamilton's *Anthony Burns: The Defeat and Triumph of a Fugitive Slave.* Anthony Burns was a slave who escaped from Virginia and settled in Boston in 1854. His putative master followed him, and under the Fugitive Slave Act, sued for his return. The case became a cause célèbre among abolitionists of the day. Burns' chief lawyer was Richard Henry Dana, author of *Two Years Before the Mast.* In spite of Dana's best efforts, and even with the cooperation of Franklin Pierce and others in high places, Anthony Burns was returned to slavery. Eventually his freedom was secured, and he went to Canada where he lived a few years, triumphantly free.

And so we come full circle, from *Johnny Tremain* to *Anthony Burns,* both concerned with the individual freedom. But the freedom of *Johnny Tremain* was denied the Anthony Burnses of this nation, so almost a century after Rab died on a Massachusetts battlefield, Boston was again the setting for a fight for liberty. And there are, as Hamilton points out in her acceptance speech, many parallels between the United States of Anthony Burns and the United States of today. Hamilton calls *Anthony Burns* "liberation literature" because it not only frees the hero of the book, but the reader as well. The reader, she says, becomes part of the struggle. We take our position then, rightly, as participants alongside the victim. We become emotionally involved in his problem; we suffer and we triumph, as the victim triumphs, in the solution of liberation. Thus, past and present are revealed as one through freedom of the individual. (1989, 185)

All seven books I have discussed have had the potential for making social contributions.

Louise Rosenblatt forcefully reminds us that the text on the printed page is merely a potential, that only in the transaction between the reader and the text is the work of art created. Further, there is no single, generic interpretation of the text. Each reader creates his or her own, depending on the background and experiences that reader brings to the transaction.

I have chosen to focus on important texts for elementary school students because I believe that *what* those students read makes a difference. I believe that if we want to begin to consider making literary experiences the "very core of the kind of educational process needed in a democracy," we ought to help young people to choose literature that can engage them in the kind of thinking and feeling and imagining that will help them grow into decent, contributing members of this society. Building literary experiences on books that deal with individual freedom, love, friendship, loyalty, courage, and hope, can be a powerful beginning. That, in my view, is the legacy of the last fifty years of children's books.

References

Durrell, Ann. 1982a. "If There Is No Happy Ending: Children's Book Publishing—Past, Present, and Future." Part I. *The Horn Book Magazine* 58:23–30.

———. 1982b. "If There Is No Happy Ending: Children's Book Publishing—Past, Present, and Future." Part II. *The Horn Book Magazine* 58:145–50.

Forbes, Esther. [1943] 1968. *Johnny Tremain*. Reprint. New York: Dell.

L'Engle, Madeleine. [1968] 1976. *A Wrinkle in Time*. Reprint. New York: Dell.

Hamilton, Virginia. 1988. *Anthony Burns: The Defeat and Triumph of a Fugitive Slave.* New York: Knopf.

———. 1989. "*Anthony Burns*: Acceptance Speech for the 1988 Boston Globe–Horn Book Award for Nonfiction." *The Horn Book Magazine* 65:183–85.

Huck, Charlotte S., Susan Hepler, and Janet Hickman. 1987. *Children's Literature in the Elementary School*. 4th Ed. New York: Holt, Rinehart and Winston.

Paterson. Katherine [1977] 1978a. *Bridge to Terabithia*. Reprint. New York: Avon.

_____. 1978b. "Newbery Award Acceptance." *The Horn Book Magazine* 54: 361–67.

Rosenblatt, Louise M. [1938] 1976. *Literature as Exploration*. Rev. Ed. New York: Noble and Noble.

Smith, Dora V. 1963. *Fifty Years of Children's Books*. Urbana, Ill.: National Council of Teachers of English.

Steptoe, John. 1969. *Stevie*. New York: Harper.

Taylor, Mildred D. 1976. *Roll of Thunder, Hear My Cry*. New York: Dial.

_____. 1977. "Newbery Acceptance Speech." *The Horn Book Magazine* 53: 401–09.

White, E. B. [1952] 1969. *Charlotte's Web*. Reprint. New York: Dell.

2. Fifty Years of Literature for Young Adults

Kenneth Donelson
Arizona State University

No matter what anyone says at present, life and literature and honesty about both didn't begin with Louise Rosenblatt. A few teachers and critics had previously made some of the same points she would score in *Literature as Exploration* in 1938. In the February 1905 *School Review,* Samuel Thurber worried about the gap between the voluntary reading of young people and the literary tastes of their English teachers:

> Teachers, to be sure, have put away childish things; they have cultivated literary tastes; they are scholarly. Yet I fail to see how they can make any use of that voluntary reading, no matter what their other tastes are, until they have at least a speaking acquaintance with it; or how they can interest their pupils in what *they* like, until they show them that their teachers are also interested in what *they* like and naturally enjoy. (175–76)

and a year later, Arlo Bates (1906) warned that

> no teaching is effective unless the interest as well as the attention of the pupils is enlisted; but whereas in other branches this is a condition, in the case of literature it is a prime essential. (3)

And only a few years before the first edition of *Literature as Exploration,* Howard Mumford Jones (1933) lamented that the methods and materials of English teachers were turning young people away from great books:

> Why do people read trash? The answer is, of course, that they don't know any better, but one of the reasons why they don't know any better is that our system of introducing them to better books in school and college and library is pretty well calculated to frighten them off. We have all got into the rut of thinking that the main reason for reading the Better Books is to improve the mind. We feel that we must do our duty by the classics, and so we have fits of moral betterment when we take up *Emerson's Essays* and *The Faerie Queene* and piously labor away while the moral fervor is

upon us. But it is also not uncommon, a day or so later, to find that the volume of Emerson remains unopened while the latest thriller is being devoured, and then there are the movies, and bridge, and conversation, and other distractions, and we shamefacedly put Emerson back on the shelves until we have another fit of moral betterment. (590)

If the sound development of literary taste did not begin with Rosenblatt, it did begin in lots of ways in the 1930s, and three teachers/ educational critics were involved. One was, of course, Louise M. Rosenblatt with her first edition of *Literature as Exploration* (1938). She gave us an approach to working with literature. Another was Dora V. Smith, who in two articles in the *English Journal* in 1930 and 1937, and in coursework at the University of Minnesota, made us aware that adolescent literature could no longer be ignored. She gave us a body of literature to work with. Finally, Lou LaBrant (1936) brought free reading to the Ohio State University Laboratory School in the last half of the 1930s. She gave us an effective way to bring Rosenblatt's response-centered approach to literature and Smith's adolescent literature together.

In addition to working well together to the advantage of young people, literature, and the English curriculum, these three educators have something else in common—each demands an act of faith on the part of English teachers. And because some English teachers have not—or cannot—make that leap of faith, the work and the accomplishments of Rosenblatt, Smith, and LaBrant still go unacknowledged and unaccepted by some educators.

Uncomfortable Freedoms

Let me briefly comment on these acts of faith and why they appeal to so many of us and do not appeal—or frighten—so many others. In all the editions of *Literature as Exploration*, Rosenblatt raises two particular issues that were certain to alarm some English teachers and antagonize others: (1) She assumes that literature ought to be enjoyable, at some level and in some way, to young people; indeed, to all readers. And (2) she assumes that such literature may influence readers:

> The power of literature to offer entertainment and recreation is, despite the pedants and moralists, still its prime reason for survival. Books read solely for entertainment satisfy, after all, definite needs and answer definite preoccupations. Such works have therefore a potential capacity to influence the reader's personality and behavior, perhaps even more than those he may read in the course of the school routine. (1968, 183–84)

Rosenblatt also assumes what most of us associate with her name, that each of us reads the literary work uniquely:

> No one else can read a literary work for us. The benefits of literature can emerge only from creative activity on the part of the reader himself. [The reader] responds to the little black marks on the page, or to the sound of the words in his ear, and he "makes something out of them." (1968, 278)

Allowing Reader-Response in the Classroom

We hardly need to be reminded that many English teachers fear the unknown involved in getting kids to open up and to respond with heaven-knows-what. How much more comfortable it is to use the teacher's guide and the end-of-the-selection questions and all those wonderfully glib answers we've picked up in those graduate seminars.

Even so, most English teachers would likely agree that one of their major responsibilities is to free students from the teacher, to help students to learn how to make meaning out of all those marks on paper when the teacher is no longer around. That seems obvious enough, yet it is among the most difficult of acts to carry through, especially since students themselves sometimes do not seem to want to be cut free. If freedom can be invigorating, it can also be uncomfortable. In the last few years, I have noticed that my students, undergraduate and graduate, have grown increasingly ambivalent about the freedom to respond as they see fit to literature. On the one hand, they take honest pleasure, as far as I can see, in honest response. But they also share horror stories of English teachers, secondary or college, who force-fed them a party-line interpretation and who denied them the right to wonder or question or doubt. As they do all of this, I find them sometimes most uncomfortable with their freedom and the lack of clear-cut answers—not responses—answers that may be provided in other classes. I do not pretend that I can always keep my mouth shut, and more often than I should admit, words have come from me that I meant as personal responses but my students took as holy writ. That was painfully obvious about a year ago when one of my sophomore students in the first required English course for English majors stayed behind to talk about a work that was giving him trouble. I asked some questions just to get him going—at least that's what I thought I was doing—and he tried this answer—not a response, but an answer—and then that one. Before I could reestablish contact with the literature and what I was trying to do, he broke in with an exasperated, "You really don't know what you want me to say, do you? Please, just tell me what you want to hear." So much right then for the response-centered literature curriculum.

Robert Scholes (1985) restates Rosenblatt's point elegantly and simply:

> Our job is not to produce "readings" for our students but to give them the tools for producing their own. Our job is not to intimidate students with our own superior textual production; it is to show them the codes on which all textual production depends, and to encourage their own textual practice. (24–25)

Sounds easy, but it isn't. And most of what I hear does not resemble Scholes. Most of it resembles something I heard a few months ago from a high school teacher in a teachers' lounge. After some heated talk about the pros and cons of teaching a modern author in the coming year, one teacher announced, "I'm not up to teaching him, not for awhile anyway. I haven't read the criticism and I've never taken a course on him. Come to think of it, are you sure they offer a course on him at ASU?" When someone looked my way, I muttered that as far as I knew no one had yet offered such a course, and I looked at the first teacher, who smiled at me and said with perfect sincerity, "Well, that takes care of that, doesn't it?" And I was not the least bit surprised.

Including "Popular" Literature in the Curriculum

In 1937, Dora V. Smith worried about the gap between the literature required in the English curriculum and the literature that appealed to young people. She also worried about young English teachers trained to teach only "the best" who would soon meet reality in the form of nonreading students, or students who read nothing more than bestsellers, much as we continue to worry about young teachers several generations later. She wrote:

> We must provide teachers who know books first-hand and recognize their place in the lives of boys and girls. It is fair neither to young people nor to their teachers to send out from our colleges and universities men and women trained alone in Chaucer and Milton and Browning to compete with Zane Grey, Robert W. Chambers, and Ethel M. Dell. At the University of Minnesota we have instituted a course in adolescent literature which aims to supplement the necessary training in the classics given by the English department with this broader knowledge of good books, old and new, for boys and girls and for intelligent, cultured men and women— books not commonly judged worthy of academic consideration. (111)

The literature Smith proposed for inclusion in the English classroom and curriculum was, by absolute standards, inferior to the classics, but it had one great advantage: young people read it and enjoyed it. Underlying Smith's apparently populist spirit, of course, was the belief that the aim of English teachers is to raise the taste of all students, and adolescent literature—just as mysteries and science fiction and fantasies are frequently used by some English teachers today was one way of getting many students out of their intellectual morass. But no matter how much snobbery lay beneath teachers' reluctance to accept adolescent literature as a way of raising tastes, it nonetheless picked up respectability and acceptance, albeit slowly. By the 1950s adolescent literature was frequently available in school and public libraries, particularly authors as good as Mary Stolz, Maureen Daly, John Tunis, Esther Forbes, and Florence Crannell Means.

The paperback industry made adolescent literature widely accessible, though much of the field was made up of hot-rod books and unsophisticated and simple-minded romances. By sheer coincidence, several books that changed the course of adolescent literature in the United States by injecting touches of a roughened reality came upon the heels of the Dartmouth Conference in 1966. The following year, S. E. Hinton's still-popular *The Outsiders* appeared, along with Robert Lipsyte's gritty little novel about prizefighting, *The Contender*. In 1968, Paul Zindel's *The Pigman* appeared, and adolescent literature seemed on its way.

The way to quality adolescent literature was rockier than most early critics might have guessed, but since 1968 some fine adolescent novels (along with the predictable and inevitable literary trash) have been published. For example,

1969	Barbara Wersba	*Run Softly, Go Fast*
1972	Robb White	*Deathwatch*
1973	Robert Newton Peck	*A Day No Pigs Would Die*
	Alice Childress	*A Hero Ain't Nothin' but a Sandwich*
1974	Robert Cormier	*The Chocolate War*
	William Sleator	*House of Stairs*
1976	Sue Ellen Bridgers	*Home Before Dark*
	Mildred D. Taylor	*Roll of Thunder, Hear My Cry*
1977	Robert Cormier	*I Am the Cheese*
1978	Robin McKinley	*Beauty*

	Walter Wangerin, Jr.	*The Book of the Dun Cow*
1979	Harry Mazer	*The Last Mission*
1980	Katherine Paterson	*Jacob Have I Loved*
1983	Cynthia Voigt	*A Solitary Blue*
1985	Paula Fox	*The Moonlight Man*

And the titles could go on and on, not all of them great, but all of them more than merely respectable; all of them readable and worth reading; all of them books that young people might enjoy and that adults would not feel a waste of their time.

And all that ignores the many fine adult novels not published specifically for young people, books that young people respond to because the authors do not write down to readers and because the characters are alive and puzzled by being alive, just as we are. Here are a few titles that I know work with young people, mixed with a few that I suspect would work if someone tried them, five novels and one curiosity:

Bernard Malamud	*The Assistant* (1957)
Howard Fast	*April Morning* (1961)
Margaret Craven	*I Heard the Owl Call My Name* (1973)
William Wharton	*A Midnight Clear* (1982)
P. C. Jersild	*Children's Island* (Sweden, 1976; U.S., 1986)
Toni Bentley	*Winter Season: A Dancer's Journal* (1982)

In *Winter Season*, Bentley gives vivid little glimpses into what it means to be a professional dancer not quite good enough to get to the top.

Rosenblatt (1940) wasn't talking about adolescent literature when she wrote the following, but she sounds as if she could have been:

> The valid test of what books should be read by youth is, not what adults or critics of the past have found good, but what is good, meaningful, effective, for this particular young human being at this stage of his emotional and intellectual development.

Or in the words of one of my favorite Wallace Stevens epigrams, "Literature is the better part of life. To this it seems inevitably necessary to add, provided life is the better part of literature" (1957, 158).

Encouraging Free Reading

Free reading is, for me, the best way to bring books and honest responses together. While Lou LaBrant codified much of what we now refer to as free reading—it is sometimes called individualized reading as well—I am responsible and culpable for what follows.

My rationale for free reading is simple. We spend too much time talking about the pleasures of reading, but we rarely allow the young to experience that pleasure, particularly in high school. We seem to say, "Reading is fun. Please do remember that, because I know that if you ever have time to read for the fun of it, I'll bet you'll enjoy yourselves. I know I do. Meanwhile, back at the text. . . ." I have heard that increasingly tiresome maxim, "It takes two to read a book." What is often left out is that it also takes *time,* and many of our young people have neither the time nor the place to read outside of school; nor do many of them have the inclination. If they do not learn from us, as models, how much fun reading is—and I mean the excitement, the satisfaction of choosing our own books and settling in for a good read—many of them, maybe most, will never learn. We may mouth our belief that individualized instruction is vital, but we do almost none of it.

Free reading gives us a fair chance to individualize reading and put the responsibility for selection on the young—with our help, of course. In many schools, this means a block of time, perhaps three to five weeks, when students are given the assignment to read—then read some more, and then read more after that—all the time, of course, while the teacher is reading as well (and occasionally wandering around the room, helping one student to find something more interesting, helping another to consider a point in the book that is troubling the young person).

Difficult as it can be, the most satisfying part of free reading is talking about the books with young people. I ask students two questions when they are ready to talk about their books: "What do you think is *worth* talking about when we talk about this book?" and "What questions do you have about this book for which there are no answers?" I use those questions as frames for most of the work my classes do, whether undergraduate or graduate. They annoy some students, many of whom want the security of certainty, but I continue to insist, no matter how loud their objections, that literature ought to be about life, and life is not riddled with certainties. Rosenblatt, Smith, and LaBrant notwithstanding, sometimes I have the uncomfortable feeling that one reason some students become English majors is for the security provided by professors who know the answers to the big questions and v/illingly pass them along to students.

A few months ago, I ran across a line by the former Secretary of Education, William J. Bennett. He had apparently heard that his old high school was dropping Latin as a requirement. His response? "I went through it. I want them to suffer, too."

Well, I do not want people to suffer, neither through required Latin nor through English classes where teachers pick all the books for all the students, where they tell the meaning of every piece of literature (and students better memorize it since it will be on the test), where they speed merrily and madly through the text, knowing that the most "important" part of the literature curriculum is based on coverage, coverage, coverage. Despite my best efforts, I know that some students will suffer in my English classes, but that will not be because I did not listen to Louise Rosenblatt, Dora V. Smith, and Lou LaBrant.

References

Bates, Arlo. 1906. *Talks on Teaching Literature*. Boston: Houghton Mifflin.

Jones, Howard Mumford. 1933. "The Place of Books and Reading in Modern Society." *ALA Bulletin* 27: 585–93.

LaBrant, Lou. 1936. *An Evaluation of the Free Reading in Grades Ten, Eleven, and Twelve*. Contributions to Education, no. 2. Columbus, Oh.: Ohio State University Press.

Rosenblatt, Louise M. [1938] 1968. *Literature as Exploration*. Rev. ed. New York: Noble and Noble.

_____. 1940. "Moderns among Masterpieces." *English Leaflet* 39: 98–110.

Scholes, Robert. 1985. *Textual Power: Literary Theory and the Teaching of English*. New Haven, Conn.: Yale University Press.

Smith, Dora V. 1930. "Extensive Reading in Junior High School: A Survey of Teacher Preparation." *English Journal* 19: 449–62.

_____. 1937. "American Youth and English." *English Journal* 26: 99–113.

Stevens, Wallace. 1957. "Adagia." In *Opus posthumous*. Samuel French Morse, ed. New York: Knopf. Reprint 1982. New York: Vintage Books.

Thurber, Samuel. 1905. "Voluntary Reading in the Classical High School." *School Review* 13: 168–79.

Weinstein, Else. Nov. 6, 1988. "High School Teacher." *New York Times*. Educational Life supplement.

3. Students Exploring Literature across the World

John Dixon

A poem, novel, a play . . . is an event in the life of a reader. It is an experience she or he lives through, part of the ongoing stream of life. Thus, each reading is unique and personal.

For fifty years these simple truths have been at the heart of Louise Rosenblatt's message to students and to fellow teachers. It has taken all her original intelligence and tenacity to sustain them—and their rich implications—against entrenched fallacies of the academy and its inherited practices.

Reading as a Personal and Social Event

The struggle is by no means over, either; yet today I can offer evidence from students and teachers across the world that those truths and their implications are being taken seriously. Let us start then with the voice of a student from Tasmania, Michelle Sims (1984), bringing the text of Lear to life in her imagination as she constructs a scene, line by line:

> REGAN: Go thrust him out at gates
>
> *(loudly, commanding, perhaps pointing with outstretched arm and finger toward the doorway. She bends and brings her face close to his and in a voice that is powerfully quiet . . .)*
>> and let him
>>> Smell his way to Dover.
>
> *(emphasizing every word, especially "smell." Very calm, but very cruel.)*

What is Michelle engaged in here as she writes these notes? She is taking the patterned symbols of the text and weaving from them an utterance, sensed as a particular voice of a particular kind of persona (57).[1] She is constructing a speaker—and her speech acts. She is calling up sounds on the ear (13).

It is evident, is it not, that the text is a necessary, but not a sufficient, condition for such work (83). To create that horrifying calmness, that menacing power, Michelle has had to dig into her past experience of life (and of literature), selecting and activating elements that she feels to be appropriate. That is her primary purpose.

Before moving on to her further purposes, let us turn aside for a moment, alerting ourselves here to a warning from Louise Rosenblatt. We have started from a personal act of reading, but we must recall that in part this is an illusion: "Any reading event in isolation is a useful fiction for analysis" (20). Michelle's current constructions from the text—like those of many similar British students I have observed—are likely to arise from some joint effort to bring the text to life, with a framing, and with expectations, set up by a teacher. So we must bear in mind that "any reading act is the outcome of a complex social nexus," a nexus that we could follow back through our personal histories to reading bedtime stories, snuggled up to our parents, or turning the same stories into make-believe dramas without friends in the yard. The personal event is unique, but it is socially formed too.

Indeed, ideally, I believe, reading is not merely done alone. A videotape from Canada, recently made by Patrick Dias (1987) and his friends in Montreal schools, shows groups of four or five students reading poems not singly, but together, and talking the experience over as a group. We can see them critically scrutinizing the "poems"— the unique personal events—each of them is evoking. And as we observe that process, we can recognize times when they are organizing the experience according to acquired social habits, assumptions and expectations (17), and times when they are engaged in a joint process of selection, revision, and expansion of relevant experiences. The text, they are learning, offers both constraints and openness. On the one hand, there may be very delicate cues to note; on the other, the sharing of potentially relevant experiences may alert a reader like Michelle to her tacit knowledge of even harder, more venomous, possibilities in Regan.

Besides, even in the act of reading, there is a new classroom tradition emerging internationally. Group readings of a "poem," group discussion of how a text is to be rendered orally, group conversations following such rehearsals and readings—all these social activities help to alert each individual student to potential cues in the text and latent potentials in the experiences that can be drawn on as they construct a human "event." Rehearsing in a group—and with a teacher to call on—they learn to become critical of the relevance of personal experiences that are activated (11), to scrutinize what they are jointly evoking, to seek out even more delicate cues by which the author directs the attention of the reader (86). As each reader's primary transactions with the text are directly communicated by the spoken voice, by gesture and by action, it is possible for a sympathetic group to produce a joint construct. This is a powerful site for cooperative teaching and learning, and in the coming years I hope that many teacher-researchers will be recording and analyzing these promising practices.

The Event as an Object of Further Thought

So much, briefly, for the primary purpose, bringing the text to life. But as Louise Rosenblatt shows in her wonderfully precise analysis, there is a secondary purpose, too, of equal importance, for the experience of the poem—the event you have lived through—may become the object of thought like any other experience (23). Indeed, it is often the case that alongside the poetic event, "a concurrent stream of feelings, attitudes and ideas is aroused" (48).

For a first glimpse, let us return to Michelle. As she noted the force of that word "smell"—"let him smell his way to Dover"—Michelle reflected in a separate column:

> *Regan may have thought this a bit of a joke. She was playing on words. . . . She may be likening him to a dog or an animal—which is ironical, because both Regan and Goneril have been referred to by Kent as the King's "Dog-hearted daughters."*

Already, as you can see, Michelle is doing more than imagining a speech act: she is tacitly judging the person who uttered it, and calling on cues elsewhere in the play to fortify her sense of an appropriate judgment. It is characteristic of works of literature that they should invite this kind of reflection on what has been evoked. And frequently such reflections are accompanied by—and become—a reenacting of the primary experience, "often simultaneous, often interwoven, often interacting" (69).

The contemplation of a possibility in human experience—that is what a poem invites. It puts a big demand on us as people. And there is no guarantee that someone like me, who is good at scholarly, critical analysis, is any more capable of meeting that demand than a young student. Indeed, there is a danger that my analytical work—my efferent readings—will actually become a substitute for the construction of the poem and the personal response that follows. To guard against that, it may be a help to listen to the fresh, spontaneous voices of some junior high school students.

Here, for example, are snatches from two fifteen-year-old English girls, Janice and Christine, who have been reading a short text about a skinny boy with burnt-out little eyes—an incendiary who had set farm buildings ablaze with flame-fanged tigers. Janice begins by reenacting the power of the flames:

> The poem gives the impression that the fire were great and it had spread all over the farm, its flames spread quickly, as quickly as a tiger hungrily coming towards you, the noise of the fire was as deafening as the roar of a tiger whilst tearing flesh. The brightness of the red and gold flames made the sky look red and fierce, and as persons choked, you could imagine the stars up in the sky being choked by the thick black smoke rising into the sky.
>
> My impressions of the small boy are that he was lonely and needed some attention just to tell him that he was still loved. All he wanted was just one warm kiss which would make him content, but there was no one in the world who would offer him this. The last two lines of the poem, "He would have been content with one warm kiss had there been anyone to offer this," *made me feel sorrowful for the child.* I wanted to reach out, pull him close and give him the one warm kiss that he so much wanted, that no one else would give him. (Dixon and Stratta, 16; my italics)

"Made me feel sorrowful for the child." It is interesting, isn't it, how a not-very-literary student, as she contemplates this experience— manifestly very real to her—finds a language to express both the seriousness of her concern and the natural spontaneity of her impulse. That is Janice's way. But each significant response is unique, because it is personal. Consider the differences in these three short extracts from Christine:

> The fire was huge to compare with what his heart needed. His need for love was "brazen, fierce and huge." That one small boy "with a face like pallid cheese" seems almost under other circumstances to be an angel, but the fire of hatred in his heart for not being wanted has burnt out his eyes. . . . The fiery colour suggests life and fierce reactions. I don't feel it is true of the boy. He is almost ash in his feelings. Almost dead and gone. . . .
>
> And it is frightening that such a small child shall carry such pain in his heart. That such a child should as the poem says "set the sky on fire and choke the stars to heat such skinny limbs." It is frightening *that we can allow such people to exist in such a state.*
>
> And then we are offered the remedy. So simple as remedies usually are. So pure a feeling and action "one warm kiss." We are not allowed to linger long on this, but to quickly realize what could have prevented this and then we are drawn quickly back to the reality and fear that there was no one there to give this remedy. No

one there to care. "Had there been anyone to offer this." (Dixon and Stratta, 19; my italics)

If Janice sees the person, Christine finally sees a world—"that we can allow such people to exist in such a state." Her concurrent stream of feelings and thoughts first carries her deep into the heart of this burnt-out child, interpreting his pain, then helps her stand back to see him as a type, an emblem, set in an uncaring world. We can see that this poem is becoming part of the life experience with which she will encounter the future (142). Already, it is "questioning her assumptions about human behavior" perhaps?

Had we space, I should have liked to show students "bringing to the work a very active present, with all its preoccupations, anxieties, questions and aspiration" (144)—to follow the "interplay of two cultures," the reader's and the writer's, to illustrate how the "differing value systems of readers" change the significance of the unique poems they experience. All this, and more, is part of Rosenblatt's rich modeling. But I must be satisfied with one more student's voice, so I have deliberately chosen Sam McClure, who had struggled the previous year to get through the class novel—only managing finally because his Australian teacher, Peter Adams, put most of it on tape for him. Indeed, as far as reading and writing went, Sam felt "stupid" and "hopeless," as he told his teacher (Adams, 151).

His breakthrough as a writer—and reader—came when he was invited to continue "Z for Zachariah"—to live on, that is, in the world of the poem. This was his preparation for what follows: an epilogue to *Lord of the Flies* (Adams 151–52). Within this work, I believe that he has found room not only to reenact the poem—the lived-through experience—but also to bring to bear the fruits of his own contemplation and human understanding. I offer it here as a fitting tribute to Louise Rosenblatt's work, to teachers, and to our students' never-ending capacity to learn.

Jack

Jack sat in an old cane chair on the verandah of his beach-shack. He looked down towards the beach and moved his eyes up to the horizon. The water was smooth and glassy and seemed to be repeating itself all the way to the skyline. His two young children ran up the steep winding path that led from the beach to the house. The youngest of them ran up to her father.

"Daddy, look what I found!"

She held a large shell in her outstretched hands.

"And Dad, if you hold it to your ear, you can hear the sea."

She handed him the shell. Jack put it to his ear. He listened to the familiar echoing sound of the air moving in and out of the shell—constant, soothing, peaceful—like water breaking on a distant reef, with the sound of the smaller waves lifting and dying on the sand.

Then, slowly and faintly, another sound appeared, just barely audible. The sound began to get louder, as if it was growing in the shell, starting from the middle and winding itself around the spiral cavity. After a few seconds he could recognize the sound: "Kill the beast! Cut his throat! Spill the blood!"

Jack began to shudder.

And out of the chant came the three most horrifying words Jack had heard on the island.

"I meant that!"

Jack began to cry.

Notes

1. All page references, unless otherwise indicated, are to Louise M. Rosenblatt's *The Reader, the Text, the Poem: The Transactional Theory of the Literary Work* 1978. Carbondale, Ill.: Southern Illinois University Press.

References

Adams, Peter. 1987. "Writing from Reading—Dependent Authorship as a Response." In *Readers, Texts, Teachers*. Edited by Bill Corcoran and Emrys Evans. Upper Montclair, N.J.: Boynton/Cook. 119–53.

Dias, Patrick. "Developing Independent Readers of Poetry: Thirteen-year-olds Read and Discuss Ted Hughes's *The Thought-Fox*." 1987. Videotape presented at the annual conference of the Canadian Council of Teachers of English, Winnipeg, Canada.

Dixon, John, and Leslie Stratta. 1987. "Examining Poetry—the Need for Change." Southampton, England: Southern Regional Examination Board. ERIC Document Reproduction No. ED 278 011.

Mallick, David, and Michelle Sims. Dec. 1984. "Writing about a Shakespeare Scene." *English in Australia*, 70: 48–9.

B. *Literature as Exploration* and the Classroom Tradition

How does the teaching of literature change when focus shifts from pedanti-cally teaching a literary work to enhancing the responses of young readers to that work? As Robert Probst clearly indicates, new teaching strategies must be employed if interaction of text and reader is to be central in the literary education of young people. Mary A. Barr next describes how the State of California is moving to establish response-oriented teaching in the classrooms of that state. And Stephen Dunning concludes by describing a brilliant classroom lesson that engages young people with poetry.

4. *Literature as Exploration* and the Classroom

Robert E. Probst
Georgia State University

It is remarkable that a book written fifty years ago should still look more to the future than the past. As I reread *Literature as Exploration* over the past months, preparing for what I thought would be a retrospective, a look at the influences of the text on literature classrooms during the past half-century, it slowly dawned on me that the book demands thought about the next fifty years at least as much as the last fifty. It insists that we think about implications yet to be examined, implementations yet to be devised, possibilities yet to be realized. It entertains questions, suggests possibilities, that are just now being realized, and so it is an eminently current book—it could have been published first in 1988 as easily as in 1938.

That is not to say that the book doesn't already have a notable history, but rather, that it is impossible to extract it from the continuing evolution of critical theory and teaching practice and speak only of what it has done, not of what it has yet to do. But *Literature as Exploration* has done, already, a great deal for literature teachers.

Conception of Literature

Literature as Exploration suggested, first of all, a conception of literature and the literature classroom likely to reawaken our first feelings for books, those feelings that drew us to them before we became professional readers and teachers:

> Certainly to the great majority of readers, the human experience that literature presents is primary. . . . The reader seeks to participate in another's vision—to reap knowledge of the world, to fathom the resources of the human spirit, to gain insights that will make his own life more comprehensible. (7)[1]

Rosenblatt proposed that this essential experience of reader-meeting-text could be the heart of the literature classroom. To draw students too soon away from those fundamental pleasures, substituting for them, rather than building upon them, the scholarly approaches (i.e., attention to biography, technique, history) would be, she argued, to drain the literature of its vitality, reducing it to a mere exercise in analyzing and memorizing. A student so encouraged to ignore his or her own transactions with a text is unlikely to participate fully in the "human experience" of the literature:

> Instead of plunging into the work and permitting its full impact, [the student] is aware that he must prepare for certain questions, that his remarks on the work must satisfy the teacher's already crystallized ideas about it.
>   The teacher of college freshmen literature courses is often perturbed to find this attitude affecting the work of even the most verbally proficient students. They read literary histories and biographies, criticism, introductions to editions, so-called study guides, and then, if there is time, they read the works. (62–63)

Rosenblatt insisted that reading the works, rather than studying them, should come first. We will not, she said,

> further the growth of literary discrimination by a training that concentrates on the so-called purely literary aspect. We go through empty motions if our primary concern is to enable the student to recognize various literary forms, to identify various verse patterns, to note the earmarks or the style of a particular author, to detect recurrent symbols, or to discriminate the kinds of irony or satire. Acquaintance with the formal aspects of literature will not in itself insure esthetic sensitivity. One can demonstrate familiarity with a wide range of literary works, be a judge of craftsmanship, and still remain, from the point of view of a rounded understanding of art, esthetically immature. The history of criticism is peopled with writers who possess refined taste but who remain minor critics precisely because they are minor personalities, limited in their understanding of life. Knowledge of literary forms is empty without an accompanying humanity. (52)

Literary Reading

In *Literature as Exploration* Rosenblatt suggested that the reading of literature might respect that human element. It is not, she argued, simply the study of literary technique and terminology, not the acquiring of information about writers, texts, genres, movements, styles. What, then, is it? What is the process by which we participate in another's vision, learn something significant about the world, acquire the insights that make our lives more comprehensible?

Rosenblatt suggested that reading is not a matter of simply extracting from texts. The meaning, she argued, was not hidden within or beneath the words, to be found, unearthed, and exhibited. It was not appropriate to suggest that the reader merely submitted to, or stole from, the text. Rather, she suggested, the reader performs *with* the text. The symbolic dance of words on paper awakens memories, arouses feelings, evokes thought, conjures images, but all those memories, feelings, thoughts, and images are the reader's as much as—even more than—they are the writer's or the text's:

> Through the medium of words, the text brings into the reader's consciousness certain concepts, certain sensuous experiences, certain images of things, people, actions, scenes. The special meanings and, more particularly, the submerged associations that these words and images have for the individual reader will largely determine what the work communicates to *him*. The reader brings to the work personality traits, memories of past events, present needs and preoccupations, a particular mood of the moment, and a particular physical condition. These and many other elements in a never-to-be-duplicated combination determine his response to the peculiar contribution of the text. (30–31)

The poem is the reader's, created not from the words on paper alone, but also from the associations and memories brought to the text. Reading, then, is a process of creating rather than simply receiving. It is active, not passive. And it requires readers to attend not only to what is on the page, but also to what they have brought with them to that page.

The Role of Readers

Literature as Exploration defines a much more responsible and demanding role for students than they would have in a system dedicated simply to supplying them with information and skills. Students are now charged not with acquiring and remembering knowledge, but with making it, with crafting it out of the raw material of their experience, the text's, and their discourse with other students, teachers, and writers.

They do not have the luxury of waiting to see what the teacher thinks or sees, of simply taking and reproducing notes on someone else's thought. Instead, they are burdened with—and freed by—the obligation to make sense themselves out of their experience. That makes their work in the literature classroom more difficult, more interesting, and more significant than it would otherwise be, because it requires them to perform—they cannot simply receive, accept, absorb, as if the literature were a vaccination injected into the bloodstream.

Further, Rosenblatt broadens the range of material that students must take into account. They must consider not only the text, but also what they bring to the text—their own histories, beliefs, biases, prejudices, experiences, hopes. And they must consider, too, the contributions made by other readers, along with the shaping effects of the context in which they encounter the text. Whatever meaning comes of literary experience is an amalgam of all those elements.

The Role of Literary Texts

The role of texts in the literature classroom changes, too, in Rosenblatt's vision:

> Much that in life itself might seem disorganized and meaningless takes on order and significance when it comes under the organizing and vitalizing influence of the artist. (42)

And earlier:

> Whatever the form—poem, novel, drama, biography, essay— literature makes comprehensible the myriad ways in which human beings meet the infinite possibilities that life offers. (6)

Literature becomes a reservoir of conceptions of human possibilities, out of which the students must forge their own visions. Literary texts are not, however, the repositories of meaning; rather, they are the source of intellectual, emotional, and aesthetic experience, out of which meaning may be made by the individual reader. Rosenblatt warns us (as will others, years later), that we must not be reverential before texts. She observes that

> it is often hard for the student to realize in a vivid or personal way that the ideas and behavior he accepts most unquestioningly derive their hold upon him from the fact that they have been unconsciously absorbed from the society about him. (253)

The reader, Rosenblatt says,

> can begin to achieve a sound approach to literature only when he reflects upon his response to it, when he attempts to understand

> what in the work and in himself produced that reaction, and when
> he thoughtfully goes on to modify, reject, or accept it. (76)

All of those ultimate judgments are possible. Thoughtful readers will expect sometimes to find their thinking reaffirmed, sometimes to discover a need to revise visions, to rethink conceptions with which they confront the world, perhaps to refute and abandon notions they have harbored. But they will not approach texts in awe, prepared to accept them uncritically; thoughtful readers do not submit to texts, but rather expect texts to submit to them. And in that process they are likely to come to better understand themselves, the others with whom they work, the texts, and their culture:

> The attempt to work out the author's system of values and assumptions about man and society should enable the student to discover the unspoken assumptions behind his own judgment. His conclusions about this particular work imply the unarticulated theories of human conduct and ideas of the good that shape his thinking. (120)

Implicit in this vision of reader and text is the teacher's role.

The Role of Teachers: Principles of Instruction

Throughout *Literature as Exploration,* Rosenblatt insisted upon attending to the human element. In doing so, she suggested several principles by which teachers might allow their students to find, in texts, those human satisfactions readers typically seek. First, she argued, *students must be free to deal with their own reactions to the text* (66; italics, unless otherwise stated, are mine). It is inappropriate and unprofitable to ignore or bypass those reactions, whatever they may be. Words are symbols; thus they function only in the mind, and as any teacher knows, all those minds are different, sometimes frighteningly so. How the words will function must depend in part upon what minds they strike. Readers cannot ignore their own associations with words, deny their existence, and attempt to replace them with dictionary definitions, or with the associations and connotations of other readers.

If readers are to learn from their reading, they must begin with the visions it awakens in them and work from there. Teachers, abiding by this principle, have begun to ask students what they see, feel, think, and remember as they read, encouraging them to attend to their own experience of the text. And teachers (those who accept the responsibility transferred to them) find students testing the literature in the light of their own experience, and rethinking their own experience in the light of the text. The questions initiate talk, not just about the text, but about reader-and-text. They invite consideration not just of what the text presents, but also of its significance in the intellectual and emotional life of the reader.

Consider just such a first reaction to this text, by Mark Van Doren:

January Chance

All afternoon before them, father and boy,
In a plush well, with winter sounding past:
In the warm cubicle between two high
Seat backs that slumber, voyaging the vast.

All afternoon to open the deep things
That long have waited, suitably unsaid.
Now one of them is older, and the other's
Art at last has audience; has head,

Has heart to take it in. It is the time.
Begin, says winter, howling through the pane.
Begin, the seat back bumps: what safer hour
Than this, within the somnolent loud train,

A prison where the corridors slide on
As the walls creak, remembering downgrade?
Begin. But with a smile the father slumps
And sleeps. And so the man is never made.

One student responded immediately, "This is about ice-fishing in Minnesota." Now, on the one hand, it is clearly, demonstrably *not* about ice-fishing in Minnesota. We could point to lines 11 and 12 as fairly conclusive evidence that the setting is a train; and that—combined with the absence of references to fishing, to ice, to lakes, to Minnesota—should be enough to carry the day, demolishing the reader's groundless assertion and exposing her careless reading.

On the other hand, as the student was able to explain vividly, it *was* about ice-fishing. In Minnesota, she said, parent and child would go out onto the ice, pitch a tent, crank up a small heater, cut a hole in the ice, and spend the hours quietly together, perhaps seldom talking, but nonetheless bound together for a short time in an event that they shared. Van Doren was wrong, she said—the traditional father-son talk wasn't necessary to make the man; it was being there together that did that.

Allowed to explore and explain her first, uncensored reaction to the text, the student began to bring her life and the text together, so that each could shed light on the other. She was invited into dialogue with the text about the human issues, the values and beliefs implicit in the text and in her reading of it. For her to do that, of course, she had to feel able to take the risk.

Rosenblatt's second principle speaks of the conditions necessary for students to deal with their reactions: *"The classroom situation and the relationship with the teacher should create a feeling of security"* (66). It must become a comfortable, non-combative place, where half-formed ideas may be explored, where personal, even private, matters might occasionally creep to the surface to be addressed with delicacy and kindness. It must not, above all, have winners and losers. It must not value correctness above investigation, conformity above exploration, answers above questions.

Teachers abiding by that principle have instituted procedures that diminish the potential threat of the classroom. They have taught their students to respond humanely and gently to one another; they've encouraged tentative, probing, uncertain statements; they've broken the class into smaller, safer, more intimate groups; they've avoided debate as the model for classroom talk. They've tried teaching works, provided by colleagues, that they have not seen until the moment they walk into the room, so that they can themselves model the tentative, questioning exploration of a text. Teachers who do this have joined the class as another reader, and that change in roles seems to increase the significance, in the students' minds, of their own readings.

Teachers committed to allowing students to explore their own responses to work must also—a third principle—*provide time and opportunity for "an initial crystallization of a personal sense of the work"* (69). It is too easy for students to report, "I think what he said. . . ." Not only is it easy; it is often encouraged. At the college level, professors who demand adherence to an established critical stance on work or author imply to their students that they are to think what the critics have thought. At the secondary school level, teachers who run a competitive classroom imply a hierarchy of answers, some best, some good, some bad, and students quickly learn who produces the best and, if they care, will defer to them. Students need periodically to be thrown onto their own resources, at least long enough to articulate their own first readings.

Some teachers have begun, consequently, to rely heavily upon journals, reading logs (in various forms), response statements (brief freewritings immediately after reading), and other similar strategies designed both to elicit first responses and to isolate students from one another for a long enough time so that their sense of the work might take shape.

Students invited to deal with their own responses must, of course, not only articulate them, but examine them—at least some of them— at greater length, and thus they must write. Rosenblatt's fourth principle argues that we must *avoid undue emphasis upon the form in which the students' reactions are couched* (67). To prescribe too narrowly the style or structure of the response is to strangle it. Students compelled to write the traditional book report, or forced into the mold of the five-paragraph theme, are unlikely to see self-discovery as the point of the exercise.

And so teachers have experimented with alternatives to comple-ment the analytical essay—papers drawing upon ideas recorded in logs or journals, fully developed response papers (longer explorations of one's own reading of a text), and other designs. The reader who responded with the memory of ice-fishing might find herself writing an autobiographical narrative about her own childhood. Or she might write about her rejection of the ideas she saw implicit in Van Doren's poem—a more traditional textual analysis, perhaps. It is even possible that she might find the appropriate form, the one most suited to making meaning of her transaction with the text, to be a letter.

An awareness of the range of possibilities, and the freedom to choose among them, is essential. If that reader can best make sense of her reading of the text by writing to her mother or father, then the five-paragraph theme is hardly the ideal genre, and to be forced into it is to be shackled by form.

Fifth, *Literature as Exploration* suggests that the teacher must try to *find points of contact among the opinions of students* (71). That is the fundamental principle for discussion in the classroom. Rosenblatt has pointed out that literature serves a socializing function—it integrates us into the society. If it is to do that, the first step for a reader is likely to be that of talking with the student at the next desk. If teachers can find, or help students find, the similarities and differences in their readings, then they may be able to encourage productive talk about experiences, assumptions, values, beliefs. They may then be able to lead students to more critically aware readings.

Teachers experimenting with this notion have tried such schemes as having students develop the agenda for discussion. They may put students in groups for five or ten minutes to compare the notes in their reading logs and identify one major issue to be discussed. Those issues, one from each group, then become the topics for full class discussion. Or, on another day, students might be asked to write freely for five minutes in response to a text. Then, while the class quietly reviews the reading, the teacher will hastily, and probably intuitively (since time permits little reflection) sort the responses (and thus the students) into four or five groups which become the discussion groups for that day. Each group might then be charged with exploring its reactions and ultimately reporting back to the full class.

Sixth, Rosenblatt suggests that the *teacher's influence should be "the elaboration of the vital influence inherent in literature itself"* (74). That is to say, teachers must not substitute extrinsic matters for the real effects of the literary work. "Literature," Rosenblatt says, "provides a *living-through*, not simply *knowledge about . . ."* (38; italics in original). It offers not just information, but experience, with its complex array of elements, intellectual and emotional. "January Chance" did not inform that one reader about the relationship of parent and child, but rather, awakened feelings and evoked memories of her own childhood; pleased her with its rhythms and its images; and provoked objections to, and then some analysis of, Van Doren's assumptions. The vital influence of the work was complex, and the teacher's job was to help her find her way through it. Providing that help is essential.

Although free response is necessary—a seventh principle of instruction—*it is not sufficient*—*students must still be led to reflection and analysis* (75). The approach is not indulgent, not permissive, despite the respect it shows for the primary responses, the first reactions of readers. A student

> can begin to achieve a sound approach to literature only when he reflects upon his response to it, when he attempts to understand what in the work and in himself produced that reaction, and when he thoughtfully goes on to modify, reject, or accept it. (76)

Rosenblatt remarks that "The danger is in the unquestioning adoption of the general attitudes toward human nature and conduct that permeate the very atmosphere we live in" (15), and she would not want the teaching of literature to encourage that uncritical acceptance of texts. To absorb attitudes unthinkingly from the literature would be as indefensible as to absorb them unthinkingly from soap operas or political speeches. Students must be encouraged to assume intellectual responsibility for the conceptions with which they face the world:

> The more conscious the individual is of the nature of the cultural forces with which he is interacting, the more intelligently can he accept or resist them, and the more intelligently can he modify their power and their direction. (155–56)

The Future

The conception of literary experience and the principles of teaching Rosenblatt articulated for us in *Literature as Exploration,* available to us for fifty years, continue now to instruct teachers, to suggest innovation and experimentation in the classroom, and to raise questions about the purpose and the practice of literature teaching. We are beginning now, for instance, to look far more intently at the relationship between reading and writing, as Rosenblatt suggested we should. If the reading of literature is a performance, if it is the active creation of meaning, then attention to students' texts, as well as to the novels and the poems, is inevitable, because it is in those student texts that the most sustained performance can take place.

Literature as Exploration suggests that we might broaden still further the range of forms students are invited to try. Acknowledging the desire of teachers to awaken students to the subtleties of technique, it says that

> one of the best ways of helping students to gain the appreciation of literary form and artistry is to encourage them to engage in such imaginative writing. (48)

Most literature programs, however, continue to treat literature as something to be received, rather than as something to be produced. Few students, I suspect, are regularly asked to write poetry, drama, or fiction. Massive changes in curriculum might result simply from exploring the possibilities inherent in that one suggestion.

Rosenblatt's emphasis upon literature as performance suggests not only that students be asked to write more, and in more widely varied modes, but also that we might spend more time dealing directly with their texts. Those texts could be the most immediate and significant accounts possible of literary experience. Few teachers, however, have begun to give much class time to the study of texts that students have produced in response to literary works, despite their great potential for revealing how we make meaning.

Literature as Exploration suggests also that we have yet to conceive of adequate curricula. We still depend upon the features of texts, rather than upon the features of transactions with texts, to organize our literature programs. Thus we continue for the most part to work with courses arranged either historically or by genre. Even those programs organized around themes seem to draw their inspiration from the content of the great texts, rather than from consideration of the potential readings young students might produce. *Literature as Exploration* suggests that we should at least consider the possibilities of other arrangements, designed with attention, perhaps, to the patterns of psychological development in childhood and adolescence, and to the expressed interests and concerns of the students, as well as to the great literature.

There is quite likely a strong correlation among those three elements, anyway. One of the tasks of adolescence, for example, is attaining some independence of parents, some autonomy and self-direction; clearly that is also one of the issues adolescents are most eager to read about; and equally clearly, "coming-of-age" is one of the significant themes in our literature. It might be possible for us to develop curricula that capitalize upon such convergences, and by doing so make our literature instruction more powerful and significant.

Rosenblatt has offered us a conception of literature and its teaching that we have yet to explore fully. It is a conception that respects the student, the teacher, the text, and the culture, and suggests a sensible relationship among them. Above all, it is a democratic vision, sustaining the freedoms of the individual. It argues

> that the human being is recognized as having value in himself and that anything which reduces him to the status of a thing, instrument, or automaton is condemned. It sets up as an ideal the social situation in which each member of society is given the opportunity for the greatest fulfillment of those culturally valued satisfactions of which he is potentially capable. (166)

Note

1. All citations are to: Rosenblatt, Louise M. [1938] 1976. *Literature as Exploration,* 3rd edition. New York: Noble and Noble.

5. The California Literature Project

Mary A. Barr
California Literature Project

The California Literature Project (CLP) is a statewide (but regional and local) project, a top-down *and* bottom-up project, devoted to putting the critical theory of Louise Rosenblatt to work for all California students, K–12. The CLP is part of a broad-based, statewide curriculum reform effort known as the California Reading Initiative.

The California Reading Initiative

In response to public criticism of schools, the California Reading Initiative was launched in 1985 by an aggressive, articulate state superintendent of public instruction, with the cooperation of a strong, business-minded governor, and a legislature determined to improve instruction in California schools. The Initiative consists of four facets: public relations, materials development, state and district assessment revision, and staff development.

Public Relations

The public relations drive is aimed at creating public support for the reading of literature by *all* students. Supermarkets, for example, now feature displays of children's literature at checkout counters. Thanks to this consciousness-raising effort, the business community and parents now see literature as deserving of its high priority in school reform.

Materials Development

The materials development facet of the Reading Initiative explains and illustrates the nature of the curriculum reform, for educators as well as for textbook publishers. A blizzard of documents in the form of handbooks, guidelines, advisories, and reading lists, has issued forth from the State Department of Education—all to interpret and make concrete for specific grade levels and categorical programs the central document: the *English Language Arts Framework, K–12*.[1] Written over an eighteen-month period by a group of language arts educators who surveyed hundreds of responses to drafts circulated throughout the state, the *Framework* sets forth the philosophy and rationale for a literature-based, integrated language arts program for *all* students. Essentially, the tenets of the *Framework* are these:

1. A focus on the meanings in high-quality literature. A literature-based program is required because of literature's

   capacity to move the human spirit in any age, to involve students and motivate learning with its appeal to universal feelings and needs, and to elevate common experiences to uncommon meaning. (6–7)

2. The interrelated use of the language arts:

   As the human mind seeks unity among the parts for a wholeness of understanding, so do the English language arts require integrating all the elements of language. (6)

3. The use of instructional strategies which help students from diverse backgrounds relate textual experiences to their life experiences:

   The activities and processes involved in reading good literature, writing about important ideas, and discussing topics which have meaning to their lives help all students, regardless of their heritage or language skills. . . . Teaching strategies that allow students to take active roles in their learning, share ideas with partners and groups, ask questions about what they want to know as well as about what the teacher intends, and write and discuss and make presentations for the class, develop in students the skills they must take with them from school into the rest of their lives. (14)

4. Respect for the teacher as the one who chooses and uses instructional materials:

   The role of the teacher must be highlighted. The whole instructional edifice must be directed to making their complex jobs possible, more worthwhile, easier, more enlightened, and more satisfying while promoting the teachers' natural gifts, insights and skills. (38)

Test Revisions

The third component of the Reading Initiative is the review and revision of all tests used in California schools, beginning with those of

---

1. See the annotated list of publications available together with ordering information at the end of this article.

the California Assessment Program. As teachers shift from a skills-based language arts curriculum to one that is meaning-centered, the assessment of student achievement has had to change. Consequently, revisions are leading us away from multiple-choice tests that use fragments of language toward assessments that call for student response (both oral and written) to whole texts, including complete works of literature.

The writing assessment is well under way, and teachers are supporting it enthusiastically. With the California Assessment Program's unique system of matrix sampling, students write to one of eight different kinds of writing at Grades 8 and 12 (New *Framework*-friendly tests for Grades 3, 6 and 10 are being developed.) The students' writing echoes the kinds of writing found in literature as well as in efferent text. Their writing ranges from the autobiographical incident to the problem/solution paper, from the interpretive to the reflective essay. Writing prompts are used to create communicative situations that call forth the kinds of thinking that define the genre. For example, a prompt for writing an evaluation at Grade 12 might set up the following situation:

> Think about all the literature—stories, novels, poems, plays and essays—you've read this year in your English class. Choose the one you've enjoyed the most.
>
> *Directions for Writing*
>
> Write an essay for your teacher evaluating your favorite literary work. Give reasons for your judgment. Tell your teacher why this work is valuable or not valuable for most high school seniors. Your teacher will use your evaluation in selecting literature for next year's class.
>
> —*Writing Assessment Handbook,*
> *Grade 12,* California Assessment
> Program

Staff Development

The fourth facet of the Initiative is staff development. Since 1985, the CLP has supported a network of teachers, K–12, as they put their interpretations of the *Framework* into practice. The program of professional development for these teachers consists of attendance at a four-week summer institute, located originally at UCLA. (Last summer four of these institutes were held on California State University campuses. Next summer we will again hold four.) Approximately 100 teachers participate in each institute in groups of 20–25. A CLP teacher-leader guides each group.

Who are these teachers? They come from urban, suburban and rural schools throughout California. They teach in neighborhood schools and magnet schools. Their students are in advanced placement classes, in special day classes for the handicapped, in migrant education and Chapter 1 programs. They have been to the Writing Projects and National Endowment of the Arts institutes. They belong to the National Council of Teachers of English, to the International Reading Association, to the National Association for Bilingual Education, or to Teachers of English to Speakers of Other Languages—or their local affiliates.

During the institutes, teachers of students, K–12, read both adult and children's literature, respond to it in a variety of ways, examine their responses, read and discuss literary theory, and construct their own interpretations of the theory and of relevant research findings. The *Framework* and other State Department of Education documents become, in this setting, useful resources. The teachers leave the Institute with the draft of a curriculum plan which embodies their own beliefs about teaching and learning, a plan which they field-test with their own students in the fall. These plans are typically focused on ideas, concepts about human motivations, and dilemmas. The literature that students read and discuss, the stories they write and tell, the field trips they take, the hypotheses they form— all furnish rich, multitextured grist for learning more.

Follow-up support consists of six days over each of the next two school years. The teachers come together regionally during these days to solve problems of implementation, to share results, and to modify teaching strategies in order to improve the chances for student success. Collaboratively, they also seek ways to inspire others throughout their schools and districts with the desire to make reforms.

The Growing Influence of CLP Teachers

As workshops develop and materials multiply and travel across the network, the teachers' influence grows. CLP teachers this past year served on state committees dealing with assessment, selection of textbooks, use of technology, and reviews of the quality of school programs. This year, CLP teachers are developing a series of monographs on issues besetting K–12 teachers of language arts. These will be distributed to the now 744 CLP teachers for use in their work within their own classrooms, schools and districts. Although plans are under way to edit these monographs for a broader readership, they are not yet available to the general public. Instead, they are intended to support CLP teachers by keeping them in touch with each other, by publishing the results of CLP teacher research, and by ensuring that this group of teachers remains informed about current professional developments.

The first of the monograph series is the work of eighteen CLP teachers (Barr 1988). It addresses the issue of buying and using K–8 textbooks recently approved by the State Board for local adoption. Although more publishers heeded the call to include literature in their basal readers, CLP teacher-reviewers found that all of them used literature only as a vehicle for teaching subskills, instead of providing literature as experience, with skills used to make that experience sensible. The monograph describes the features of these texts collectively and specifically and suggests ways to use each constructively; e.g., by using reading logs instead of worksheets, by provoking real student questions rather than using predetermined ones, by using collaborative groupings within a heterogeneous class rather than separating students into achievement-level groups.

Other monographs under development this year will deal with portfolio assessment in a literature-based, integrated language arts classroom; the question of "classics" for *all* students; the ways teachers across the span of levels provide classroom contexts for personal response to literary texts; and emerging literacy.

The Influence of Louise Rosenblatt on the CLP

With the increasing cultural diversity in California classrooms, literature as "lived-through" experience holds special promise. With reading no longer a subject consisting of vocabulary-controlled snippets and stories followed by intrusive, Bloom-taxonomied questions, CLP teachers report that students of all achievement levels are now doing more sustained reading *and* writing *and* discussion when they read literature. Sally Thomas, in the just-published monograph, explains how it works in her sixth-grade classroom:

> I find that *all* students are successful when I teach a core work using "into, through and beyond" activities. Inexperienced and LEP [Limited English Proficiency] students don't need to be sidetracked into skill sheets or extensive reteaching cycles which keep them from the interesting projects or "enrichment" activities. All students actually read in a variety of formats—sometimes I read, they listen or follow along, sometimes the whole class reads,

sometimes pairs read, all students (not just the lower achieving) have turns reading aloud with me or adult volunteers, and students read individually. I try to give choices but still watch that students keep a balance.

All students come to a small group reading session prepared to read aloud a particularly meaningful passage and to share with group members their reasons for choosing that passage. (The resource specialist for special education introduces the reading to her students so that they, too, are prepared for discussion.) I make sure students have many opportunities to keep up with the literature we're reading as a core work, regardless of whether they've actually read every word, through collaborative enactments or visualization activities.

The use of units focused on a theme helps meet the needs of a wide range of students. In selecting the small group extensions, I try to find good literature ranging from easy to challenging. I *never* actually assign an easier selection to a student, but I do make suggestions or give them the opportunity to try out the various choices. Our class discusses what it is that makes a good book. And because the books relate to a central theme, every student contributes to the growing body of information, concepts, and understandings related to that theme.

About assessments of student progress: my students keep writing folders which include drafts of work in progress and finished pieces. I also keep samples and evidence from activities other than writing—story boards, story maps, Venn diagrams, illustrations. Students evaluate finished pieces, using criteria we set together, and occasionally write about overall progress. In folders, students and I maintain a running summary of the writing completed, the strengths and goals for the next assignment. I duplicate samples from reading logs several times a year to illustrate growth. Students, of course, keep their whole logs, and they keep a record of the books they read. (Barr, 10)

As Sally Thomas has explained, the California Literature Project owes much of its success to the work of Louise Rosenblatt, whose theory underpins and continues to inform our efforts. Rosenblatt's emphasis on personal response to the literary experience respects the diversity of human experience present in all classrooms. By trusting the validity of their own experiences, students learn to compare their responses to those of others, thereby widening their worlds. With the meanings of texts understood to grow out of their transactions with them, not in answer keys or their teachers' minds, we know that all students can equip themselves to engage in grand conversations about the humane values and issues only literature evokes.

Pertinent Materials Available from the California State Department of Education

Celebrating the National Reading Initiative. 1988. ISBN 0-8011-0760-1. $6.75

Practices and activities that can be used to promote reading among preschoolers, school-age children, adolescents, and adults are featured. Suggestions for parents, teachers, librarians, and community volunteers are included.

English-Language Arts Framework for California Public Schools, Kindergarten Through Grade Twelve. 1987. ISBN 0-8011-0041-0. $3.00

This document is the pivotal one, and all others are aligned with it. It is designed to provide philosophical direction and perspectives on curriculum and instruction in English-language arts to teachers, school administrators, curriculum planners, and parents throughout the state.

English-Language Arts Model Curriculum Guide, Kindergarten Through Grade Eight. 1988. ISBN 0-8011-0731-8. $3.00

This guide includes information and model lessons for teachers as they design their curriculum plans.

Model Curriculum Standards, Grades Nine Through Twelve, First Edition. 1985. ISBN 0-8011-0252-9. $5.50

The standards in required high school subjects were revised to begin the far-reaching reform called for in 1983 state legislation. These standards are included in this 320 page publication.

Recommended Readings in Literature, Kindergarten Through Grade Eight, Annotated Edition. 1988. ISBN 0-8011-0754-8. $4.50

Compiled by teachers, administrators, curriculum planners, and librarians from throughout the state, this publication contains more than 1000 titles, representing works of fiction, nonfiction, poetry, and drama. Each entry is briefly described.

Note

1. In ordering, make checks payable to California State Department of Education. Remittance or purchase order must accompany order. Purchase orders without checks are accepted only from governmental agencies. Mail to California State Department of Education, P.O. Box 271, Sacramento, CA 95802-0271.

Reference

Barr, Mary A., ed. 1988. The Inside Story about the New K–8 Textbooks and What To Do About Them. No. 1. *CLP Teacher-Leaders Speak Out* Series. Los Angeles, Calif.: California Literature Project.

6. Exploring a Poem

Stephen Dunning
University of Michigan

Sentiment is not a feeling outside the spirit of our honoring of Louise Rosenblatt's *Literature as Exploration*. Nor would I have been asked to join the celebration had I no history with this wonderful book.

My sentimental history, then, begins in 1951 when first I read *Literature as Exploration*. I did so because Dora V. Smith at the University of Minnesota told me to. Perhaps she meant it as a corrective for the annotated bibliography I had just turned in to her course in literature for adolescents. The main work of that course, as I remember, was the reading of a zillion junior books. The written work for that course, as I remember, included what Dora V. called "a book ladder"—a range of books, from easy to difficult, on a given subject or theme; I also remember preparing a lengthy bibliography, numerous books annotated in what I recall as my promising (if yet undeveloped) critical style. If in fact the course and the work were as I remember, then I feel sure I went to Dora V.'s office hour to discuss my bibliography. Reconstructing my probable motives, I presume that with that clock congenital in all grade-grubbers, I was aware that quarter's end and the day of judgment were nigh.

The Appleton-Century-Crofts edition of *Literature as Exploration* was on Dora V.'s desk. Soon it was in my hands. Surely Dora V. thought it might enrich some of my critical judgments. "Read this," she said, gently, firmly. "It's a wonderful book. Borrow my copy, if you don't find it elsewhere."

I found that wonderful book in the library and read it for the first time. I remember being excited and surprised that anyone dared to raise questions about the New Criticism, as though that Truth were revealed by mere mortals. Indeed, even as I read I was getting text-as-text gospel in my English courses. Who is this Rosenblatt? Some kind of subversive?

Still, I read *Literature as Exploration* less well then in 1951 than later in 1957 when the book appeared on a bibliography in Dwight Burton's course at Florida State, whence I had migrated. In the telegram I keep even today among my memorabilia, Professor Burton had asked me, "Come to Tallahassee and head up the Florida High English Department." I arrived in Tallahassee not only to head up, but to be, the English department. (As I remember, there is one woman, Mary Ann Plant, who has had me as her teacher of English six or seven times— eighth through twelfth grades in Tallahassee plus a year at Duke. Ponder how well-educated that woman must be.)

Shortly, in Tallahassee, I was writing that longest of term papers under Dwight Burton's patient direction. The pedagogical shadows of my dissertation were lightened by my second reading of *Literature as Exploration*. Those of you who still cherish copies of my dissertation will want to look again at pages 40 to 42, where, in an effort to describe outstanding practices in English teaching, I characterize Rosenblatt's book as "deeply, perhaps uniquely informed" by both the social sciences and by literary criticism. Of course I quoted lavishly from Rosenblatt. Professor Burton wondered whether my dissertation should be credited to Dunning and Rosenblatt—or in less generous frame of mind, to Rosenblatt and Dunning.

Literature as Exploration was then, for me, as still it is for later readers, a genuinely liberating text. It seemed to argue coherently and convincingly for practices that we young teachers only dared to suspect might greatly improve our teaching of literature.

No wonder I read the book better that second time. As Rosenblatt says in her introduction:[1]

> what readers make of a work will vary with different situations
> and at different times, as they bring diverse preoccupations and
> interests to the text. (vi)

Preoccupied I was, with finishing my dissertation, and interested I was, in borrowing Rosenblatt's authority for my work.

I remember *not* rereading *Literature as Exploration* in the seventies. Oh, I looked at it, and I *should* have reread it, for I had assigned it to students in my master's level course at Michigan. Consider my alibis: I had read the book twice. Moreover, I had my very own copy now, sweet with marginalia. At the same time, I was suffering from excessive professional activity, mainly with NCTE. After all, a person could not do everything. Still, I remember feeling left out from the enthusiastic and rich reading given the book by my students. (Was I, as student, ever so well-prepared?)

Now to this celebration of *Literature as Exploration*. Knowing that the occasion required me to forego sentiment and history in favor of inference and demonstration, I reread Rosenblatt's book, the third edition (1976) and, I think, read the text better than ever I had. What a wonderful and wise book! How well it stands up to slow reading and study! Fifty years since first publication, and it is still fresh and useful—artfully designed to guide the thoughtful reader to good practices in the teaching of literature.

There are no clearer messages in *Literature as Exploration* than that readers must be helped to bring their own responses to the text, that the teacher's first job is seeing that that happens, and that it is in the interaction between the reader and the page that the real text is written. My focus now is on the implications of these messages for the teaching of poetry. (I believe Louise Rosenblatt would agree that there are as many texts of *Literature as Exploration* as there are readers of that text.)

So what text did I write in rereading *Literature as Exploration?* The book weaves together ideas from pedagogy, from the social sciences, and from literary criticism. Remember:

> A poem . . . remains merely inkspots on paper until a reader transforms them into a set of meaningful symbols. [The poem] exists in the live circuit set up between reader and text: the reader infuses intellectual and emotional meanings into the pattern of verbal symbols, and those symbols channel his thoughts and feelings. Out of this complex process emerges a more or less organized imaginative experience. (25)

Does that sound like fifty years ago, during the heyday of the New Criticism? Rereading *Literature as Exploration* for this paper, I transformed those inkspots like crazy, infusing intellectual and emotional meanings all over the place.

True? Yes, and for good reasons. For one, during the last ten years of my teaching at Michigan I regularly taught the introduction to poetry course; for another, I practiced writing poems, almost daily, for a good long stretch; and for a third, the real reason, I had an early November date to teach poetry to a third grade in Oakland County. Why not try to *do Literature as Exploration* with those third graders? They could not damage me, could they? Much? I mean, eight years old?

From all there is to feed on in *Literature as Exploration*, I most relish Rosenblatt's pedagogic principles. I put this quote from her in front of me and went to work, preparing for the third graders and for you.

> The interest in inductive methods of teaching at that time also led me to differentiate between the old method, whereby leading

questions were aimed at preordained conclusions, and my view, that "the most fruitful inductive learning arises out of the involvement of the student ... which leads him to raise personally meaningful questions ... [and] to seek in the text the basis for valid answers and the impetus to further inquiry." (ix–x)

Then I found this quote, in the middle of a restless night:

The problem that the teacher faces first of all, then, is the creation of a situation favorable to a vital experience of literature. (61)

Some Transactions in a Third-Grade Classroom

Truly, had I space, I would attempt to explore with you instead of reporting on my exploration with third graders. But captive in this tiny space of a handful of pages I am forced to report:

The scene: Scotch Elementary School in Oakland County, Michigan, a couple of weeks ago. Two third-grade teachers are sitting in with the students of one of them. The other teacher is, fortunately for me, taking notes, ostensibly so that she can share my, uh, techniques with other teachers. Supposedly, I am "model teaching."

Me (smiling): "Early this morning I drove by farms coming here. I saw barns and farmhouses and animals. What animals do you think I saw?"

Most students: Garble, garble, shout, shout.

Me: "Whoa! One at a time. Someone whose hand is up."

Individual students: Horses. Cows. Pigs. Chickens. Horses.

Melissa: "I already said that."

Me: "Remember, I need hands. Any other animals?"

Charles: "Wasn't it too dark to see?"

Me (thinking): Bingo, little rascal

(Aloud): "Well, yes, it was dark. What animals might I see on a farm now, when it's light?"

Students give a good list, including cats, dogs, ducks, geese, and a goat. Melissa tells about her brother shooting crows on her Uncle's farm. Cheyenne says that we're having meatloaf for lunch. Another girl tells about a donkey ride. She can't remember the word for donkey, but classmates help her. Then it turns out that the donkey ride was at a carnival. Charles points out that a carnival isn't a farm.

Me: "Let me ask a different question. Answer courteously now, giving everyone a turn. When I was eight or nine I had a chicken named Eleazor. I'd feed Eleazor and talk to him. Do any of you talk to animals? Do they ever talk back?"

Students: Many answers. One said, "I can tell what they're thinking."

Me: "Did the pets ever talk back?"

Students: "Yes." "No." "Not really."

Me: "Have you ever been to a zoo?"

Significant error. The whole class had made a field trip to the zoo two weeks earlier. So we had five minutes of talking-to-animals-at-the-zoo testimony. I hung in there, interrupting with questions. "What noises did the animals make? Do animals talk to each other? To themselves?"

They turned themselves back to conversations with their own and their neighbors' pets. Cats and dogs figured most prominently, but the range of child-animal conversations included those with ants and fish. Taking turns without my calling on them, half the class told stories.

I led them back to the farm. My main interruptions were such specifying questions as, "What exactly did you say to the frog?"

Then I put this poem on the overhead:

When Did the World Begin?

"When did the world begin, and how?"
I asked a lamb, a goat, a cow:
"What's it all about and why?"
I asked a hog as he went by.
"Where will the whole thing end and when?"
I asked a duck, a goose, a hen:
And I copied all the answers too:
A quack, a honk, an oink, a moo.
       —Robert Clairmont

We read the poem several ways—me aloud, first. Then me reading the questions, and the children in casual unison reading the other five lines. I asked them to tell me what this poem reminded them of. I had probably blunted their responses here, lingering too long on their "talking with animals" stories. But they forgave me, and, keying off the last line, I presume, talked interestingly about the sounds of various animals. We weren't sure we could distinguish some sounds. What sound does a lamb make? Now what sound does a goat make? It is also true that we were hard pressed to differentiate all the honks, quacks, and other cluckings of various barnyard fowls.

Someone (not Melissa): "Not all the animals answered questions."

Me (alert to the chance): "Oho! Good noticing. How many animals are in the poem?" (Six. Four. Seven.) "Name the animals." (They did.)

Charles (bored, to the boy sitting alongside): "Baa, baa."

Me (looking closely again): "How many animals are there? And how many answers?"

Melissa: "Do you count the person?"

Another girl: "The person isn't an animal."

Melissa: "Well. . . ." (General discussion.)

A boy: "Animals can't answer those questions."

Me: "What do you mean about the questions? What are they like?"

General discussion: "The questions are dumb." "The questions are hard." "They sound like questions in church." (I highlighted *it* and *the whole thing* in the second and third questions of the poem. These were first said to be "a farm" and then later, "life.")

Children soon lost interest in the questions posed in the poem. They remained quite interested in how many animals were in the poem, in my contention that "I" (the character who asks animals those dumb questions) need not be the poet, Robert Clairmont, and most of all in the fact that only four animals gave answers.

The children's regular teacher (alert to the clock): "Everybody copy the poem, so we can read it later, if we want. Try to get it exactly right."

Nine children in chorus: "Do we have to do cursive?"

Charles (prepared to be bored, to the boy sitting alongside): "Baa, baa."

Teacher: "Cursive or print. But copy it exactly, so we can talk about it some more."

Me (aside to teacher): "Do you have gold stars, or smiley faces?" (Yes)

Me (to children): "Boys and girls, after you've copied the poem, how about naming the animals that don't give answers? Is that clear?"

Eleven children: "No."

But they helped me make it clear, and they liked the detective work. Together we read the poem aloud; those finished with their copying read from their own texts. And suddenly time *was* gone.

At the door I got notes from five or six children. My favorite was from Cheyenne. "Dear Mr. Dunning. (My name was on the board.) I like the way you moo. Call me on the telephone."

> "What then happens in the reading . . . ?" [asks Rosenblatt]
>
> [T]he text brings into the reader's consciousness certain concepts, certain sensuous experiences, certain images of things, people, actions, scenes. The special meanings and, more particularly, the submerged associations that these words and images have for the individual reader will largely determine what the work communicates to *him*. (30)

What were the better "special meanings" of our lesson? I would claim that most students were significantly involved and had a pleasurable time with a poem. At least I did not make the poem, in Rosenblatt's words,

> something to summarize or analyze or define, something to identify as one might identify the different constellations on a star map or define the qualities of a particular chemical element. (59)

I agree with Rosenblatt that "emphasis on abstract verbalization, on intellectual concepts cut off from their roots in concrete sensuous experience, is destructive of responsiveness to literature" (50–51). Nor am I one of those teachers who would deny that the individual's ability to read and enjoy literature is the primary aim of literary study (65).

The worst aspect of the lesson? My inability, under the gun, to divorce myself from what I realized too late was my agenda. Rosenblatt says:

> First is the necessity not to impose a set of preconceived notions about the proper way to react to any work. The student must be free to grapple with his own reaction. (66)

My agenda required that students react, and so I insisted on their providing reactions. Certainly I moved the discussion toward the questions in the poem—an aspect less interesting to the children than to me. Had I set aside my preconceived notions, there would have been more baa-ing and quacking. And had I had the wit, we might have had interesting conversations on how we humans represent animal talk in writing. That is, in cursive.

My ineptness aside, what other "special meanings" were "communicated" to these children? Baa-baa Charley learned that chickens do not say cock-a-doodle-do. Ann, even more into animal sounds than Charley, certainly upgraded the sonority of her bleat over the course of the hour. Less frivolously, I suspect that in the future several class members might somewhat more confidently face visits to farms and to poems.

I move to conclusion through Louise Rosenblatt's fifty-year-ago adumbration of my recent effort to explore with third graders:

> The teacher . . . must be ready to face the fact that the student's reactions will inevitably be in terms of his own temperament and background. Undoubtedly these may often lead him to do injustice to the text. *Nevertheless, the student's primary experience of the work will have had meaning for him in those personal terms and no others.* No matter how imperfect or mistaken, this will constitute the present meaning of the work for him, rather than anything he docilely repeats about it. (51, italics added.)

I seek a metaphor. We learn much, comparing the unknown to the known. Our first question about almost anything foreign is, "What is it like?" My surest beliefs about poetry writing are metaphors: Writing is swimming the Australian crawl. Starting a poem is starting a car on ice. To transform experience into poetry, one abandons the hometown and wanders the triggering town. To write a poem is to invent a jungle and inhabit it.

Exploring "Other Towns," Experiencing Other Texts

My failure to find a perfect metaphor, here, is in part Louise Rosenblatt's fault. For indeed it is she who explains why the word "exploration" is part of her title:

> The word *exploration* is designed to suggest primarily that the experience of literature, far from being for the reader a passive process of absorption, is a form of intense personal activity. (v)

Moreover, Rosenblatt insists on the connections between literature and its origins in the social sciences. It is a special quality of *Literature as Exploration* that it is resonant with understandings from the social sciences. Louise Rosenblatt reminds teachers of their responsibilities to be somewhat informed and to be fully authentic as students translate their responses to literature, as surely students will, into their own social and cultural terms. So from Rosenblatt's gloss on exploration and from her concern for the social sciences, I am going to say that reading *Literature as Exploration* well is, for me, like working with a perfectly scaled map.

I think first of the text as a highway map. This small-scale map, one inch to thirty-five miles, gives highways, cities, major bodies of water, and occasional national parks. I notice some subtleties: the thick highways seem designed to go directly from here to there; the skinny ones tend to curl and roam around. I can tell from focusing in down here that if I stay on Interstate 80, I need not go into downtown Youngstown at all.

A good map for a fast trip. Not wonderful for exploring.

The map of Metro Detroit has a somewhat larger scale. One inch to less than four miles. Here's Metro Airport. And tiny Grand Prix airport, too. Tiger Stadium. Up here near Southfield, Sarah Fisher Children's Home. Right about there, Scotch Elementary School. Melissa, and her meatloaf. Charley. Cheyenne. I read this map about as well as I read *Literature for Exploration* at the time of my dissertation.

A map of a section of Ontario province is yet of grander scale. One inch to less than a mile. Here is the lake known as Bobbiwash, heaven on earth. I have explored, responded to, experienced this text. There, a hundred yards below the deserted fire tower, is where we saw fresh scat of bear. And the mile-long portage from Ten Mile to Dollyberry? Our fifth portage that Tuesday. Day-long drizzle. The parka my son-in-law lent me leaked down both arms and in back. Pete and I were whipped. Well, I was whipped. Mud up to my butt, my right shoulder sliced in two by the strap from the food pack.

"How come I always get the food pack, Pete?" (He stares, uncomprehendingly.) "OK, OK, you always carry the canoe."

Pete never seems to tire. How is that? He must be tired. Ah, but he can't show it, eh? "Is that it, Pete? You're dying inside, so naturally you smile like a Buddha." Right here, where we slid our canoe down the face of the rock, we met the two Canadians. The only humans we'd seen in a week. Fishing, they say.

Oh, really? They aren't fishing, Pete. Nor have they fish, so far as I can see. The slender one, Pete, his eyes don't focus. Are your afraid, too? Pete, answer: Are you afraid?

Now, reading *Literature as Exploration* is, for me, like reading the map that gets me to Bobbiwash. Having experienced that trip to Bobbiwash, I respond fully to its map. Having been there, trying to teach literature, I feel the truth of *Literature as Exploration*. It has that generous scale I need in order to teach literature well.

Alan Purves says that *Literature as Exploration* is "a timely warning." Purves is afraid that the teaching of literature may pull back to where "the individuality and creativity of the teacher will be stifled, where the emotions will be neglected, where the detachment will replace commitment" (iv).

Is that a danger? A present reality?

Why aren't all of us paying closer attention?

So hurry! Everybody! Read and reread *Literature as Exploration*. Spread the word! For fifty years this accurate, richly scaled guide, working the topographies of principle and practice, has been in our glove compartments. It is time we get it out again. Walk it. Do a little exploring. And time we took our students along.

Note

1. All page references are to Rosenblatt, Louise M. [1938] 1976. *Literature as Exploration*. 3rd Ed. New York: Noble and Noble.

C. *Literature as Exploration* and the Research Tradition

More than any other work, save possibly I. A. Richards' *Practical Criticism, Literature as Exploration* alerted scholars and researchers concerned with literary education to the importance of analyzing the responses of readers—not of placing focus on the text itself, or on the author, or on the cultural epoch in which it was written, not even on teaching strategies, but on the responses of readers. First educational researchers, then developmental and cognitive psychologists, finally literary theorists have studied responses from many points of view, with the result that a substantial body of knowledge has become available to guide classroom practice. In the papers that follow, Richard Beach summarizes findings from more important studies, while Arthur Applebee and Alan C. Purves discuss research either presently under way or presently contemplated. Two annotated bibliographies from The Center for the Learning and Teaching of Literature are provided at the end of the monograph, following Louise M. Rosenblatt's reminiscences on the early history of her volume.

7. Fostering Literary Understanding: The State of the Schools

Arthur N. Applebee
University at Albany
State University of New York

On the occasion of this 50th anniversary of *Literature as Exploration*, we need to ask what our schools are doing to foster the kinds of literary understanding that Louise Rosenblatt called for in 1938. Yet when we turn to look at instruction in literature, we find that the last systematic examination of school programs was Squire and Applebee's national study, conducted between 1963 and 1965 and published in 1968. We know little about how literature instruction has fared through the succeeding decades.

To provide a fuller picture of the state of literature instruction, the Center for the Learning and Teaching of Literature is carrying out a series of studies of various aspects of the curriculum. These studies will include examination of the book-length works that are taught, analyses of high school literature anthologies, and surveys of current practice and approaches.

One of our first studies for the Center for the Learning and Teaching of Literature was designed to provide an initial context for framing the most pressing questions in the teaching of literature (Applebee, 1989a). To do this, we examined the teaching of English in the classrooms of teachers whose departments have local reputations for excellence as perceived by other teachers, by university professors concerned with education, and by other education professionals. Such departments have usually built their reputations over many years and are likely to reflect the best of conventional theory and practice, though they are not necessarily centers of experiment and change. The issues that

Preparation of this article was supported in part by grant number G009720278 from the Department of Education, Office of Educational Research and Improvement, and from the National Endowment for the Arts, to support the Center for the Learning and Teaching of Literature. However, the opinions expressed do not necessarily reflect the position or policy of the funding agencies, and no official endorsement should be inferred.

emerge in such programs should help to define how well current theory and practice in the teaching of literature work, as well as areas that may need further development.

To briefly summarize our approach, we solicited the cooperation of colleagues in different regions in the United States to visit seventeen schools that had been identified as having local reputations for outstanding programs in English. In each area we identified schools that served differing populations (e.g., urban, suburban). During the spring and fall of 1988, each school was visited by two observers, one of whom was based in English or in Education at a local university, the other of whom was a local teacher who could provide a practitioner's perspective. Both observers were selected for their expertise in, and commitment to, the teaching of English.

To guide the observations and provide for structure and consistency across the school sites, we developed a large collection of instruments which built upon, but did not seek to directly replicate, the instruments used by Squire and Applebee (1968). The instruments included classroom observation schedules; teacher interview questions; department head interview questions; questionnaires for department heads, teachers, and librarians; checklists of library titles; and questionnaires that asked twelfth-grade students about their reading experiences and their courses in English. The observations were structured so that they could be completed in approximately two days of visits at each school, involving a total of 145 hours of classroom observation, 200 English teachers, and 600 students.

As we had intended in our selection of schools, we found that all of the schools had a well-trained and professional staff of English teachers, some 69 percent of whom had an MA or higher degree. The teachers averaged over fifteen years of teaching experience and reported regular conference attendance and professional reading. As a group, they had clearly given thought and attention to their curriculum in English. Hardly "representative" of English departments nationally, the departments in these schools should reflect how current theory and approaches in the teaching of literature work themselves out in actual practice. At the same time, the issues raised by the teachers, students, and observers in these schools should help to define important issues that need to be addressed as we plan for further improvement in the teaching of literature.

Issues in the Teaching of Literature

The various instruments used in this study provided a wealth of detailed information about instruction in the seventeen schools.

Looking across the broad set of results, however, one sees that a series of issues emerged that were noted by observers, teachers, and department heads alike.

1. *We need to revitalize literature and instruction for nonacademic students.* It was clear from the teachers' comments as well as the observers' reports that the classes that impressed them most were those targeted at the college-bound. These were the programs cited with most pride by teachers and department chairs; these were the classes that produced the award-winning students and high SAT scores; these were the students who earned newspaper reports and favorable publicity for the school and department. When there were successes with the nonacademic students (and we saw a number of highly successful classrooms in our visits), they tended to be attributed to individual outstanding teachers—not to the structure and organization of the curriculum that had been developed for the students.

The students for whom programs were most successful were those most like their teachers. College-bound students' suggestions for books to read and for titles that they had found personally significant, paralleled their teachers' tastes. The nonacademic students, on the other hand, diverged from their teachers in the newspapers, books, and magazines they preferred to read. Thus the two most popular authors for the college-bound students were Shakespeare and Hemingway; for the nonacademic, Stephen King and Judy Blume.

The net result is that the students who need the most help get the least attention in curriculum planning and curriculum revision.

2. *We need to reconcile approaches to literature with approaches to composition.* In the schools we studied, recent discussions of process-oriented approaches to writing instruction were widely recognized. Teachers were familiar with the issue, and had developed a new technical vocabulary to discuss them. This led to a vitality and liveliness in discussions of approaches to writing instruction, even when teachers had ultimately decided that process-oriented approaches were not appropriate for their classes.

At the same time, there was widespread adherence to traditional approaches to literature: this included continuing attention to the traditional canon of texts, emphasis on New Critical techniques of textual analysis, and a pattern of classroom discussion that usually involved leading students toward a received, canonical interpretation. This traditional approach to literature seemed overly text-centered to many teachers and observers, but the profession has offered few clearly worked out alternatives to consider. Indeed, Rosenblatt's (1938) proposals remain the most frequently cited alternative.

In many classrooms, the result was a conflict in orientation and approach, with student-centered, process-oriented writing instruction coexisting with teacher-centered, text-oriented literature instruction. Teachers often recognized the conflict, but there are few models to sharpen the debate about literature instruction in the way that process-oriented approaches have sharpened the debate about writing instruction. Teachers lacked an accepted vocabulary to talk about the process of literary understanding and its relationship to instruction.

3. *We need to strike a more appropriate balance in our selections of texts to study.* In the majority of these schools, instruction was dominated by the literary anthology. At all grade levels and for all genres, the curriculum emphasized traditional selections of British and American literature, with only token attention to world literature, contemporary literature, minority literature, or selections by women. The narrowness of the curriculum was particularly obvious in a separate study of book-length works taught in a national sample of public schools, grades 9–12 (Applebee, 1989b). The most popular titles were:

Romeo and Juliet

Macbeth

The Adventures of Huckleberry Finn

Julius Caesar

To Kill a Mockingbird

The Scarlet Letter

Of Mice and Men

Hamlet

The Great Gatsby

Lord of the Flies

All but one of these selections was written by a white, Anglo-Saxon, male author.

4. *We need to develop a theory of the teaching and learning of literature to guide the rethinking of high school instruction.* Recent developments in literary theory have for the most part ignored pedagogical issues, and teachers in these schools have found little in current theory to revitalize their instructional approaches. Most remain largely unaware of movements such as structuralism, feminist criticism, deconstruction, or recent developments in reader-response theory. Instead, they rely, in planning the curriculum as well as in day-to-day instruction,

on genres and periods as organizing devices, sometimes integrated with broad "themes," and on New Critical approaches to individual texts.

The teachers' neglect of contemporary critical theory may be appropriate, since most of these movements have given little attention to pedagogical issues, even at the college level. Yet the neglect creates an unusual disjunction between scholarship and instruction, leaving a need for a broader theory of literature learning and instruction to fill the current void.

5. *We need to provide supportive institutional contexts for our programs in literature.* The teachers in these successful English programs did not work alone. The best programs were characterized by strong departmental leadership and by administrators who trusted the professionalism of the teaching staff. Most of the schools could also boast of abundant materials and resources, both within the departments and within the schools as a whole. When resources were lacking, as they were in some of the inner-city schools we studied, the problem of how to obtain them came to dominate almost all discussions.

The issues being raised here define a large and important agenda for the profession. When we can offer programs which more effectively engage our nonacademic students, which reconcile currently conflicting approaches to literature and composition, which are based on a richer theory of the learning and teaching of literature, and which exist within a supportive professional environment, we will have come a long way toward the goals that Louise Rosenblatt articulated so well so long ago.

References

Applebee, Arthur N. 1989a. *The Teaching of Literature in Programs with Reputations for Excellence in English.* Technical Report 1.1. Albany, N.Y.: Center for the Learning and Teaching of Literature.

———. 1989b. *A Study of Book-Length Works Taught in High School English Courses.* Technical Report 1.2. Albany, N.Y.: Center for the Learning and Teaching of Literature.

Squire, James R., and Roger K. Applebee. 1968. *High School English Instruction Today.* New York: Appleton-Century-Crofts.

8. New Directions in Research on Response to Literature

Richard Beach
University of Minnesota

I ask you to envision the typical literature classroom of 1938. The teacher is lecturing on the moral virtues implicit in a Shakespeare play. The students are gazing longingly out the window, recalling the last Tom Mix western, or an ominous newsreel film of Adolf Hitler at the local Bijou.

It was in 1938 that Louise Rosenblatt produced her book *Literature as Exploration.* Despite the innovative rhetoric of the Progressive era and the Hatfield Experience Curriculum, much of literature instruction at that time was based on the desire to present didactic lessons regarding good behavior and to impart the virtues of literary classics—methods that emphasized the teacher's priviledged interpretation at the expense of students' expression of their own responses.

Given this somewhat antiquated context, *Literature as Exploration* was both pioneering and iconoclastic. It is in the spirit of our honoring the innovative nature of Louise M. Rosenblatt's work that I review some of the current research in response to literature.

In compiling with Susan Hynds the annotative bibliography, *Research on Response to Literature: A Selected Bibliography,* I noted a number of distinct trends that reflect certain assumptions about the nature of response, assumptions that first saw the light of day in the 1938 *Literature as Exploration.* In this chapter, I will summarize some of these trends, cite some studies illustrating each trend, and draw some possible implications for teaching literature.

Response as a Process of Discovering Meaning through Talking and Writing

Much of literature instruction assumes that "meaning" occurs at defined "snapshot" moments at the completion of a text. In this "read-

and-respond" scenario, students complete the text and then state some definitive meaning for it.

However, recent response research, paralleling composition research, finds that students have difficulty generating sudden "snapshot" insights about a text. Rather, they gradually discover insights through articulation, reflection, and application of related experiences or texts (Beach, in press; Marshall 1987; Rogers 1987). Through informal writing or discussion, particularly with others, students use their initial reactions, conceptions, or autobiographical connections to lead them to discover novel insights about a text.

Consistent with the idea of talking- or writing-to-learn, this research documents both readers' use of oral and writing strategies to define meanings as well as their recognition of the value of these strategies.

Think-Alouds Encourage Complex Thought

Susan Lytle's (1982) research on students' think-alouds, for example, documents the complex thought-processes involved in orally exploring meanings. In doing a think-aloud, a student goes through a text on a line-by-line basis, and expresses his or her responses much as a sports commentator describes the events of a game. The teacher or peer, as audience, provides verbal and nonverbal encouragement.

One of Lytle's essential findings is that students need ample time to explore initial responses to texts, particularly more difficult texts. Prior to making any interpretations, students in their think-alouds often devoted considerable time to expressing their emotional reactions, sorting out and clarifying their conceptions, or coping with difficulties in understanding meanings. And the more students were willing to explore their own responses, the more insightful were their interpretations. Moreover, as they learned to use the think-alouds, less able students developed a sense of self-confidence in their ability to express their own thoughts, and, more importantly, to trust the validity of those thoughts.

Think-alouds with pairs of students, conducted prior to small- or large-group discussion, may help students articulate their initial responses in preparation for the discussion.

Oral Interpretation Enhances Language Articulation

Oral interpretation of literature also serves to foster response. In particular, by assuming the voice of a narrator or character, a reader adopts a "literary" use of language, through which he or she discovers meanings. In his analysis of readers' retelling or recalling of stories, Jerome Bruner (1986) focused on instances of shifts in verb tense to the subjunctive mood as well as on other transformations of language that occurred through retelling or recalling (Labov 1972; Pratt 1976). For example, rather than recalling an action as "The boy sat on the front porch," a reader would recall that act as, "The boy was sitting on the front porch," a shift in tense that mimics the writer's initial intention to "set the scene" in a narrative, as in, "I was just sitting there minding my own business, when all of a sudden . . ." In making these shifts and transformations, readers were incorporating, according to Bruner, the language of the text into their own language. In an analysis of three children's retellings, Daniel Hade (1988) found similar evidence of extensive transformations, suggesting that the children were acquiring literary language through recalling or retelling.

Extended Writing Fosters Higher Levels of Interpretation

Extended writing about texts also fosters response. In his 1987 study, James Marshall found that writing a series of extended essays about some Salinger short stories fostered higher levels of interpretation than did short-answer questions or no writing. A key factor here was time. By writing a series of essays over time about the same stories, students were able to formulate and test out their hypotheses about the stories across the essays.

Interestingly, the students in a group which did no writing did better than those students in a group which wrote responses only to short answer questions. Marshall argues that these short answer questions—"Who is the main character?" "What is the setting?" and so forth, tend to fragment students' attention, sending them off in different directions. In contrast, continuous writing about the same ideas may help students consolidate their ideas.

Writing in the Personal Mode Produces Higher Levels of Interpretation

Within the extended writing essay group, Marshall found no significant differences between the formal and the personal analytic essays. To compare the effects of those two different kinds of writing, Newell, Suszynski, and Weingart (1989) asked tenth-grade students to write essay responses to two short stories in either a personal, "reader-based" mode or in a formal, "text-based" mode. In the personal essays, students elaborated on their personal interpretations, using their own experiences and text elements, while in the formal mode they interpreted only the text elements. Students writing in the personal mode produced essays judged to be significantly higher in quality in terms of level of interpretation than students writing in the formal mode. In writing in the personal mode, students were more likely to address the teacher in terms of a teacher/learner dialogue, adopting a tentative, exploratory stance. In contrast, in writing in a formal mode, students were more likely to perceive the teacher as examiner, adopting a more definitive stance consistent with conveying the "right interpretation." Thus, writing in a reader-based mode encouraged students to consider the meaning and significance of story elements, resulting in some elaboration of their point of view. And, because they could explore their thoughts in a less definitive manner, the students were more willing to entertain optional perspectives and possibilities of meaning.

Autobiographical Responses Enhance Discovery of Meaning

Readers may also discover meaning by relating their own autobiographical experiences to texts. In my own research (Beach, in press), I examined college students' journal responses to determine the degree to which students' autobiographical responses were related to the students' level of interpretation of a series of short stories. Confirming the results of Petrosky's (1981) study, I found that the more students elaborated on their own evoked autobiographical experiences in their journals, the more likely that they would explore the significance, or point, of their autobiographical experience. In some cases, students would simply recall a related experience in abbreviated shorthand—for example, in responding to Updike's "A & P," "This reminds me of the time I worked in a grocery store." In other cases, by elaborating on their narratives, they began to define their own attitudes and beliefs about that experience. Having defined the personal significance or point of their own experience, they were then able to use that experience to illuminate the significance or point of the story.

All of this suggests that informal, personal writing fosters insights into literature. One limitation of formal essay writing is that it lies a predetermined stance or hypothesis; for example, "Prove that Willy Loman is a tragic hero." In contrast, informal writing, by implying a tentative, spontaneous, and exploratory stance, encourages students to discover meaning through their writing.

Emotional Response as Related to Interpretation

It is often assumed that students' emotional responses are irrelevant to understanding a text, a superfluous frill that has little to do with the cognitive, hard-nosed business of interpretation. However, some recent research suggests that readers' emotional responses are essential to understanding a text (Golden & Guthrie 1986; Nell 1988; Sadoski, Goetz, & Kangiser 1988). Literary texts evoke meanings associated with familiar emotions—desire, envy, sorrow, fear, jealousy, remorse, anger, and so forth (Opdahl 1988). For example, in reading a description of a character experiencing the death of a spouse, readers imagine that character's grief, thus gaining an understanding of the nature of bereavement. At the same time, by relating their own emotional experiences of grief to the text, they gain insight into the character's grief.

Differences between Male and Female Response

For various reasons, readers differ considerably in their ability to empathize. Research on gender differences and response by Bleich (1986), Flynn (1986), and others, suggests that females are often more likely than males to empathize with characters' experiences. Consistent with Carol Gilligan's (1982) research on moral reasoning, females often consider the consequences and the implications of actions on social relationships. They may therefore adopt a range of different characters' perspectives in order to apply what Gilligan calls an "ethics of relationships." In contrast, males are more likely to want to "dominate" the text, placing the text at arm's length without empathizing with different characters' perspectives.

To help students, particularly males, to learn to empathize with a text, teachers could model or demonstrate ways of entertaining characters' perspectives, as well as the differences between their own and the characters' perspectives. Adopting characters' roles in role-playing sessions, and then discussing their feelings about assuming those roles, can help students learn to empathize with characters' perspectives (Heathcote 1980).

"Text-Bound" versus "Intertextual" Meaning

Much literature instruction assumes that readers experience texts as discrete, autonomous entities. However, some research suggests that readers understand texts in terms of evoked "intertextual" literary knowledge (Beach, Appleman & Dorsey, in press; Lehr 1988; Rogers 1987). With each new text, readers apply an evolving literary "data-bank" of prior literary experiences, learning to "read resonantly" (Wolf 1988). By learning to conceive of texts as representative of certain types or genres ("poems," "allegories," "mysteries," and so on), or of text aspects in terms of prototypical concepts ("villain," "happy ending," "foreboding event," and so forth), readers learn to evoke prior knowledge of related literary experiences. However, in her dissertation research, Rogers (1987) found that ninth-grade students employed few, if any, intertextual links—nor had their teachers encouraged such links.

Freewriting, Reading, and Small-Group Discussions
Encourage Intertextual Links

In our own research with eighth graders (Beach, Appleman, & Dorsey, in press), students did some freewriting about a story and then drew a map portraying their conceptions of the story. They then connected parts of the map, defined the nature of the similarities, and used these links to explain the characters' actions. We found that the more students elaborated about related character attributes in their free-writing and on their maps, the higher the quality of their final explanations of the characters' actions in the current text. Defining similarities between the past and current stories helped the students apply knowledge of prototypical literary meanings.

We also found that the more stories they read, the richer their intertextual links, which, in turn, related to the quality of their interpretation of the story. These results are consistent with studies by Svensson (1985) and Thomson (1987) who found that the amount of prior reading of literature is related to secondary students' level of interpretation.

Students may learn to define intertextual links in small-group discussions. Analysis of fifth-grade discussion groups indicated that mention of one text often triggered recollections of related texts according to similarities in genres, topics, or emotional experiences (Cox, Beach & Many, in preparation). Students were also motivated to contribute their own recollections by the need for social membership in the group.

This research on intertextual linking suggests the value of continually relating current texts to past texts so that students build a sense of their own histories as readers (Wolf 1988). Students could also use a journal, index cards, or even a computer datafile, such as the Macintosh Hypercard system, to develop their own personal or class "literary databank" or "hypertext" (Barrett 1988; Tchudi 1988).

Attitudes and Response

Researchers have also been examining the relationship between readers' attitudes and their responses. For example, I examined the influence of attitudes about education on responses to a story (Beach 1983). Students who held more "traditional" attitudes towards instruction responded more negatively than did "liberal" students to a teacher character employing "liberal" teaching methods.

In another study examining how attitudes towards police power influenced responses to "Corner" by Frank Conroy, a poem portraying a young man's reactions to a policeman's observation of his behavior, responses of members of a suburban police department were compared with those of a group of university students (Beach & de Beaugrande 1987). As a group, members of the police force espoused, as expected, more positive attitudes towards police power than did the students. In responding to the poem, the police frequently used a bureaucratic style typical of a crime report: "Vagrant loitering on street corner. Intercepted by patrolman on duty." In contrast, the students couched their response in language such as "heavy-duty pig cop harassing poverty-stricken street person," conceptions that reflect the differences between the two groups' attitudes.

Using Attitudes to Judge Characters' Behavior
Promotes Textual Understanding

Dorfman (1985) and Jose and Brewer (1984) have examined how readers use their attitudes to infer the point of a story, research described as "just-ending" research. As illustrated by the example of "The Tortoise and the Hare," a reader attributes positive and negative meanings to the tortoise and the hare—positive ones to the tortoise for his persistent, prodding attitude and negative ones to the hare for his cocky arrogance. Similarly, a reader attributes positive and negative meanings to the story's resolution—positive ones to the fact that the tortoise wins through persistence and the hare loses through indolence—a just ending. From equating a positive character trait with a positive resolution, a reader then infers the point or message: persistence pays off. Thus, learning to apply one's attitudes to judging characters and resolutions helps readers understand stories.

Response to Characters Reinforces Attitudes

In addition to examining how readers apply their attitudes, researchers are also interested in how the act of responding, as a cultural
process, serves to shape, reaffirm, verify, or challenge attitudes.

In an important study entitled *Reading the Romance,* Janice Radway
(1984) examined women readers' response to romance novels. Some of
these women were reading four or five romances a week. As reflected
in interview responses, these women's positive response to the
"nurturing" heroine roles served to verify their attitudes towards their
own culturally-constituted roles as housewives. In these novels, the
heroine transforms the impersonal, cold, sometimes violent male hero
into a more caring type, all, of course, within the confines of a
patriarchical cultural context. Empathizing with the sex-role portrayals of women found in most romance novels serves to reinforce rather
than challenge women's traditional attitudes. (In a replication of the
Radway study with adolescent females, Willinsky and Hunniford
[1986] found similar results.) Radway's findings provide one explanation for the enormous popularity of movies such as *Dirty Dancing,* an
idealized version of the female-transforms-male story line that verifies
the female as nurturer. This research suggests that through responding, we define our attitudes and beliefs and ultimately ourselves. As
Rosenblatt has consistently suggested, response is a cultural act or event.

Readers' Responses as Constituted by
Varying Stances and Orientations

In responding to texts, readers are constantly shifting their stances or
orientations, depending on the social relationship with the text. For
example, in responding to the romance novel, readers with a feminist
orientation may adopt a critical stance, rejecting the world view and
values implied by the romance novel.

A series of studies (Hunt & Vipond 1985; Vipond & Hunt, in press)
have examined the influence of "information-driven," "story-driven,"
and "point-driven" orientations on response. From an "information-
driven" orientation (similar to Rosenblatt's efferent reading), a reader
reads primarily to extract information. From a story-driven orientation, a reader reads primarily for the enjoyment of the text, the
vicarious experience of living through the story. And, from a point-
driven orientation, a reader reads for the point. By "point," Hunt and
Vipond do not mean the gist, theme, or moral. They mean the social
activity of collaborating or making contact with a narrator or author in
order to understand the teller's motives.

Hunt and Vipond (in press) found that, in responding to the John Updike story "A & P," many students who had adopted a "story-driven" orientation responded negatively to the story because they had difficulty understanding the descriptive details, which they tellingly viewed as "pointless." In contrast, students who read the story from a point-driven orientation could infer the purpose for Updike's use of description. Readers may also vary orientations, from adopting a story-driven orientation while reading, to assuming a point-driven orientation after reading.

Hunt and Vipond find that many secondary and college students read from a story-driven orientation. As a result, they may have difficulty entering into a "dialogic" relationship with a text, one in which they define their own response and purpose as related to their perception of an author's or speaker's purpose or motives (Vipond, Hunt, Jewett, & Reither, in press). At the same time, many secondary students perceive a disparity between their own "story-driven" orientation and the "information-driven" orientation implied by worksheet/short-answer questions (Hynds 1989).

Response as a Learned Social Activity

It is often assumed that response is a private, solitary matter. However, taken collectively, the research by Radway, Hunt, and Vipond (1987) and others suggests that response is a social, cultural activity that occurs, in Rosenblatt's words, as "a unique coming-together of a particular personality and a particular text at a particular time and place under particular circumstances" (Rosenblatt 1985, 104). Through sharing their responses in "particular circumstances," readers establish membership in a social community; i.e., a community of "mystery buffs," "science fiction freaks," or avid romance novels readers. To participate as members in these communities, readers learn the particular ways of responses, attitudes, interests, and roles unique to their communities.

Teacher Agendas Dictate Classroom Discussions

The classroom itself ultimately becomes a community of responders whose agenda is shaped by the teacher. In a recent study sponsored by the Center for Learning and Teaching of Literature at SUNY, Albany, James Marshall (1989) analyzed teachers' and students' responses in six teachers' "high-ability" classes over several weeks of class meetings. One of the major findings of that study was that the six teachers' own agendas consistently dictated the direction of the discussions. The teachers dominated the discussions. The floor was generally returned to the teacher after each student's contribution. Seventy percent of the teachers' questions focused on eliciting textual knowledge, while only 12 percent of the questions elicited students' general knowledge. These were teachers who rarely let go of the reins. Marshall found that

> the general pattern seemed to be one of the students' contributing to an interpretive agenda implied by [the teacher's] questions. Their response tended to be relatively brief and unelaborated; their questions relatively few. Both individually and as a group, they cooperated with the teacher in organizing and sustaining an examination of the text, but the direction and content of that examination was usually in the teacher's control. The students' role was to help develop an interpretation, rarely to construct or defend an interpretation of their own. (42)

Marshall's research suggests that, if response is a learned social practice, students have little opportunity to practice articulating their own responses according to their own intentions. In contrast, activities such as collaborative learning, dialogue-journal writing, book club discussions, and computer bulletin boards, motivate students to share responses as members of a social group.

And the ambience of the social context is essential—as can be attested to by those who recall the pleasure of intimately sharing in a casual bar or restaurant their late-night responses in a "particular time and place under particular circumstances." By creating the opportunity for moments of intimate sharing in a classroom, teachers enhance the pleasure of sharing responses.

Ways to Enhance Classroom Response

In summary, this cumulative research on response to literature suggests that teachers can enhance the quality of classroom responses by the following:

- Employing informal oral or writing that encourages a tentative, exploratory stance.
- Eliciting engagement responses.
- Helping students relate prior texts to current texts.
- Relating students' attitudes to their reading.
- Recognizing students' "story-driven" orientation.

- Encouraging sharing of responses to build a sense of community.

References

Beach, Richard, and Susan Hynds. 1988. *Research on the Learning and Teaching of Literature: A Selected Bibliography.* Albany, N.Y.: Center for the Learning and Teaching of Literature.

———. (In press). "Research on Response to Literature." In P. David Pearson, Michael Kamil, and Peter Mosenthall, eds. *The Handbook on Reading Research.* White Plains, N.Y.: Longman.

Response as the Discovery of Meaning Through Talking and Writing

Beach, Richard. In press. "The Creative Development of Meaning: Using Autobiographical Experiences to Interpret Literature." In Stanley Straw, and D. Bogdon, eds. *Beyond Comprehension and Communication to Response.* Portsmouth, N.H.: Boynton/Cook.

Bruner, Jerome. 1986. *Actual Minds, Possible Worlds.* Cambridge, Mass.: Harvard University Press.

Hade, Daniel. 1988. "Children, Stories, and Narrative Transformations." *Research in the Teaching of English* 22: 310–26.

Labov, William. 1972. *The Language of the Inner City.* Philadelphia: University of Pennsylvania Press.

Lytle, Susan. 1982. *Exploring Comprehension Style: A Study of Twelfth-Grade Readers' Transactions with Text.* Dissertation, Stanford University.

Marshall, James. 1987. "The Effects of Writing on Students' Understanding of Literary Texts." *Research in the Teaching of English.* 21: 30–63.

Newell, George, Karen Suszynski, and Ruth Wingart. 1989. "The Effects of Writing in a Reader-Based and Text-Based Mode on Students' Understanding of Two Short Stories." *Journal of Reading Behavior* 21: 37–57.

Petrosky, Anthony R. 1981. "From Story to Essay: Reading and Writing." *College Composition and Communication* 33: 19–36.

Pratt, Louise. 1976. *A Speech-Act Theory of Literary Discourse.* Bloomington, Ind.: University of Indiana Press.

Emotional Responses as Related to Interpretation

Bleich, David. 1986. "Gender Interests in Reading and Language." In Elizabeth Flynn and Patrocinio Schweickart, eds. *Gender and Reading.* Baltimore: Johns Hopkins University Press.

Flynn, Elizabeth. 1986. "Gender and Reading." In Elizabeth Flynn, and Patrocinio Schweickart, eds. *Gender and Reading.* Baltimore: Johns Hopkins University Press.

Gilligan, Carol. 1982. *In a Different Voice.* Cambridge, Mass.: Harvard University Press.

Golden, Joanne, and John Guthrie. 1986. "Convergence and Divergence in Reader-Response to Literature." *Reading Research Quarterly.* 21: 408–21.

Heathcote, Dorothy. 1980. *Drama as Context.* Aberdeen, Scotland: Aberdeen University Press.

Nell, Victor. 1988. "The Psychology of Reading for Pleasure: Needs and Gratifications." *Reading Research Quarterly* 23: 6–50.

Opdahl, Kate. Spring 1988. "Imagination and Emotion: Toward a Theory of Representation." *Reader* 19: 1–20.

Sadoski, Mark, Ernest Goetz, and Susan Kangiser. 1988. "Imagination in Story Response: Relationships between Imagery, Affect, and Structural Importance." *Reading Research Quarterly.* 23: 320–36.

"Text-Bound" versus "Intertextual" Meaning

Barrett, Edward, ed. 1988. *Text, Context, and Hypertext.* Cambridge, Mass.: M.I.T. Press.

Beach, Richard, Deborah Appleman, and Sharon Dorsey. In press. "Adolescents' Use of Intertextual Links to Understand a Story." In Richard Beach and Susan Hynds, eds., *Becoming Readers and Writers during Adolescence and Adulthood.* Norwood, N.J.: Ablex.

Cox, Carole, Richard Beach, and Joyce Many. In preparation. *Students' Intertextual Links in Group Discussions.* Long Beach, Calif.: Long Beach California State University Press.

Lehr, Susan. 1988. "The Child's Developing Sense of Theme as a Response to Literature." *Reading Research Quarterly* 23: 337–57.

Rogers, Terry. 1987. *Students as Literary Critics: The Interpretive Theories, Processes, and Experiences of Ninth-Grade Students.* Doctoral dissertation, University of Illinois.

Svensson, Cai. 1987. 'The Construction of Poetic Meaning." *Poetics* 16: 471–503.

Tchudi, Steven. 1988. "Invisible Thinking and the Hypertext." *English Journal* 77 (1): 22–30.

Wolf, Dennie. 1988. "Reading Reconsidered: Students, Teachers, and Literature." Princeton, N.J.: Report to the College Board.

Attitudes and Response

Beach, Richard. 1983. "Attitudes, Social Conventions and Response to Literature." *Journal of Research and Development in Education* 16: 47–54.

Beach, Richard and Roberte de Beaugrande. 1987. "Authority Attitudes in Response to Literature." *Pszichologia.* 7: 67–92.

Dorfman, Marge. August 1985. "A Model for Understanding the Points of Stories: Evidence from Adult and Child Readers." Paper presented at the Seventh Annual Conference of the Cognitive Science Society, Irvine, Calif.

Jose, Paul, and William Brewer. 1984. "Development of Story Liking: Character Identification, Suspense, and Outcome Resolution." *Developmental Psychology* 20: 911-24.

Holland, Norman. 1985b. *I.* New Haven: Yale University Press.

Radway, Janice. 1984. *Reading the Romance: Women, Patriarchy, and Popular Literature.* Chapel Hill, N.C.: University of North Carolina Press.

Willinsky, John, and R. Mark Hunniford. 1986. "Reading the Romance Younger: The Mirrors and Fears of a Preparatory Literature." *Reading-Canada-Lecture* 4: 16-31.

Readers' Response as Constituted by Stances and Orientations

Hunt, Russell A., and Douglas Vipond. 1985. "Crash-Testing a Transactional Model of Literary Learning." *Reader* 14: 23-39.

Hynds, Susan. 1989. "Bringing Life to Literature and Literature to Life: Social Constructs and Contexts of Four Adolescent Readers" *Research in the Teaching of English* 23: 30-61.

Vipond, Douglas, and Russell A. Hunt. 1989. "Literary Processing and Response as Transaction: Evidence for the Contribution of Readers, Texts, and Situations." In Dietrich Meutsch & Reinhold Viehoff, eds. *Comprehension of Literary Discourse: Results and Problems of Interdisciplinary Approaches.* Berlin, Germany: de Gruyter.

Vipond, Douglas, Russell A. Hunt, Joy Jewett, and James Reither. In press. "Dimensions of Reading." In Richard Beach and Susan Hynds, eds. *Becoming Readers and Writers during Adolescence and Adulthood.* Norwood, N.J.: Ablex.

Response as a Learned Social Activity

Hynds, Susan. In press. "Reading as a Social Event: Comprehension and Response in the Text, Classroom, and World." In S. Straw and D. Bogdan, *Beyond Comprehension and Communication to Response.* Portsmouth, N.H.: Boynton/Cook.

Marshall, James. 1989. *Patterns of Discourse in Classroom Discussions of Literature.* Albany, N.Y.: SUNY at Albany, The Center for the Learning and Teaching of Literature.

Rosenblatt, Louise M. 1985. "Transaction versus Interaction: A Terminological Rescue Operation." *Research in the Teaching of English* 19: 96-107.

Vipond, Douglas, and Russell A. Hunt. 1987. "Shunting Information or Making Contact? Assumptions for Research on Aesthetic Reading." *English Quarterly* 20: 131-36.

9. Can Literature Be Rescued from Reading?

Alan C. Purves
State University of New York at Albany

Many who have seen Robin Williams as Mr. Keating in the film *Dead Poet's Society* have said that things aren't that way now, that schools don't treat literature as a set of dead facts that can be weighed and measured. Mr. Keating was a voice in the wilderness of the 1950s but, thanks to the Dartmouth Conference and the resurgence of Louise Rosenblatt, things are changed now.

Or are they? If you look at the tests that face today's students, you would see that the Keatings of this world have been thoroughly routed from the schools. Such are the findings of a recent report of the Center for the Learning and Teaching of Literature at The University at Albany (Brody, DeMilo, and Purves 1989). These tests contribute, I believe, to the serious decline of cultural literacy among our students.

The Triumph of Reading over Literature

The nation's testing programs devote a great deal of energy to testing reading and writing, but they fail to treat literature and cultural literacy seriously. The artistic aspects of literature and the cultural heritage of our society are not reflected in the nation's tests and, as a result, lead to neglect by the schools. The tests focus on literal comprehension and on the reading of prose fiction. Poetry and drama are seldom included. If literature and its artistic aspects are not made important in those tests which affect students' lives and influence teaching, no wonder that students' knowledge and appreciation of literature are as poor as critics of the schools—such as E. D. Hirsch, Jr., Diane Ravitch, and Allan Bloom—claim they are.

The Brody, DeMilo, and Purves report contains a census of state assessment programs to find out each state's policy towards literature learning and its testing. In it, we found that the testing of learning in literature is not emphasized as a separate topic by most states, but instead is treated as an aspect of reading. What this means in practice is that reading assessments either include some passages from literary works in their mix of textual sources, or include a literature section as a subtest within a reading assessment. Only two states have a humanities assessment and thus include literature as an aspect of general cultural and intellectual history. Fewer than a quarter of the states (mostly in the Northeast) measure student knowledge of specific authors and titles, literary terminology, or general cultural information, and only two of the states report that these particular measures are used to help determine promotion or graduation. Although reading is important in state assessment or competence tests, literature plays only a minor role.

Next, we analyzed all of the published tests produced for secondary school students (including those used in the state assessments) in order to see what sorts of knowledge and skill were measured. The sample of tests included proprietary language arts batteries, reading tests, and literature tests; the major entrance and placement programs of the College Board and American College Testing programs; and the tests associated with literature text series and with grade-7 basal reading series. Almost universally, these tests employ multiple-choice questions that focus on the comprehension of content, particularly on the meaning of specific parts of the text or of the main idea or theme of a passage which is given to the student to read (see Figures 1 and 2). Only in the college placement tests is there some emphasis on knowledge, primarily of authors and titles. Relatively scant attention is paid to aspects of the text other than content, and notably absent from the tests are any items dealing with such artistic characteristics of literature as language, structure, and point of view.

When one turns to the critical skills demanded in these tests, a similar pattern emerges. The vast majority of the items in all tests focus on recognition and recall and on the application of knowledge to the given text. There is relatively little attempt to deal with such complex mental operations as analysis, interpretation, and generalization. There are virtually no questions dealing with the evaluation of the work as an aesthetic object, or with attitudes, beliefs and interests, and no questions dealing with the nature of the aesthetic transaction. A typical test will, for example, include a two-paragraph excerpt from a novel or story and follow it with three or four questions such as the following fictitious examples.

> In line 10, the word *rogue* means: a) stranger, b) out of control, c) colored with red, d) falling apart.

Figure1

Content of Literature Items in Proprietary Tests

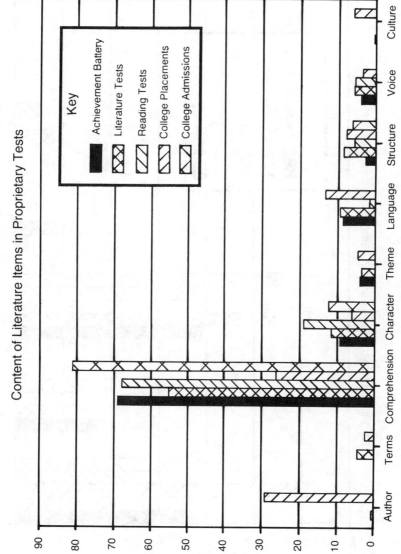

Figure 2

Cognitive Demand for Literature Items in Proprietary Tests

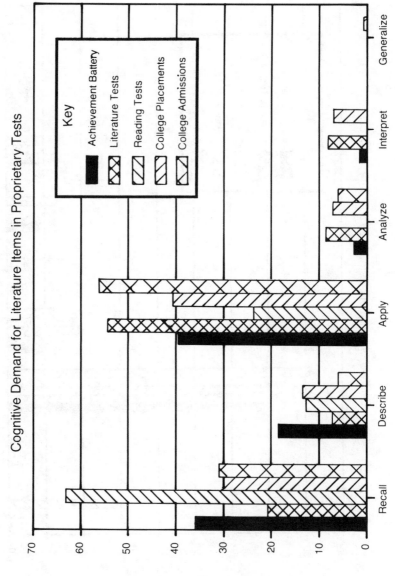

The two people are: a) father and son, b) brothers, c) husband and wife, d) strangers.

This selection is about: a) the end of an adventure, b) the relationship between people and animals, c) the climax of a journey, d) the break-up of a family.

Such questions hardly tap the imaginative power of fiction or drama; in fact they reduce it to the level of those textbooks where knowledge is factual. Some of the published tests go so far as to ask true or false questions, such as: *Huckleberry Finn is a good boy*, or *Hamlet is mad*. As a result, students find that they do not have to read the original works, they can turn to plot summaries or simplified study guides instead.

In summary, we found that the nation's testing programs focus their attention on textual comprehension at a relatively low level of understanding. They do so without a clear differentiation between reading a literary selection and reading a nonliterary one—*any* text is viewed as having a content that can be easily summarized into a single main idea, point, gist, or theme. The power of literature to capture the imagination of the reader remains unexplored. In most tests that affect high school students, literary texts are treated as if they were no different from articles in encyclopedias or research reports. Against this, Louise Rosenblatt and those who accept her ideas would argue that literature is a complex use of language to stimulate the readers' imaginations about the world and themselves, and to make readers aware of the beauty and power of our language as well as of the richness of our multicultural heritage.

Student Perceptions of Achievement in Literature

The effect of the tests on instruction and students can be seen in the earlier work of Purves et al. (1980), which showed how response preferences were learned in secondary schools. More recent evidence can be seen in Brody, DeMilo, and Purves (1989), a pilot study of student perceptions of achievement in literature which analyzed a set of compositions written by secondary students on the following topic:

Write a letter of advice to someone two years younger than yourself who is intending to attend your school and who has asked you to explain how to do well in literature classes in your school. Write a friendly letter and include in it five specific pieces of advice.

In the pilot study, responses of 500 students from five secondary schools in and around two urban centers (in New York and in Ohio) were analyzed by using four general categories of advice: reading strategies, writing strategies, classroom strategies, and general admonitions. These, in turn, were subdivided into from three to nine subcategories (e.g., under reading strategies: physical setting, reading procedures and routines, complementary activities to reading, reading habits, use of alternative sources, mental strategies, and literary foci). Each of these was further divided into up to twelve individual item classes. The results of the pilot study indicate that the largest proportion of responses dealt with reading strategies, followed by classroom strategies, particularly test-taking strategies.

Reading Strategies

Responses in the reading strategies category dealt with such procedures as reading on an empty stomach, how to sit while reading, where to read, whether or not to skim first, and whether to underline or to take notes. The second most frequent category of advice dealt with various ancillary aids. Some of the writers advised calling a friend who has read the book, talking to one's parents, or, most frequently, using Cliffs Notes.

Classroom Strategies

The second largest category of advice dealt with classroom politics, with particular emphasis on such strategies as where to sit or whether to be called on or to volunteer. Much of the advice in this category refers to homework strategies (you should get it in on time), and test taking (it's better to have English second period so you can get the questions from the first-period students). All of this advice is eminently practical, although the students are at times facetious (suggesting that the teacher can be bribed). It seems clear from this evidence that the tests have had a negative impact on classrooms and on students.

Misunderstanding the Nature of Literature

I would argue that this situation has come about to a great extent as the result of the pressure of the reading establishment, which from my observation, has little sympathy with the work or ideas of Louise Rosenblatt, and little understanding of the nature of literature. It is this group which has come to dominate the world of tests and to influence the world of textbooks. In making these claims, I realize that there are many in the reading establishment who have come to call for something named "whole language," and who have attacked the basal reader. Many of them have even used the term *transaction* in their discussion of reading (Goodman 1984; Pearson and Tierney 1984), but despite their seeming adherence to a view of texts and reading that has been advanced by Louise Rosenblatt, they have generally missed the point—they would put literature into the primary school curriculum but still focus on an efferent view of comprehension. It is the bottle that has changed, not the wine.

As a result, the majority of reading experts sees nothing wrong with the sort of questions that appear in these tests, although they might cavil at the multiple-choice format. I have sat in a meeting of reading people who fail to understand that a question that neglects the author's title such as, "Which of the following would be the best title for the selection?" does violation to the transactional view. I have heard some reading people refer to all texts as "stories." I have worked with some who have been perfectly happy to change a text to accommodate a readability formula. I have argued with some who insist that literature tests should treat the text as contextless and ahistorical, and who cannot admit that a text might be ironic or ambiguous.

What emerges from this view is a set of tests that treat literature as did the textbook of Mr. Pritchard in *Dead Poet's Society*. Literature exists not to stir the emotions or the mind, not to set the feet moving or the reader humming or drawing or musing or comparing one text with another, but instead to be weighed and measured on a standardized score—just as a student can be measured by one of the tests. This view has come into the literature textbooks and permeates the study questions and the teachers' guides. Such a view of literature neglects any sort of comprehensive view of the domain by selecting from that domain a set of objectives that are easy to measure with objective questions—questions that accord with a simplistic cognitive view of reading. Such a view allows reading to become a monolith in a curriculum in which any teacher can teach reading because the view of the text never changes.

Three Current Views of the Domain of Literature

In order to see how this situation might be changed, the research team then turned to an examination of experimental measures and measures that had been used in other systems of education around the world. From this assortment as well as from an analysis of curricular statements, the group began to establish a broader depiction of the domain of literature learning in secondary schools. This review showed that there were three complementary or competing views of the domain: (1) literature is an adjunct of the language arts; (2) it comprises a distinct body of knowledge; and (3) it is an aspect of aesthetic perception. Thus literature is seen alternatively as a stimulus for reading and writing, as an aspect of the humanities, and as one of the arts.

Literature as Part of the Language Arts

School literature has often been fitted, rather uncomfortably, into "the language arts," (i.e., reading, writing, speaking, and listening). Since literature involves texts that people read or write, and since students who read literature often write about what they have read, literature is often seen as simply a subset of reading and writing (with an occasional nod to speaking and listening). Literature thus fits into the program as something pleasant to read and perhaps as something interesting to write about. This view seems to prevail in the basal reading approach to elementary schools (Walmsley 1989), and it carries on into the secondary school curriculum and its tests. Literature is but one of the content areas like science or social studies that, depending upon the ideology attached to the language arts, can be mined to promote skills in reading and writing or to promote individual growth. In the current world of tests, literature is usually a vehicle for testing reading comprehension or for measuring writing skill or proficiency.

Literature as an Independent Subject

A second perspective shows literature as a school subject with its own body of knowledge consisting primarily of literary texts, perhaps classified by genre, date, theme, author, and so on. Particular texts are set in part by experts, in part by those who purvey textbooks, and in part by teachers and curriculum planners.

Another system of classification identifies three other broad areas of literature content: (1) historical and background information concerning authors, texts, and the times in which they were written or that form their subject matter; (2) information concerning critical terminology, critical strategies, and literary theory; and (3) information of a broad cultural nature, such as that emerging from folklore and mythology, which forms a necessary starting point for the reading of many literary texts. Although this perspective on the domain has been criticized as focusing too much on things external to the text, many have argued that such knowledge is crucial to the acts of reading and writing. In the world of testing, however, there are only a few current commercial tests (usually at the college level) that concentrate on this sort of knowledge, even though it formed the basis of the 1987 study of cultural knowledge by Ravitch and Finn.

Literature as an Aspect of Aesthetic Perception

Yet another group sees the domain of literature learning as the development of a kind of reading different from that used with other texts. This kind of reading is called "aesthetic" and is opposed to the reading that one does with informational texts. Recent literary theory has come to view literature less in terms of the writer and more in terms of the reader, for it appears to be the reader—particularly the informed and trained reader—who defines a text as "literary" and reads it not for information but for the nuances of the text itself. Such a definition follows from the strand of thinking that developed from I. A. Richard's *Practical Criticism* (1929), which gave cogent voice to the idea that the reader helped form the meaning of the text. The summary of that position is best expressed by Rosenblatt, who, in *The Reader, the Text and the Poem* (1977), reminds us that literary texts are grounded in the real world of writers who may intend them to be seen poetically or not. Once written, the texts become alive only when they are read, and they become literary only when a sufficient body of readers chooses to read them as aesthetic objects rather than as informational documents. These readers bring to the text a great deal of background knowledge concerning substance, structure, and style in order to ascertain its meaning and its significance. The meaning of the text is that which can be verified by other readers and by recourse to the historical grounding of the text, if such is available. The significance of the text is personal or, perhaps, communal.

Rosenblatt's book primarily discusses the nature of aesthetic reading, that which goes on within the reader. Although her writing subtly demonstrates what happens when this reading is brought into the realm of discourse, she does not directly address the ways by which aesthetic reading becomes articulated in a classroom discussion or in an essay—such is not her purpose. It is here that Rosenblatt must be supplemented by the work of those critical theorists who discuss less the nature of reading and more the nature of the public discourse concerning that reading. The assumption of these critics, particularly those in the "reader-response" group, would seem to be that practice, particularly of critical discourse, would have a positive effect on the ways students read. Support for their position can be found in the negative evidence of the report cited in the first part of this chapter.

Thus a major function of literature education is the development of what one might call "preferences," or "habits of mind" in reading and writing. One must learn to read aesthetically and to switch lenses when one moves from social studies to poetry. In addition, literature education is supposed to develop something called "taste" or the love of "good literature," so that literature education goes beyond reading and writing; it inculcates specific sets of preferred habits of reading and writing about that body of texts termed "literature."

Integrating the Domain of Literature

As I have suggested earlier, the problem of current assessment in literature is that it has a limited view of the domain. If one is to have a full assessment of learning at the classroom or the state level, one must broaden the perspective. Rather than being forced to choose among the three views, I would argue that the domain of school literature can be divided into three interrelated aspects: knowledge, practice, and habit. In this sense literature learning is similar to the domains of reading and writing (Takala 1983; Purves 1985). The interrelationships are complex in that the individual uses knowledge in the various acts that constitute the practice and habits, and that the practices and habits can have their influence on knowledge. At the same time one can separate them for the purposes of curriculum planning, and, as we shall see, testing. We may schematize the three subdomains as indicated in Table 1.

Cultural knowledge can be contained in texts like myths, songs, and folk tales or it can exist outside particular texts and in history. Under the heading *Practice* I have used *Responding* to cover reading, watching, and listening. Responding includes *decoding* (making out the plain sense of the text or film) as well as that mental *re-creation* of the text that Rosenblatt refers to as "the poem"—which is to say the cognitive, emotive, and aesthetic experience in a totality. Responding may thus be seen as encompassing a great number of cognitive components and as bringing to the reading a vast array of knowledge (Purves, 1987; 1990).

I use *Articulating* to cover a wide variety of ways by which students let people know what their response is. In many ways, this is the key to the curriculum. Articulating is not just reading in a closet but

Table 1

SCHOOL LITERATURE

Cultural Knowledge		Practice		Preferences & Habits	
Textual	Extra-Textual	Responding	Articulating	Aesthetic Choice	Habits
Specific Text	History	Decoding	Retelling	Evaluating	Reading
Cultural Allusion	Author	Re-creating	Criticizing single works	Selecting	Criticizing
	Genres		Analyzing	Valuing	
	Styles		Interpreting		
	Critical Terms		Personalizing		
			Generalizing across works		

bringing the re-creation of what is read out into the open. Like any school subject, literature involves public acts in which the student must be more articulate about procedures and strategies, and conclusions than might be true of the subject outside of school. (Proofs are not necessary in mathematical applications outside of school; essays about one's reading of a text are not required after reading every library book.) In school, these public articulations are the stuff of learning. They can deal with individual works or they can range across groups of works found to be related by genre, author, style, period, culture, or theme. As such, public articulations must be the objects of instruction and testing, and it is here that the tests can have (and have had) such a deleterious effect. Thus far, the articulations in school have focused on the easily testable and that which is "right" or "wrong." They have inculcated a view of reading literature that sees the poem as a work which is to be read efferently, for there is a body of knowledge that can be extracted from the reading and made subject to examination. This limited focus of the articulation redounds upon both the reading and the response. In order to prevent this kind of effect, assessment and the curriculum must attend to the third strand—*Preferences and Habits*.

In order to preserve the aesthetic nature of the text, and treat a work of literature such as *Moby Dick* as literature and not as a treatise on whales, the curriculum seeks to inculcate a set of habits. If literary works are not read and talked about as other kinds of texts are, students must learn how to perform aesthetic reading, and they must be encouraged to read that way voluntarily. The curriculum, then, must seek to promote habits of mind in reading and writing. One of these habits is to make aesthetic judgments about the various texts read and to justify these judgments publicly. Personal preference is not sufficient for the curriculum; one must learn to be a critic in the sense of a judge. In some cases it is desired that specific criteria be used, usually formal or thematic rather than personal.

Since literature education is supposed to develop something called "taste" or the love of "good literature," it goes beyond reading and writing to encompass specific sets of preferences and habits of reading and writing. It may include the development of a tolerance for a variety of literature—a willingness to acknowledge that many different kinds and styles of work can be thought of as "literature," and an acceptance that just because we do not like a certain poem, it does not mean that the poem is not "good." It can even lead students to distrust the meretricious or the shoddy use of sentiment. Experienced readers of literature can see that they are being tricked by a book or a film even when the trickery is going on—and they can enjoy the experience.

I should note that these habits and preferences are culture-specific. A dramatic example of the clash of cultural values has occurred over Salman Rushdie's *Satanic Verses*. It is clear that the literary and aesthetic habits of mind of most of the West are not shared by many in the Islamic world. It is also clear that writers such as the Nigerian Wole Soyinka are themselves torn when they defend Rushdie on Western terms, only to find themselves the targets of another group. This issue writ large in a global scene also divides the citizens of a country, as the many censorship cases in the United States have attested.

Saving Literature from the Reading Specialists

The domain of literature learning, then, is a complex and multifaceted one. It is clear that the current tests that face secondary school students, dominated as they are by the perspective of reading comprehension, cover only a small part of the actual domain and do so at a fairly unimportant level. In order to make a comprehensive assessment of literature learning, a testing program needs to cover the whole of the domain—or at least a larger sample from it. In order to make the best sample and to cover the domain effectively and efficiently, we need to extend our knowledge of the relationships among the segments of the domain. It is this issue that the current work of the Center for the Learning and Teaching of Literature is addressing in the development of prototype measures for assessment. Draft tests using measures for the various subparts of the domain were piloted in 1989, in order to look at what might be a good combination of measures. The results validate the model in showing that knowledge, practice, and preference are related—but not highly interrelated—aspects of the construct of literature learning.

A comprehensive measure of student performance, therefore, would address each of the three areas. It would appear that within the "knowledge" domain, textual knowledge and knowledge of critical terms are distinct, particularly in their relationship to the practice of reading and responding. Within the "practice" domain, more than one passage is needed to get some estimate of a student's performance across text-types. It seems to make little difference whether one uses open-ended or multiple-choice questions, but open-ended questions present somewhat more of a challenge to students and would therefore be a more exacting measure of the ability to read and shape a response to what is read.

It is also clear that an extended response is desirable, but that the phrasing of the question might be such as to allow the student some preparation for the setting forth of a fully articulated composition. A stark question is less preferable than a question that builds upon another sort of task, one that gets the student to consider the text in question (Hansson 1990).

In the realm of "preference", it is important to separate determining the student's criteria for judging a text from the actual judgment. It would also appear to be important to get a depiction of the general attitudes towards literature, including censorship.

From these conclusions one may derive a set of specifications for an assessment of student learning in literature that would include the following:

1. Measures of background knowledge; i.e., terminology and cultural information. These may include matching and supplying or generating items.

2. Measures of the ability to read and articulate a written response to at least two texts that differ in genre. The measures should include both supplying and constructing items, with the latter taking the form of extended discourse.

3. Measures of preference, including aesthetic judgment of specific texts and general habits and beliefs concerning literature and its place in the world.

Such an assessment would give a more comprehensive picture of student learning and program effectiveness than would a measure of any one taken alone. A recent study that used a more comprehensive measure showed that a complex measure served best to validate a model of instruction that made the classroom exploration of literature more open and used more "real" and thought-provoking questioning than normal instruction (Ho 1987). It is the trial of such an assessment package that will form the next phase of this area of research. If successful, the package might well serve as a model of assessment at the state or district as well as the classroom level. Such a package may also contribute to the saving of literature from the reading specialists and allow the Keatings of the world their chance. Perhaps it may also affect curriculum and instruction and the students' perceptions of achievement, but that may be too much to hope.

References

Brody, Pamela, Carol DeMilo, and Alan C. Purves. 1989. *The Current State of Assessment in Literature*. Report Series 3.1. Albany, N.Y.: Center for the Learning and Teaching of Literature.

Goodman, Kenneth. 1984. "Unity in Reading." In *Becoming Readers in a Complex Society*. Edited by Alan C. Purves and Olive Niles. Chicago: Chicago National Society for the Study of Education, 79–114.

Hansson, G. 1990. *Reading and Understanding Literature*. Report Series 3. Albany, N.Y.: Center for the Learning and Teaching of Literature.

Ho, B. 1988. *An Investigation of Two Methods of Teaching Poetry to Secondary-One Students*. Unpublished Master of Education thesis. Singapore: National University of Singapore.

Pearson, P. David, and Robert J. Tierney. 1984. "On Becoming a Thoughtful Reader: Learning to Read Like a Writer." Purves, A.C. and Niles, O. eds. In *Becoming Readers in a Complex Society*. Edited by Alan C. Purves and Olive Niles. Chicago: Chicago National Society for the Study of Education, 144–74.

Purves, Alan C. 1985. "The Potential and Real Achievement of U.S. Students in School Reading." *American Journal of Education* 93: 82–106.

_____. 1987. "Literacy, Culture and Community." In *The Future of Literacy in a Changing World*. Edited by Daniel A. Wagner. Oxford: Pergamon Press.

_____. 1990. *The Scribal Society*. White Plains, N.Y.: Longmans.

Purves, Alan, Dalwin L. Harnisch, Donald Quirk, and Barbara Bauer. 1980. *Achievement in Reading and Literature: The United States in International Perspective.* Urbana, Ill.: National Council of Teachers of English.

Ravitch, Diane, and Chester E. Finn, Jr. 1987. *What Seventeen-Year-Olds Know.* Boston: Houghton Mifflin.

Richards, I. A. 1929. *Practical Criticism.* New York: Harcourt Brace.

Rosenblatt, Louise M. 1977. *The Reader, the Text, and the Poem.* Carbondale, Ill.: Southern Illinois University Press.

Takala, Sauli. 1983. "Achievement and the Domain of School Writing." Urbana, Ill.: IEA Written Composition Study.

Walmsley, Sean, and Trudy Walt. 1989. *Teaching Literature in Elementary School.* Report 1.3. Albany, N.Y.: Center for the Learning and Teaching of Literature.

D. Reaffirming *Literature* as *Exploration*

In the next chapter, Louise M. Rosenblatt recalls the major influences on her writing the pioneering, iconoclastic, and innovative book, *Literature as Exploration*. Liberated from traditional late Victorian attitudes about gender, class, and ethnic differences by her "progressive" upbringing and an eclectic education in literature, anthropology, and the social sciences, Rosenblatt rejected the prevailing elitist approaches to the study of literature because, in a new age of mass communication, they did not prepare her to help the average reader to discover why one should read literary texts. In her classes at Barnard College and later at New York University she formulated the reader-response study method, and in *Literature as Exploration* she published a new philosophic/theoretical foundation for making personal response the basis for a balanced, self-critical, and knowledgeable interpretation of literature. (Recognition of the importance of the reader did not come into most universities until the late 1960s.)

In this important essay, Rosenblatt reaffirms the transactional nature of her reader-response theory and measures it against those theories that have come after her, explaining why the recognition of the reader's stance as an integral part of the reading transaction is vital to the survival of the reading of literature as an active part of American culture.

10. Retrospect

Louise M. Rosenblatt

The theme of *Literature as Exploration*—that the work exists in the transaction between reader and text—leads me to think gratefully of all those who have kept the book alive over the years. Fifty years! It boggles the mind! I recall a similar reaction in 1922, in my sophomore year at Barnard College. Returning from a class in Victorian literature, I staggered into my dormitory room, hand on brow, exclaiming to my roommate, "Professor Hubbard *saw* Matthew Arnold in 1888!" Today, I am further from the young woman who wrote *Literature as Exploration* than I was then from Matthew Arnold.

The editors have asked me to explain how that young woman of 1935-36 came to write the book. What prepared her to present ideas in diverse fields that in some instances have only recently been generally accepted? How was the book received? How does it relate, they ask, to what she has written in subsequent years? When I seek to respond, I find that various aspects of her experience before 1935—family background, undergraduate years at Barnard College, doctoral work at the University of Paris, postdoctoral study of anthropology at Columbia University, teaching at Barnard College—converged to provide the matrix for the book.

Family upbringing was of overarching importance. Intellectually influenced mainly by ideas drawn from anti-authoritarian European sources and such American writers as Emerson and Thoreau, it would at a later date have been called "progressive." Accordingly, I was saved from acquiring lingering Victorian attitudes—especially about gender, class, and ethnic differences. Instead of the social Darwinism of "struggle for survival," I was introduced to Peter Kropotkin's ideas about "mutual aid" even in the animal world. At Barnard College also, my experience was not conventional. As part of an experiment probably modeled on the British universities, I became an "honor student" during my last two years and was released from the

97

traditional liberal arts English program, with its array of period courses. Reading mainly on my own, intensively in English and American literature and widely in the social sciences, I conferred once a week with a professor. A week-long series of written examinations at the end of the senior year rendered the usual work for the M. A. superfluous.

Returning to my files in connection with these reminiscences, I came upon a paper written in my junior year that may have some interest in this context. Having come across an article by the philosopher Horace Kallen which found tragedy to reside mainly in the destruction of values, I went on to discuss what this meant in terms of the relationship between writers and their readers or audiences! I argued that Shakespeare could take for granted that he and his audience shared the same value system, whereas Ibsen had to build into his plays a way of changing his audience's values before they could share his tragic vision.

My choice of graduate specialization also involved important preparation for later concerns. At graduation from Barnard, I had hesitated between continuing the study of literature and electing graduate work in anthropology, a lively interest since my sophomore course with Professor Franz Boas, the great founder of American anthropology. My compromise was to study in France and ultimately to seek acceptance as a doctoral candidate in Comparative Literature at the University of Paris. My dissertation, *L'idée de l'art pour l'art*, published in 1931, on the espousal by English and French writers of the idea of "art for art's sake," foreshadowed *Literature as Exploration* by its concern with the relationship between writers and society in the context of comparative cultures and the philosophy of art. After I had received the doctorate from the Sorbonne, and while I was teaching at Barnard, I enrolled in graduate work in anthropology with Professor Boas and Professor Ruth Benedict, whose *Patterns of Culture* (1934) is still widely read. The combination of training in literature and in anthropology and other social sciences led in 1935 to my being appointed to the Commission on Human Relations.

The title page of the first edition of *Literature as Exploration* contained, after the author's name, the phrase, "for the Commission on Human Relations, Progressive Education Association." The relationship between the book and those agencies was not, however, as simple as the title page might suggest. Much as I was in sympathy with their general aims, the book was largely the product of other connections, and, in a sense, was written on the rebound from completing the work for which I was appointed to the Commission.

For several years a group of social scientists at the forefront of their fields had been meeting for interdisciplinary discussions, and had conceived the idea of two commissions, one on secondary education and the other on human relations. Since the General Education Board of the Rockefeller Foundation, which funded the projects, did not subsidize individuals, the grant was administered through the Progressive Education Association. The task of the Commission on Human Relations was to produce a group of books addressed to older adolescents—late high school and early college students—on important subjects such as human development and the family. My contribution was to draw on my literary and social science background for the planning of the books. Others, skilled at popularizing the social sciences, were to do the actual writing.

The work with the Commission, for which I took a leave of absence from Barnard, gave me the opportunity to meet with the social scientists who had initiated the project, to read widely, and to visit some schools and colleges—especially those seeking to innovate. This was perhaps the heyday of the progressive education movement. I had been aware of its existence, and, because of the influences mentioned earlier, was already imbued with the "progressive" point of view. John Dewey's *Human Nature and Conduct* and *Art as Experience* confirmed my sympathy for that general approach. My completely "liberal arts" education and work had not, however, brought me into contact with schools or with specialists in education. I entered enthusiastically into the work for the Commission under the progressive rubric, but perhaps because the roots of my thinking were elsewhere, I maintained a certain objectivity.

The Commission agenda contained no plans, and no commitment for, a book by me or for a book on the teaching of a particular subject. Given my role, my work was completed when the responsibility for producing the books on the various areas of human relations was turned over to the writers. As I reflected on the books planned, I felt that their expositions of the latest developments in the social sciences would be valuable contributions toward students' understanding. But I also came to the conclusion that the kinds of discussion of human relations that went on in my own literature classes could also perform a unique and vital function.

My teaching experience had made me increasingly disillusioned with the discipline represented by university departments of English. Even introductory literature courses were geared to the needs of future majors in English and reflected the approaches dominating the graduate curriculum, which in turn reflected the pseudoscientific model of the German universities. Literary history, philology, or a watered-down, moralistic didacticism mainly constituted the "study of literature." My training—excellent, I must admit, in its terms—had prepared me for historical and theoretical research, but had not prepared me, I felt, for helping the average student discover why one should read literary texts, given all the other interesting things in life. Although the lecture method prevailed at Barnard—sometimes in a rather relaxed form, it is true—and I gave some advanced "lecture courses," I had been able to develop in my introductory courses what has come to be called the "reader-response" discussion method.

The reading of texts such as the Commission proposed—texts that expounded, even though in popular style, sociological and psychological ideas about, say, family relationships—was, I decided, very different from the reading of *Romeo and Juliet* or *Great Expectations*. The informative texts were ultimately needed, perhaps essential, but they were to be read impersonally and objectively. In contrast, my work for the doctorate had taught me, and Dewey had confirmed, that literary works of art exist in unique personal experiences. The reader attends not only to the formal aspects of the work, but also, perhaps primarily, to the situations, thoughts, and emotions called forth during the reading. Generational conflicts and tensions over family loyalties lived through in reading *Romeo and Juliet*, for example, can give rise to personal responses that can be reflected on and expressed. Thus the literary experience provides the opportunity to help students to think rationally about issues with which they are emotionally involved. When the desire arises to hear what others, such as social scientists, have to say, it can influence, and be assimilated into, personally felt attitudes and expectations.

I had visited classes in schools and colleges where the teachers had thoroughly eliminated the traditional exposition of standard interpretations of literary works for students to echo on examinations. There was lively expression of opinion, and the excitement of freedom from conventional methods. Yet I felt that I could contribute something constructive—a philosophic or theoretical foundation for revising the teaching of literature, a foundation for setting up a process that would make personal response the basis for growth toward more and more balanced, self-critical, knowledgeable interpretation. Moreover, I could draw on my literary and interdisciplinary studies to provide students with frameworks for thinking about the social, psychological, and aesthetic assumptions implied by the literary work and by their own and others' responses. Much as I agreed with rejection of the traditional methods, my approach, especially in its emphasis on growth based on personal experience, constituted an implicit criticism of what I had observed in some experimental classes. I later discovered in John Dewey's *Experience and Education* (1938), published in the same year as my book, an explicit criticism of the divergence of some so-called progressive educators from his own broader vision.

I dictated a first draft of the book, much of it while on vacation in Connecticut, and completed it after returning to teaching at Barnard. Since I had received secretarial assistance, I gave the book to the Commission. When the Progressive Education Association disbanded in 1955, whatever royalties were produced went to designated professional organizations. The copyright reverted to me in 1965. The second edition appeared in 1968 (1970 in England); the third edition in 1976; the fourth edition (Modern Language Association publication) in 1983.

Various people have recently expressed satisfaction that the book has "finally" received recognition, but they underestimate the strength of the progressive current in educational thinking at the time of its publication. Actually, in 1938, *Literature as Exploration,* despite its challenge to accepted practices and philosophies, received a surprisingly wide favorable response. A leading authority on American literature at Harvard (who gave the book high praise) and the Shakespeare authority at Columbia invited me to join with them in writing a statement for an MLA committee on the teaching of literature. At a meeting during the convention of the Modern Language Association, a group of eminent scholars voted to approve the statement, which was published in the November (1938) issue of *PMLA.* This was the very university establishment whose influence on the teaching of literature in colleges and schools I was seeking to combat!

Equally astonishing to me was the fact that at the national meeting of the National Council of Teachers of English in New York, I found myself on the stage of the Manhattan Opera House, addressing thousands of teachers. (After the book had appeared, Dora V. Smith, then president of NCTE, had asked me to have lunch with her, and the invitation to speak had followed.) I discovered an organization that welcomed all who were concerned with the teaching of English in all its modes and at all levels, from kindergarten to graduate school. And in the NCTE I also found leaders seeking to promote an educational process aimed at developing critically minded, socially productive individuals.

The NCTE became the professional organization to which I mainly devoted my energies over the next half-century—because I felt that the teaching of English to all our people was of paramount importance, an importance that few of my "liberal arts" university colleagues recognized or felt to be their concern. Over the years, I found myself involved in many NCTE committees, commissions, conventions, and publications. In these days of articulate minority voices, I especially recall editing the June 1946 issue of the *English Journal*, devoted to furthering the concept of cultural pluralism set forth in *Literature as Exploration*. (Thomas Mann and Ruth Benedict, among other leaders in their fields, wrote essays for the issue.)

Historians of education in the post-World War II period recorded, on the one hand, the capture of English departments in the colleges by the formalist and elitist New Criticism. On the other hand, the increasing number of students and the extension of school-leaving age reflected the fact that our society had undertaken the noble—and unparalleled—responsibility for educating all of our children. The early response to mass education fostered the "life adjustment" movement. Unfortunately, this anti-intellectualistic effort to prepare pupils to serve, to "adjust" to the needs of the status quo, was confused with the progressives' concern for meeting the needs of students. The progressives sought rather to help them to develop their capacities to the full, a view of education assuming a democratically mobile society.

The historians are correct in reporting the continuing prevalence of generally conservative methods, but they fail, it seems to me, to do justice to the persistence and gradual acceptance of many of the ideas generated during the twenties and thirties. In the mid-century decades, colleges and universities simply rejected students "unprepared" to carry out their traditional programs. The teachers in the elementary and secondary schools could not evade the task created by our increasingly democratic educational system. No matter what the changes in the society and in the schools, and no matter what elitist ideas dominated in the universities, there have always been teachers, I have found, who understand the need for a new approach.

The New Criticism prevailed after World War II through the wide adoption of college textbooks such as Brooks and Warren's *Introduction to Poetry* (published, ironically enough, in the same prewar year as my own book). Surely one reason for their success was that their approach fitted in with the postwar glorification of science, fueled by fear of Soviet scientific superiority. The New Critics and I seemed to start out on the same path by deploring the neglect of literature as an art resulting from the traditional preoccupation with literary history and "the message" of the work. But we parted company in our understanding of the nature of art. The New Critics treated the poem as an autonomous entity that could be objectively analyzed. This approach suited an intellectual climate of narrow empiricism in which behaviorism dominated psychology and logical positivism reigned in philosophy.

Moreover, the methods of "close reading" that the New Critics propagated were easily merged with traditional methods of formal analysis and categorization of the text. The New Critics' dogmatic attack on the "intentional fallacy" and "the affective fallacy" diminished the importance of the author and decried concern with the reader's feelings and ideas. In the universities, recognition of the reader did not begin until the late sixties and early seventies.

Despite the hegemony of the New Criticism, whose formalistic methods of analysis are reflected in literature classes even today, I never felt completely isolated. I continued to be invited to present papers at NCTE meetings and to be active in its committees. I served on various state and national educational panels, was called on as a consultant, was one of the thirteen members of the College Entrance Examination Board Commission on English. My differences with the formalists, or my urging of a different idea of the reading process from the theory being taught by reading experts in my own School of Education, simply acted as stimulants to further thought and writing and served as the basis for a continuing and sometimes effective criticism of dominant practices. When in 1948 I joined the New York University School of Education, which included "content" courses as well as pedagogy in its programs, I was able to develop an undergraduate curriculum and a doctoral program combining English and education which reflected my philosophy. Indeed, my own courses, such as "Literature and the Crisis in Values" and "Criticism and the Literary Experience," provided the empirical basis for further refinement of my theories.

In 1968, the publication of the second edition of *Literature as Exploration* was cited as one of the signs of the growing reaction against the New Criticism. The 1970s were to see a proliferation of diverse alternative theoretical positions in the academic and critical journals. By 1980, when two anthologies of "reader-response" criticism were published, both editors cited *Literature as Exploration* as the first to set forth the importance of the reader. (For whatever reason, however, neither anthology includes my article, "The Poem as Event," published in *College English* in November, 1964—so far as I know, the first explicit attack on the New Critics that called for a criticism based on the reader's response.)

My 1978 book, *The Reader, the Text, the Poem: The Transactional Theory of the Literary Work,* was not intended as a substitute for the earlier work; indeed, I think of the two books as complementary. The earlier book not only deals with implications for teaching, but also presents more fully the cultural and social aspects of the reading event. Decades of studying student responses had led me to develop a theory of the reading process that is both general and rounded. The later book deals systematically with such questions as validity in interpretation, the nature of the literary experience, and the relationship of evocation, interpretation, and criticism.

In 1949, John Dewey had suggested that, instead of *interaction*, which implies separate entities acting on one another, the term *transaction* should be used to designate relationships between reciprocally-conditioned elements. I adopted the term because it underlines what was already present in my 1938 declaration that there are no generic readers or generic interpretations, but only innumerable relationships between readers and texts. Most reader-response exponents still seem ultimately to conceive of the reader and the text in the traditional ways—as already-defined entities acting on each other—and hence tend to situate the "meaning" of a work either "in" the reader or "in" the text, instead of recognizing the dynamic to-and-fro relationship that gives rise to "the work." The transactional phrasing places the stress on each reading as a particular event involving a particular reader and a particular text under particular circumstances.

As I explained earlier, a conviction about the difference between "literary" and other reading led to my writing *Literature as Exploration* in the first place. In *The Reader, the Text, the Poem,* I work out more fully the theoretical explanation of what the reader does in "literary," or, to use my terminology, *aesthetic* reading, as against nonliterary, or *efferent* reading. Strangely enough, this distinction has been the most difficult to communicate. The habit of explaining the literary qualities of a work by pointing to elements in the text (such as rhythm, imagery, metaphor, and departures from ordinary diction) has prevented the realization that the reader must first of all adopt what I term an "aesthetic stance"—that is, focus attention on the private, as well as the public, aspects of meaning. Reading to find the answer to a factual question requires attention only to the public aspects of meaning, and excludes, pushes into the periphery, any personal feelings or ideas activated. To call forth a literary work of art from the same text, the reader must first of all permit into the focus of attention not only the public linkages with the words, but also the personal associations, feelings, and ideas being lived through during the reading. Traditional and formalist methods of teaching literature treat it as a body of information to be transmitted, rather than as experiences to be reflected upon. I find this matter of the reader's stance toward the contents of consciousness vital not only to the solution of various persistent problems in literary theory, but, to put it bluntly, essential to the survival of the reading of literature as an active part of our American culture.

In both kinds of reading, efferent and aesthetic, the reader focuses attention on the stream of consciousness, selecting out the particular mix of public and private linkages with the words dictated by the purpose of the reading. Teachers often forget that if students know that they will be tested primarily on factual aspects of the work (often by multiple-choice questions) a full aesthetic reading is prevented, and the "mix" swings toward the efferent end of the continuum.

Why, some have asked, am I so concerned about my differences with the other so-called reader-response exponents? Don't we all start by rejecting the idea of a single determinate meaning "in" the text? Despite this agreement, I believe that the differences in epistemology, theories of the nature of language, and views of the reading process lead to very important differences in educational and political implications.

In education, the period since World War II has been in many ways a reactionary one. The authentic philosophy of progressive education as Dewey had envisioned it has, for various reasons, never been fully realized, while narrow partial versions have brought the very label into disrepute. Behaviorist psychology reinforced practices that provided what seemed like answers to the increasing demands of mass education. Yet, as I have said, many of the progressive ideas concerning human development and the learning process have persisted. Current criticisms of the schools range from misguided calls for a "literacy" achieved by rote-acquisition of facts and skills, to an elitist "classical" traditionalism, to efforts, as in the California program, to return to the humanistic ethos of the 1930s. Within the sphere of the teaching of language and literature, similar tensions prevail. Under the "reader-response" umbrella are to be found theories that, even though giving lip service to the reader, end up with positions even more remote from mine than was the New Criticism.

Looked at in terms of educational and political implications, the division in literary theories falls elsewhere than between the old historicism and formalism on the one hand and the new reader-response approaches on the other. Reader-response theories such as the psychoanalytically based ones tend to overemphasize the reader and to treat responses primarily as a means of self-interpretation according to Freudian or some other theory of personality. Poststructuralists or deconstructionists, on the other hand, range themselves with the New Critics and the traditionalists in overemphasizing the text. They are concerned with abstracting the underlying system of codes and conventions that the text possesses for a particular "interpretive community." Author and reader become mere carriers of cultural conventions, and both fade away under the extreme relativism of the deconstructionists and the "cultural" critics. Even some of those theorists who phrase the reading process in terms of an interaction between reader and text tend in practice to postulate the text as an entity ultimately determinate of meaning.

The critical processes and teaching procedures that serve this overemphasis on the text result in neglect of the personal aesthetic experience. The stress is placed on efferent analysis, whether of codes and conventions, logical self-contradictions, or ideological assumptions. The advocates of these textually orientated theories find no problem in continuing the teaching practices of the traditionalists and the formalist New Critics.

My insistence on the term *transaction* is a means of establishing the active role of both reader and text in interpretation, and ensures that we recognize that any interpretation is an event occurring at a particular time in a particular social or cultural context. *Once the work has been evoked*, it can become the object of reflection and analysis, according to the various critical and scholarly approaches.

Without accepting the notion of a single "correct" interpretation, the transactional concept provides the basis for developing, in a particular context, criteria for discriminating the relative validity of differing interpretations. The importance of the culture is recognized (here, *Literature as Exploration* is especially pertinent), but, I point out, personal choice and variety derive from the fact that cultural conventions are individually internalized. This especially differentiates my theory from the poststructuralism that sees the individual as caught in "the prison house" of language and culture.

Again, I am especially concerned with differentiating the political implications of my position from others who claim to start from "reader-response" premises. Since 1938, I have urged that students be made aware of the implicit underlying cultural and social assumptions of any evoked work, and that they be helped to make these the basis for scrutinizing their own assumptions. Those who term themselves "cultural" critics seem to share this emphasis. The difference lies in what often seems to be an overarching negative attitude toward our Western culture. Reading thus becomes a defensive action against "manipulation" by the text. My aim, instead, is to develop a discriminating attitude of mind, a readiness to question and to reject anachronistic or unjust assumptions, but a willingness also to accept and build on what is sound in our culture.

Those who claim that there is always a covert political message in teaching literary works of art often disregard their complexity. But I am ready to agree that to claim absence of any political orientation in the classroom only serves confusion. Students should be actively helped to develop criteria based on democratic assumptions about the freedom and well-being of individual human beings.

In 1938, democracy was being threatened by Fascism in Italy and totalitarian governments in Germany and Russia. This retrospect, this backward look, has not lingered on much that was dark in the intervening years. But in recent months, we have been witnessing the heartening spectacle of the liberation from within of such totalitarian states. We have seen whole peoples effect peaceful nonviolent revolutions, and we apprehensively watch their hazardous gropings toward democracy. Note that, despite their economic sufferings, their demands were first of all for freedom, for the freedoms that we enjoy.

Yet we should not be complacent over the removal of the crude opposition between democracy and totalitarianism. Much has changed in our own democracy over the past fifty years, especially in terms of the responsibilities accepted by our society toward its members. Nevertheless, we, too, are at a crucial moment in our history. Our democracy is still threatened, not by totalitarianism, but by social and economic problems that, if not solved, will prevent the education and development of a people capable of the decisions and responsibilities of a full democracy.

The political indifference of many of our citizens, their acceptance of appeals to narrow personal interests, and their vulnerability to the influence of the media are important symptoms. Also, zeal for some, often admirable, social or economic cause seems to blind others to the need to defend our basic democratic values. Much cries out for reform, but an indiscriminately negative attitude may alienate youth from the very democratic means necessary for constructive, humane change.

I am not under the illusion that the schools alone can change society. However, I can reaffirm the belief uttered so many years ago: We teachers of language and literature have a crucial role to play as educators and citizens. We phrase our goals as fostering the growth of the capacity for personally meaningful, self-critical literary experience. The educational process that achieves this aim most effectively will serve a broader purpose, the nurturing of men and women capable of building a fully democratic society. The prospect is invigorating!

Princeton, New Jersey, December 1988
Luquillo, Puerto Rico, January 1990

E. Selected Bibliographies from the Center for the Learning and Teaching of Literature

The Center for the Learning and Teaching of Literature is a research and development center located at the University at Albany, State University of New York. The Center was established in 1987 with funds from the U.S. Department of Education, Office of Educational Research and Improvement, and from the National Endowment for the Arts. The Center's mission is to improve the teaching of content knowledge and critical thinking strategies that contribute to literary understanding, particularly at the middle and high school levels.

Center-sponsored research falls into three broad areas: (1) surveys of current practice in the teaching of literature, including studies of both what is taught and how it is taught; (2) studies of alternative approaches to instruction and their effects on students' knowledge of literature and critical thinking abilities; and (3) studies of alternative approaches to the assessment of literature achievement, including both classroom-based and larger-scale approaches to testing.

The Center also promotes good practice in the teaching of literature through conferences and seminars, through the development of computerized bibliographies on research and practice in the teaching of literature, and through publications that present the Center's own research and provide other resources for research and practice. To receive a list of current publications, please write to CLTL, School of Education, The University at Albany, 1400 Washington Avenue, Albany, NY 12222.

11. Materials and Approaches to Literature Instruction

James Bradley
University at Albany
State University of New York

The following annotated bibliography was compiled from a search of the ERIC database, and from a review of other materials that have been brought to the attention of the Literature Center. The bibliography surveys professional publications concerned with literature instruction at the elementary and secondary levels. Only materials published since 1980 are included. Commercially available student materials are excluded, as are works published in foreign languages or concerning foreign curricula (except those that are applicable to study in U.S. schools). The section headings, and their corresponding page references, are:

This bibliography represents one portion of a more comprehensive bibliography of resources in the teaching of literature, which is available from the Center for the Learning and Teaching of Literature.

1. Literature Instruction–Elementary

1.1   Cullinan, B. E. (Ed.). (1987). *Children's literature in the reading program.* Newark, DE: International Reading Association.

Preparation of this report for the Center for the Learning and Teaching of Literature was supported in part by grant number G008720278, which is cosponsored by the U.S. Department of Education, Office of Educational Research and Improvement (OERI/ED), and by the National Endowment for the Arts (NEA). However, the opinions expressed herein do not necessarily reflect the position or policy of OERI/ED or NEA, and no official endorsement of either agency should be inferred.

Intended to help teachers decide which books to start with when incorporating children's literature into the reading program and to show them how to use these books with a variety of readers, this book provides a rationale and guidance for using "real books" to teach reading. The 17 articles here aim to make the subject of children's literature approachable through an informal, conversational writing style. Titles include: "Extending Multicultural Understanding through Children's Books" (Rudine Sims Bishop); "Enriching the Arts and Humanities through Children's Books" (Sam Leaton Sebesta); and "Resources to Identify Children's Books for the Reading Program" (Arlene M. Pillar).

1.2   McConaghy, J. (1985). Once upon a time and me. *Language Arts, 62*(4), 349–54.

McConaghy describes some of the discussions and writing that first-grade children engaged in as the result of their exposure to literature read aloud.

1.3   Moss, J. F. (1984). *Focus units in literature: A handbook for elementary school teachers.* Urbana, IL: National Council of Teachers of English.

Literature can and should be an integral part of helping students become thoughtful and motivated readers and should encourage them to develop critical-thinking and creative-writing skills. This book provides 13 units that focus on a wide variety of topics. Background information is provided on how focus units can be used to create a context for literacy and on how to create one's own focus units using the book's guidelines for questioning.

1.4   Poole, R. (1986). The books teachers use. *Children's Literature in Education, 17*(3), 159–80.

Using a questionnaire, a study determined the titles and authors of fiction most used by teachers in the classroom, how the books were used, and the time spent on these books.

1.5   Roser, N., & Frith, M. (Eds.). (1983). *Children's choices: Teaching with books children like.* Newark, DE: International Reading Association.

Leading educators in children's literature offer suggestions for effective classroom use of favorite children's books. The suggestions include ideas on which books and poems to use, how to structure the classroom, how to encourage writing, and how to stimulate children's responses to literature.

2. Literature Instruction–Secondary

2.1 Anderson, P. M. (Ed.). (1984). Material selection/censorship. *The Leaflet, 83*(1).

The seven articles in this focused journal issue are concerned with choosing books for teaching and the various constraints on those choices.

2.2 Armstrong, D. P., Patberg, J., & DeWitz, P. (1988). Reading guidelines—helping students understand. *Journal of Reading, 31*(6), 532–41.

The authors report on the effective use of hierarchical and nonhierarchical reading guides with John Steinbeck's *Grapes of Wrath*. What they find indicates that reading guides improve comprehension, provide transferable skills, and create positive feelings about learning.

2.3 Berger, A., & Robinson, H. A. (Eds.). (1982). *Secondary school reading: What research reveals for classroom practice.* Urbana, IL: National Council of Teachers of English.

Intended to help the secondary school classroom teacher make use of some of the current research related to reading instruction, this book contains reviews of the literature on the various aspects of secondary school reading.

2.4 Cameron, J. R. (1981). The sounds and pictorial images of literature. *English Quarterly, 14*(1), 13–19.

Cameron discusses the use of visual/aural stimuli in presenting poetry and literature. This article includes a step-by-step script for a slide/tape presentation.

2.5 Carter, C., & Committee on Classroom Practices. (1985). *Literature—news that stays news: Fresh approaches to the classics.* Urbana, IL: National Council of Teachers of English.

This book offers suggestions of fresh approaches to the teaching of books widely regarded as classics. Some of the texts included are: *Beowulf, To Kill A Mockingbird, Pride and Prejudice, Romeo and Juliet, A Tale of Two Cities, Animal Farm,* and *The Scarlet Letter.* There are suggestions for every grade level, as well as ideas for the literature-writing connection and for teaching multiple titles.

2.6 Christenbury, L. (Ed.). (1981). Developing lifelong readers. *Virginia English Bulletin, 31*(2).

The theme of this journal issue is the development of lifelong reading habits and interests. The articles address questions of what to read, how to read, and why one should read. Bibliographies are provided, novels and poems are recommended, and teaching strategies and curricula are outlined. In addition, two student essays are offered on the question of censorship.

2.7 Corcoran, B., & Evans, E. (Eds.) (1987). *Readers, texts, teachers.* Upper Montclair, NJ: Boynton/Cook.

These 11 essays "affirm the explanatory power of reader-oriented theory, and in their range of concerns invite teachers to conduct their own explorations of the transformation of real texts by real readers in their own classrooms." Essays include: "Rendering Literature Accessible" (Lola Brown); "Reading/Writing in the Culture of the Classroom" (Clem Young and Esme Robinson); "Responding to Poetry: Create, Comprehend, Criticize" (Molly Travers); and "The Hidden Life of a Drama Text" (Roslyn Arnold).

2.8 Davis, K. (Ed.). (1982). *The responding reader: Nine new approaches to teaching literature.* Urbana, IL: National Council of Teachers of English.

These nine articles on reader-response to literature mix theory, pedagogy, and specific teaching techniques. Poetry, narrative fiction, "clustering" techniques, and many other topics are covered.

2.9 Delia, M. A. (1987). Toward a more humanistic discourse in the English classroom. *Clearing House, 61*(4), 179–82.

The author discusses Stephen Tanner's model of using literary criticism as a discourse, asserting that it fails to train students to think, but only teaches them to discuss literature from an academic perspective. In contrast, Robert Scholes' model of textual studies offers both a workable methodology and a relevant curriculum.

2.10 Dias, P., & Hayhoe, M. (1988). *Developing response to poetry.* Philadelphia, PA: Open University Press.

This book is concerned primarily with presenting arguments for a reexamination of the ways in which poetry is taught in the secondary classroom. Focus is placed on reader response and teaching methods, and the implications of current theory and the authors' own research are considered.

2.11 Dominianni, R. (1984). Ray Bradbury's *2026*: A year with current value. *English Journal, 73*(7), 49–51.

Dominianni describes how Bradbury's work can be used in the classroom. He indicates how attitudes towards technology can be found in the work, and how these may be used to stimulate interest in mature students.

2.12 Donelson, K. (1982). A rationale for writing rationales: Advice to (and comments on) teachers who don't see any point in writing rationales. *Contemporary Education, 54*(1), 9–12.

In this article, reasons are discussed for requiring high school English teachers to write rationales justifying the inclusion of all books (controversial or not) assigned and read in the classroom. The reasons given include communicating with students and parents, providing evidence of the teacher's concern and knowledge, and preparing for censorship disagreements.

2.13 Duke, C. R. (1982, October). *Involving students with the short story.* Paper presented at the Annual Meeting of the Southwest Regional English Teachers' Conference, Phoenix, AZ. (ERIC Document Reproduction Service No. ED 222 919)

Although the short story is brief and seemingly simple to comprehend, experienced teachers know from painful experience that students often read without "seeing" and that the only way to get them to "see" is to isolate some of the elements of the short story and present them in a different way in order to focus attention on them.

2.14 Dyer, J. (1986). Teaching how to quote from literary text. *Exercise Exchange, 32*(1), 17–20.

In this article, the author discusses the idea of using Grimm's fairy tales to teach students how to read critically for appropriate quotations and outlines the proper style for including them in writing.

2.15 Ervin, E. S., & Eads, A. E., Jr. (1983). Instrumented team learning—a new concept for teaching twelfth grade English. *NAASP Bulletin, 67*(464), 71–75.

The instrumented team approach at St. John's High School, South Carolina, succeeds in getting general students to meet serious intellectual challenges because group learning counters the problems of poor reading ability, fear of failure, absenteeism, limited time, and underestimation of the importance of school.

2.16 Fitch, R. E. (Guest Ed.). (1981). *Literary theory in the English classroom.* Urbana, IL: National Council of Teachers of English.

Of the 19 articles in this collection, 15 focus on bringing literary theories into the classroom. All of the contributors discuss how literary theory gives creative vitality to the act of interpretation.

2.17 Fleming, M., & McGinnis, J. (Eds.). (1985). *Portraits: Focusing on biography and autobiography in the secondary school.* Urbana, IL: National Council of Teachers of English.

Using Maya Angelou's *I Know Why the Caged Bird Sings* and Carl Sandburg's *Abe Lincoln Grows Up* as their models, the authors provide specific guidelines and classroom applications for teaching biography and autobiography.

2.18 Hays, I. de la Bretonne. (1983). Using semantic clues to get at meaning in *Henry IV, Part I. Exercise Exchange, 29*(1), 7–12.

This work offers suggestions for student writing exercises before, during and after reading Shakespeare's *Henry IV*. Hays cites specific passages useful for classroom examination, followed by discussion and writing questions centered on the conflict between Henry IV and his son, a "generation gap" theme to which students can easily relate.

2.19 Herr, K. U. (1981). *Guided imagery in the classroom: An enhancement to learning.* (ERIC Document Reproduction Service No. ED 214 365)

The use of guided imagery meshes with recent insights into right- and left-brain learning. Guided imagery engages the right-brain processes such as imagination and emotion, creative and intuitive activities.

2.20 Holbrook, H. T. (1985). Keeping the human dimension in literature. *Journal of Reading, 28*(4), 368–70.

The author explores a few of the trends contributing to the apparent decline in substantive literature instruction. He suggests some teaching methods that can help restore the human element to literature.

2.21 Huband, D. (1982). Literature and the modern world: Teaching *Overkill. Use of English, 34*(1), 39–42.

Huband offers three reasons that justify the inclusion of the book *Overkill* on the British "O" level literature syllabus: (1) the nuclear bomb is the most important invention of the century; (2) the language provides a clear example of scientific writing and talking; and (3) the book is informative in helping students arrive at a decision concerning disarmament.

2.22 Karolides, N. J. (Ed.). (1983). Strategy and focus: Teaching literature. *Wisconsin English Journal, 25*(3).

The six articles in this focused journal issue are concerned with literature teaching on the secondary and college level. The titles and authors include: "Discovery: The Role of Subjective Response in Initiating the Literature Discussion" (Susan Casper); "Inquiry" (Helen C. Lee); and "The Practical Book Report" (Randeane Tetu). Reviews of selected books for children, adolescents, and teachers are also included.

2.23 Lawson, A. E., & Kral, E. A. (1985). Developing formal reasoning through the study of English. *Educational Forum, 49*(2), 11–26.

This article presents 10 practical teaching procedures to encourage students to develop formal reasoning skills. A 12th-grade English course is used as an example. Procedures include pretesting, sequencing instruction, providing students with concrete experiences, discussing reasoning patterns and forms of argumentation, assigning argumentative writing assignments, and encouraging discussion and debate.

2.24 Lindberg, B. (1988). Teaching literature: The process approach. *Journal of Reading, 31*(8), 732–35.

The author outlines a process approach to teaching literature which focuses both on meaningful writing and on the ways students respond to what they read.

2.25 Lindquist, A. A. (1982). Applying Bloom's taxonomy in writing reading guides for literature. *Journal of Reading, 25*(8), 768–74.

In this work the author describes a study guide to help students read short stories, essays, novels, drama, and poetry, according to Bloom's taxonomy.

2.26 Mackey, G. (1987). Teaching values and values clarification in the English classroom. *Exercise Exchange, 32*(2), 39–41.

Mackey presents a rationale and framework for teaching values using quality works of literature.

2.27 *Man's inhumanity to man: A case in point: The Nazi holocaust. A resource for Connecticut teachers, grades 7–12.* (1981). Hartford, CT: Connecticut State Department of Education. (ERIC Document Reproduction Service No. ED 201 586)

This teacher resource contains readings, discussion questions, and learning activities on the Holocaust for use with junior and senior high school students.

2.28 Matthews, D. (Ed.). (1982). Focus on Chicago: Four teachers tap its riches. *Illinois English Bulletin, 69*(2).

This journal issue presents teaching ideas based on the city of Chicago and the literary works of its citizens. The first article describes a combined social studies/English course based on the study of Chicago's influence on literature and history. The second article describes how Carl Sandburg's poems can be used to study the question, "What does Chicago mean?" and to teach students how to read dramatically. The final article examines the song lyrics of Chicagoan Steve Goodman, and discusses their relevance to Chicago places and people and how they illustrate the effectiveness of precise detail and apt metaphor.

2.29 Matthews, D. (Ed.). (1985). On contemporary literature: Critiques, reviews and recommendations. *Illinois English Bulletin, 72*(2).

The articles in this focused issue draw attention to works of contemporary literature with classroom potential. Four articles suggest new approaches for the reading and teaching of such established writers as Robert Frost, Kurt Vonnegut, Jr., Eudora Welty, and Saul Bellow. Two other articles examine the bestsellers *Ordinary People* and *The Color Purple*. Reviews and suggestions for teaching the fantasy writers Lloyd Alexander and Ursula Le Guin are presented. Theodore Sturgeon's *More Than Human* is also discussed, as a classic of modern science fiction.

2.30 Matthews, D. (Ed.). (1987). Getting students to read: New materials and methods. *Illinois English Bulletin, 74*(2).

Focusing on young adult reading and instruction, this issue addresses teachers' concerns about recommended recent authors and books, integrating independent reading into the reading program, and student motivation.

2.31 Members and Staff. (1983). *Idea exchange for English teachers.* Urbana, IL: National Council of Teachers of English.

This book offers over 200 ideas for activities that can be adapted for students in middle school, junior high, or high school. The ideas are grouped into 11 categories, including: Getting Ready to Write; Expressive Writing; Revision, Review, and Evaluation;

Punctuation and Grammar; Speaking and Listening; and Talking and Writing about Literature.

2.32 Miller, B. E. (1980). *Teaching the art of literature.* Urbana, IL: National Council of Teachers of English.

Part 1 of this book provides a discussion of literature as event, as object, and as message, plus consideration of what makes good reading. Part 2 details four models for teaching single works in which Miller demonstrates his encounter with the work as work, and then offers a program for teacher preparation, the use of audiovisual aids, and oral presentations.

2.33 Moore, D. W., Moore, S. A., & Readence, J. E. (1983). Understanding characters' reactions to death. *Journal of Reading, 26*(6), 540–44.

The authors suggest a structured response format for interpreting literary characters in death-related literature using Kübler-Ross's five stages of confronting death.

2.34 Morache, J. (1987). Use of quotes in teaching literature. *English Journal, 76*(6), 61–63.

This journal article describes an assignment sequence that introduces secondary school students to finding and interpreting quotes from assigned literature by having students: (1) respond in journals to a quotation chosen by the teacher; (2) analyze characterization by illustrating character traits with quotations; (3) create a collage or a mobile visually interpreting a quote; and (4) discuss in class the meaning of quotes selected in each assignment.

2.35 Neil, L. R. (1987). Imitation: Playing with language. *Exercise Exchange, 32*(2), 3–5.

Neil describes the use of imitation exercises to expose students to selections from great literature and give them opportunities to practice certain English usage or conventions. He notes that imitation improves syntax and style.

2.36 Nugent, S. M. (1984). Adolescent literature: A transition into a future of reading. *English Journal, 73*(7), 35–37.

The author describes the advantages of presenting students with novels designed for them and notes some recommended works with which students can be successful.

2.37 Holston, V. with Santa, C., & Schon, I. Open to suggestion. (1985). *Journal of Reading, 28*(5), 456–57.

These articles describe a method of writing across the curriculum that works and also identifies two Spanish-language young adult novels written by Hispanic authors.

2.38 Welker, W. A., Parrish, B., & Nichols, J. N. Open to suggestion. (1985). *Journal of Reading, 29*(3), 262–67.

This journal article provides suggestions for teaching multisyllable words to remedial readers, incorporating romantic fiction into a reading program, and using content writing activities in a biology class.

2.39 Williams, P., Miller, G. M., & Mandino, G. Open to Suggestion: Traveling through children's literature. (1987). *Journal of Reading, 31*(1), 70–73.

This journal article presents a way of interesting students in high school literature by starting with children's books. The technique involves teacher modeling, using illustrations to motivate writing, and linking a children's book with a more advanced work on a similar topic.

2.40 Otten, N., & Stelmach, M. (1987). Telling stories. *English Journal, 76*(6), 87–88.

The authors present and analyze a high school student's story about fishing. They provide study guide questions intended to amplify the reading for students. Teachers are invited to use this story and study guide in their own classrooms.

2.41 Owen, L. (1984). Dragons in the classroom. *English Journal, 73*(7), 76–77.

Owen discusses how fantasy books can be used in the classroom to provide exercises for the imagination, to allow students to see themselves more clearly, to allow them to escape, and to generate hope.

2.42 Richardson, J. S. (1980, December). *Adolescent literature as a vehicle for developing comprehension and composition skills.* Paper presented at the Annual Meeting of the American Reading Conference, Sarasota, FL. (ERIC Document Reproduction Service No. ED 201 959)

C. Smith's "read a book in an hour" procedure for the development of listening and reading comprehension and B. Beyer's "hamburger writing" procedure for the development of composition skills formed the basis of a teaching technique that provided students with problem-solving tasks, a procedure for writing compositions, and exposure to a classic adolescent novel within a limited time.

2.43   Robinson, R. (1988). *Unlocking Shakespeare's language: Help for the teacher and student.* Urbana, IL: National Council of Teachers of English.

The activities in this book are designed to help students learn to understand the language of Shakespeare by learning to recognize and translate unfamiliar words and syntactic patterns.

2.44   Rouse, J. (1988). On going to visit William Wordsworth. *English Journal, 77*(4), 16–18.

Rouse probes William Wordsworth's relationship to the young reader. He concludes that although many young people today cannot have the direct, immediate experience of nature that overawed Wordsworth, they can, in a room where they sit down together and read a poem, "learn a contemplative solitude—and respond to [a] poem in their individual ways."

2.45   Smagorinsky, P., McCann, T., & Kern, S. (1987). *Explorations: Introductory activities for literature and composition, 7–12.* Urbana, IL: National Council of Teachers of English.

The activities in this book are designed specifically to introduce students to new literature and composition assignments and to help them explore ideas that are unfamiliar and complex.

2.46   Stevens, J. H. (1981, May). *Six novels as parables: A literature unit for grades 9–10.* Paper presented at the Annual Meeting of the Canadian Council of Teachers of English, Vancouver, Canada. (ERIC Document Reproduction Service No. ED 210 698)

The unit of study offered in this paper is designed to guide the analysis of a representative sample of modern fiction from four English-speaking countries. Annotations of six novels are offered to show painful problems and also how the novels are useful for study by 9th- and 10th-grade students. *The Pearl* by John Steinbeck is an example.

2.47   Storey, D. C. (1985). A legacy of values: War in literature for adolescents. *Social Studies, 76*(2), 85–88.

By reading literature about wars, secondary students can learn about the values of different cultures and societies. Teaching approaches are suggested, and specific titles are discussed.

2.48 Strategies for teaching literature in journalism. (1986). *Communication: Journalism Education Today, 19*(4), 7–8.

This thematic journal article cites three strategies for teaching literature in journalism classes, including using literature packets as a class project and having students receive grades for the work they do on the literature packets.

2.49 Whale, K. B., & Gambell, T. J. (Eds.). (1985). *From seed to harvest: Looking at literature.* Urbana, IL: National Council of Teachers of English.

The authors of these articles view the writer as the seed of literature and the critical response by the reader as the harvest. The collection covers such topics as writing about literature, integrating language and literature, developing literary criticism, and using drama as literature.

3. Literature Instruction–General

3.1 California Literature Institute Participants. (1985). *Literature for all students: A sourcebook for teachers.* Los Angeles, CA: The California Literature Project.

This curriculum reform package seeks to find ways *"into, through, and beyond* the text." Methods, materials, and focus are concentrated on and amplified as the key factors in integrating literature into and beyond the classroom. Various methods are discussed for giving both the student and the teacher a more involved role in the appreciation of literature, and for making that literature a comprehensive, practical element in the lives of student readers.

3.2 D'Angelo, K. (1981, April). *Developing concepts of reading and writing through literature.* Paper presented at the Annual Meeting of the International Reading Association, New Orleans, LA. (ERIC Document Reproduction Service No. ED 203 290)

Based on the premise that young people's positive attitudes toward reading and writing can be shaped through the use of literature which treats those activities as valuable, a content analysis was conducted of Caldecott Medal winners from 1938 through 1981 and of Newbery Medal winners from 1922 to 1981 to determine how these books dealt with reading and writing. The results showed that 1 Caldecott and 16 Newbery award winners used reading and writing either as a main theme or as related aspects of plot or characterization. The books depicted reading and writing as important activities for survival, enjoyment, and the gaining and sharing of knowledge. Summaries of the 17 books are included, along with instructional strategies designed for use with reluctant readers and writers.

3.3 Davis, K. (Ed.). (1984). *Teaching English in a nuclear age.* Urbana, IL: National Council of Teachers of English.

This handbook suggests ways to bring into the English classroom literature that deals with the human response to a nuclear threat.

3.4 Easton, S. E., & Abel, F. J. (1985). Tearing up the book. *Clearing House, 59*(1), 5–8.

This article describes the group intermix procedure, a prediscussion strategy in which students work in groups to process the content of a single book. The author suggests various classroom applications.

3.5 Ehle, M. (1982, February). The Velveteen Rabbit, The Little Prince, *and friends: Posacculturation through literature.* Paper presented at the Annual Meeting of the Professional Clinic Association of Teacher Educators, Phoenix, AZ. (ERIC Document Reproduction Service No. ED 221 881)

"Posacculturation" (positive acculturation) is the power of literature to deepen understanding and appreciation of the self and others. Works discussed in this paper for use in a posacculturation program include *The Pigman, The Velveteen Rabbit, The Little Prince, The Door in the Wall, Charlotte's Web, All Kinds of Families, Harriet the Spy, The Outsiders, Nilda, Across Five Aprils, Blubber,* and *Grapes of Wrath.*

3.6 Elbaz, F., & Elbaz, R. (1981). Literature and curriculum: Toward a view of curriculum as discursive practice. *Curriculum Inquiry, 11*(2), 105–22.

This article identifies the contradictions in some of the existing applications of literary tools to curriculum thought, indicates some of the problematic implications for curriculum practice, and sketches an alternative conception of literature as discursive practice.

3.7 Ganz, B. C. (1982, December). *Holocaust literature: Our hope for understanding.* Paper presented at the Annual Meeting of the Eastern Regional Conference of the International Reading Association, Boston, MA. (ERIC Document Reproduction Service No. ED 251 844)

Until recently the Holocaust was largely ignored in history books and literature, leaving most students without even the basic knowledge of a historical event that can and should have meaning for them. Ganz asserts that literature, because it is concerned with feelings and conveys emotions, can move young people to an empathetic awareness of the subject.

3.8   Gauthier, M. G. (1982). Narcissus in the classroom: The pedagogical implications of subjective criticism. *Journal of Education, 164*(3), 238–55.

This journal article begins with the assertion that subjectivist literary criticism, which emphasizes readers' emotional responses to texts and adopts psychoanalytic classroom techniques, renders questionable such aspects of literature teaching as goals, evaluation, and teacher preparation. Literature teachers must abandon the scientific orientation of objectivism and subjectivism in favor of an aesthetic framework for interpreting and teaching literature.

3.9   Golub, J., & NCTE Committee on Classroom Practices (1988). *Focus on collaborative learning: Classroom practices in teaching English, 1988.* Urbana, IL: National Council of Teachers of English.

Collaborative learning activities allow students to learn through "talk": as students talk with each other and work together on various classroom projects and activities, they learn to develop their ideas, and their teacher becomes an active guide rather than just a source of information. The first section of this book provides guidelines for developing "Collaborative Learning Skills"; the second section contains activities for "Collaborative Learning and Literature Study"; the third offers ways to implement "Collaboration in Writing, Revising, and Editing"; and the final section, "Additional Collaborative Learning Activities," involves television, music, and scriptwriting.

3.10 *Handbook for planning an effective literature program, kindergarten through grade twelve.* (1987). Sacramento, CA: California State Department of Education.

Intended for teachers, administrators, consultants, parents and students who wish to review and improve elementary and secondary educational programs, this handbook provides essays discussing educational research, teaching philosophies and methods, instructional materials, and curriculum planning strategies in relation to the teaching of literature.

3.11 Karolides, N. J. (Ed.). (1985). Language learning. *Wisconsin English Journal, 27*(2).

The articles in this journal issue explore classroom methods for enhancing language acquisition. The titles of the articles and their authors include: "Using Literature to Teach Language" (Richard D. Cureton); "ERIC/RCS Report: Evaluating Language Development" (Fran Lehr); and "Language Learning through Sentence Combining" (Nicholas J. Karolides).

3.12 Karolides, N. J. (Ed.). (1987). Beyond the two R's. *Wisconsin English Journal, 29*(2).

The compendium of articles in this journal issue deals with the diverse components of the language arts, communication, and critical thinking curricula. The titles and authors of the articles include: "What to Do until the Doctor Comes: Speech in the Language Arts Classroom" (John Fortier); "Teaching and Thinking Skills: Some Practical Applications" (Mary Kay Bryan); and "Getting Children to Tune In" (Caroline G. Majek). Also included in this journal are a list of NCTE Achievement Awards winners and reviews of selected books for children, adolescents, and teachers.

3.13 Koontz, C. L. (Ed.). (1985). *Connections: Using contemporary children's literature (K-9) in the classroom*. Urbana, IL: National Council of Teachers of English.

This compilation includes many valuable ideas and teaching aids, and lists reviews of 52 popular K-9 titles to help teachers select high-quality works.

3.14 Lazarus, A., & Smith, W. (1983). *A glossary of literature and composition*. Urbana, IL: National Council of Teachers of English.

This revised edition concentrates on three major branches of English studies: literature (including criticism), rhetorical theory, and composition. Nearly 800 terms are thoroughly defined, illustrated by appropriate literary examples, and cross-referenced.

3.15 Matthews, D. E. (1983). Popular literature: Its compatibility with the basics. *Illinois English Bulletin, 70*(2).

This special journal issue contains nine articles on the subject of using popular literature in the classroom. Subjects covered in these articles include: using vernacular, supernatural literature to teach the skills of literary analysis; pairing the classics with detective fiction; using fantasy literature with students afraid of great literature; and using adolescent literature to teach value clarification.

3.16 Matthews, D. E. (1984). The English teacher and the arts. *Illinois English Bulletin, 71*(2).

Emphasizing an aesthetic approach to language arts, this focused journal issue brings together ideas for literature and writing instruction that capitalize upon opportunities provided by all the fine arts.

3.17 McLeod, A. M. (Ed.). (1983). Books still worth reading [Special issue]. *Virginia English Bulletin, 33*(1).

The 10 major articles in this special journal issue deal with literary works designated by individual educators as "still worth reading." Some of the works discussed include: *The Assistant* (Bernard Malamud), *The Old Man and the Sea* (Ernest Hemingway), *Emma* (Jane Austen), *Lord Jim* (Joseph Conrad), *The Scarlet Letter* (Nathaniel Hawthorne), and "The Rime of the Ancient Mariner" by Samuel Taylor Coleridge.

3.18 McLeod, A. M. (Ed.). (1984). Literature and its teaching [Special issue]. *Virginia English Bulletin, 34*(2).

The theme of this focused issue centers on "Literature and Its Teaching." The 15 major articles discuss a variety of topics including William Faulkner, the use of metaphor, mathematics as a literary theme in *The Phantom Tollbooth,* and the effect of war literature on an adolescent reader. In addition, the journal contains suggestions for teaching *Great Expectations, Treasure Island, Flowers for Algernon, I Am the Cheese, Walden,* and *Sounder.*

3.19 Mier, M. (1985). The New Realism in children's literature. *English Quarterly, 17*(1), 42–48.

This work cites documents from the ERIC system that may help teachers who are faced with the tasks of evaluating the New Realism and finding methods to use it effectively in the classroom.

3.20 Moss, P. (1982). Literature: The neglected situation. *English in Australia, 60,* 3–7.

Moss argues for the development of new literary texts and for the development of new and appropriate literary theories to teach those texts.

3.21 Nelms, B. F. (Ed.). (1988). *Literature in the classroom: Readers, texts, and contexts.* Urbana, IL: National Council of Teachers of English.

This book discusses the teaching of literature from first grade through senior high school within a variety of theoretical perspectives, including structuralist, psychoanalytic, Marxist, archetypal, and feminist. The three principal sections are: "Readers: Student Responses to Literature"; "Texts: Interpretive Approaches to Literature"; and "Contexts: Social Dimensions of Literature."

3.22 Nugent, S. M., & Nugent, H. E. (1984, October). *Young adult literature: From middle school to college.* Paper presented at the Annual Meeting of the New England Association of Teachers of English Fall Conference, Providence, RI. (ERIC Document Reproduction Service No. ED 251 855)

This paper begins with the assertion that learning difficult literary concepts (such as point of view and unfamiliar content) while reading difficult and often unfamiliar content prematurely places too many demands upon middle school and high school students. Young adult literature allows students to address the demands of a new concept while reading more familiar content. One specific technique found to be beneficial when teaching new concepts is the double-entry journal, which requires students to write affective responses to readings and to compare such entries with classmates. After discussion with peers and critical analysis of the literature in class discussion, students write a second journal entry synthesizing insights gained from discussion, analysis, readings, and writings.

3.23 Schimmel, R. S., & Monaghan, C. (1983). Deaf awareness through literature using deaf adults as role models. *American Annals of the Deaf, 128*(7), 890–93.

This literature program promotes students' language development, positive self-concept, and mental health skills through fluent communication with a deaf student adviser who leads weekly discussion/storytelling for students from kindergarten through high school. Teachers report, among other positive effects, that the deaf educator is an excellent role model for classroom teaching techniques.

3.24 Small, R. C., & Strzepek, J. E. (1988). *A casebook for English teachers: Dilemmas and decisions.* Belmont, CA: Wadsworth.

The 33 cases in this book have been carefully designed to present a full and comprehensive examination of the teaching of English language arts. The teaching of literature, language, and composition is explored, as is evaluation, censorship, materials selection, grouping, and a host of other aspects of the teaching of English.

3.25 Weaver, C. (Ed.). (1981). Using junior novels to develop language and thought: Five integrative teaching guides [Special issue]. *Another Day, Another Pineapple.*

This monograph consists of teaching guides for five junior novels: *Tales of a Fourth Grade Nothing; Mrs. Frisby and the Rats of NIMH; Across Five Aprils; The Lion, the Witch and the Wardrobe;* and *Harriet the Spy.*

3.26 Woodhead, C. (1982). Dream and waking: Theory and practice in the teaching of literature. *Use of English, 33*(2), 3–15.

Woodhead suggests that any attempt that the teacher makes to create a lesson where the student can engage the text runs directly counter to the whole drift of the secondary school curriculum as it exists today.

3.27 Wyman, L. (Ed.). (1984). *Poetry in the Classroom.* Urbana, IL: National Council of Teachers of English.

This book consists of a collection of 17 articles that deal with the notion that students cannot be "taught" poetry, but can be introduced to it in certain ways and can learn to love it on their own.

Author List

The following alphabetical list of authors cited in this bibliography is provided as a service to readers.

Abel, F. J., 3.4
Anderson, P. M., 2.1
Armstrong, D. P., 2.2
Berger, A., 2.3
California Literature
    Institute Participants, 3.1
California State Department
    of Education, 3.10
Cameron, J. R., 2.4

Carter, C., 2.5
Christenbury, L., 2.6
Committee on Classroom
    Practices, 2.5
Conn. State Department
    of Education, 2.27
Corcoran, B., 2.7
Cullinan, B. E., 1.1
D'Angelo, K., 3.2

12. Research on Response to Literature

Richard Beach
University of Minnesota

Susan Hynds
Syracuse University

Criteria for Inclusion

In order to be included in this selected bibliography, the studies must have employed some systematic analysis of readers' responses to literary texts, even though, in some cases, that analysis was not empirical. We excluded reading comprehension research with literary texts in which the primary interest was determining comprehension. A few studies employed nonliterary texts but were of sufficient interest to be relevant to literary response researchers. We have only included research published in English, thereby excluding a large body of research recently published in Europe, particularly in West and East Germany and in Hungary. In addition, the bibliography excluded many studies focusing on the effects of literature instruction. Finally, the research also must have been completed after 1970.

Research Reviews

For a summary of research conducted prior to 1970, see Alan Purves and Richard Beach (1972). *Literature and the reader: Research on response to literature, reading interests, and the teaching of literature,* Urbana, IL: National Council of Teachers of English.

Preparation of this report for the Center for the Learning and Teaching of Literature was supported in part by grant number G008720278, which is cosponsored by the U.S. Department of Education, Office of Educational Research and Improvement (OERI/ED), and by the National Endowment for the Arts (NEA). However, the opinions expressed herein do not necessarily reflect the position or policy of OERI/ED or NEA, and no official endorsement of either agency should be inferred.

131

For summary reviews of later research see the following:

Applebee, A. (1977). The elements of response to a literary work: What we have learned. *Research in the Teaching of English, 11,* 255–71.

Beach, R., & Appleman, D. (1983). Reading strategies for expository and literary text types. In A. Purves and O. Niles (Eds.), *Becoming readers in a complex society.* Eighty-third Yearbook of the National Society for the Study of Education. Chicago: The University of Chicago Press.

Beach, R., & Hynds, S. (in press). Research on response to literature. In R. Barr, M. Kamil, P. Mosenthal, & P.D. Pearson (Eds.), *Handbook of Reading Research, Volume 2.* White Plains, NY: Longman.

Cooper, C. (Ed.). (1985). *Researching response to literature and the teaching of literature.* Norwood, NJ: Ablex.

Galda, L. (1983). Research in response to literature. *Journal of Research and Development in Education 16,* 1–8.

Galda, L. (1982). Assessment: Response to literature. In A. Berger & A.H. Robinson (Eds.) *Secondary School Reading.* Urbana, Ill: NCRE and ERIC/RCS.

Klemenz-Belgardt, E. (1981). American research on response to literature: The empirical studies. *Poetics, 10,* 357–80.

Categories for Organization of the Research

We have organized this bibliography according to the following categories which we define at the beginning of each major section. All studies were categorized based on the primary focus of that study. In some cases, studies are categorized according to one additional secondary focus. At the end of each primary focus section, these secondary focus studies are cross-referenced by authors' names.

Reader Variables

These studies focus on characteristics of readers and/or the influences of reader characteristics on response. For purposes of this review these categories are defined as follows:

1. *Orientation:* The reader's stance, approach, personality, reading style, goals, values, beliefs, cultural influences, and knowledge.
2. *Development:* Studies which focus on differences among readers in terms of age, cognitive development, and social-cognitive abilities.
3. *Gender:* Studies which focus on the influence of gender on response.

1. Orientation

1.1 Banks, M. (1987). An analysis of nineteenth century black responses to *Uncle Tom's Cabin* as recorded in selected antebellum black newspapers: 1852–1855. (Doctoral dissertation, Rensselaer Polytechnic Institute). *Dissertation Abstracts International, 47,* 1852A–1853A.

This study examined the nature of blacks' published reactions to the novel *Uncle Tom's Cabin* appearing in black newspapers over a three-year period, from the novel's initial date of publication (1852) to 1855. While initial responses were positive, later responses were increasingly negative, expressing skepticism and anger about the inferior images of blacks as portrayed in the novel.

1.2 Beach, R. (1983). Attitudes, social conventions, and response to literature. *Journal of Research and Development in Education, 16*(3) 47–53.

This study examines the differences between high school and college students' attitudes toward literature teaching and the responses to a story portraying a literature teacher. Forty-five 11th-grade students and 45 college preservice English education majors were administered the Gallo "Attitude Towards Poetry Teaching Scale" (1968). Students also rated the appropriateness of, and responded to, specific acts in a story portraying a relatively traditional literature teacher. Students' responses were clustered according to similarity of content. The high school students had significantly more "traditional" scores on the attitude scale than the college students. Similarly, high school students responded more positively to more traditional teacher behaviors in the story than did the college students. (For the Gallo scale, see Gallo, D. [1968]. Toward a more effective assessment of poetry teaching methods. *Research in the Teaching of English, 2,* 125–41.)

1.3   Beach, R. (1985). Discourse conventions and researching response to literary dialogue. In C. Cooper (Ed.), *Researching response to literature and the teaching of literature.* Norwood, NJ: Ablex.

This report discusses examples of readers' applications of knowledge of speech-act, social, and literary conventions to make inferences about characters' traits, beliefs, goals, knowledge, and plans from dialogue presented. It also reports the results of a study of 30 high school and 30 college students' inferences in response to 16 specific dialogue acts in a one-act comic play about marriage. Students' inferences were clustered according to those representing long-term versus immediate goals. College students' inferences were ranked significantly higher than high school students' inferences for 12 of 16 dialogue acts, a difference representing the college students' knowledge of marriage and comic conventions.

1.4   Blake, R., & Lumm, A. (1986). Responding to poetry: High school students read poetry. *English Journal, 75*(2), 68–73.

This study was conducted to see how five untrained high school students responded to a new poem. The students were asked to read a new poem aloud, interpret it, and tape-record that interpretation. The taped responses were analyzed to see how different readers approached problematic parts of the poem, and an in-depth analysis of one reader's response was conducted. Results suggest that rereading is essential in poetry understanding and that individuals respond differently to the same poem.

1.5   Bleich, D. (1986a). Cognitive stereoscopy and the study of language and literature. In B. Peterson (Ed.), *Convergences.* Urbana, IL: National Council of Teachers of English.

Based on a theory of knowing texts as experiencing an intersubjective integration of different perspectives, this study asked teachers to retell and discuss a story. The responses are discussed in terms of the degree to which readers explored alternative perspectives and were aware of the influence of their own perspective on their responses. Analysis of two teachers' responses indicated that one teacher was concerned with the perspective defined in terms of power and the value of authority—a perspective she reflected on and questioned— while the other was concerned with the value of competence and duty, a perspective he accepted without self-reflection.

1.6 Cullinan, R., Harwood, K., & Galda, L. (1983). The reader and the story: Comprehension and response. *Journal of Research and Development in Education, 16,*(3) 29–38.

This research studied the responses of fourth-, sixth-, and eighth-grade students to two novels. Six students at each grade level were asked focused questions individually and in groups following the reading of each novel. The study suggested that there is a direct relationship between story preference and comprehension. Students' expectations determined story comprehension and evaluation.

1.7 Culp, M. (1977). Case studies of the influence of literature on the attitudes, values, and behaviors of adolescents. *Research in the Teaching of English, 11,* 245–53.

This report presents case-study analyses of the influence of reading literature on two college freshman students' attitudes, values, and behaviors: one who experienced a strong influence, and the other, minimal influence. Five students were selected for case studies from a larger pool of 158 students. Students were interviewed and completed a self-classification check list regarding their reading orientation (Shirley, 1966). Students most frequently cited influences on their attitudes in terms of self-image, sensitivity to others, awareness of moral/ethical issues, and social problems. Students were most influenced by novels of their own choosing. Heavy readers who could involve themselves with texts were more likely to be influenced than light readers. (For Shirley, F. [1966], see: Purves, A. & Beach, R., Case studies of the influence of reading on adolescence. *Research in the Teaching of Reading, 1*(30–41.)

1.8 DeVries, J. (1973). A statistical analysis of undergraduate readers: Responses to selected characters in Shakespeare's *The Tempest.* (Doctoral dissertation, University of Illinois). *Dissertation Abstracts International, 34,* 5906A.

The purpose of this study was to determine changes in readers' evaluative reactions as the readers moved through a play. One hundred college students applied seventeen, 15-point semantic differential scales to students' ratings of certain events. Findings indicated that as the students read through the play their perception of characters increased in complexity. Students' primary interest shifted from a focus on plot in the beginning of the play to character interactions at the end of the play. Self-concept had little influence on ratings.

1.9   Dillon, G. (1982). Styles of reading. *Poetics Today, 3*,(1) 77–88.

This study examines readers' responses to Faulkner's "A Rose for Emily," focusing particularly on how readers perceive the chronological sequence or "event chain" of the story. The study concludes that readers adopt three basic styles of reading: "Character-Action-Moral," "Digger for Secrets," and "Anthropologist." Results further indicate that readers understand life and literature in similar ways.

1.10   Faggiani, L. (1971). The relationship of attitude to response in the reading of a poem by ninth-grade students. (Doctoral dissertation, New York University). *Dissertation Abstracts International, 31*, 4004A–4005A.

Analysis of the relationship between ninth-grade students' scores on an attitude-towards-death scale and their responses to a poem about death indicated no significant relationship. Highly positive or highly negative attitudes towards death were related to the degree of involvement in the poem.

1.11   Gilman, I. (1986). Student responses to two literary passages and two paintings as they relate to the perception of stylistic complexity and the dimension of extraversion-introversion. (Doctoral dissertation, New York University). *Dissertation Abstracts International, 47*, 1223A.

This study examined the relationships between students' introversion/extraversion as measured by the Eysenck Personality Inventory and perceived stylistic complexity of two literary passages and two paintings. One hundred forty-two students responded to two literary passages and two paintings using semantic differential pairs to measure perceived stylistic complexity, interest, and pleasure. Results indicated that students who assess verbal and visual artwork as stylistically complex are more likely to give a lower pleasure rating than students assessing them as stylistically simple. Ambiverts and extraverts tend to be more similar to each other than to introverts in making pleasure assessments of paintings. Analysis of four students' written responses suggested that interest and pleasure are not meaningfully discriminated from general evaluation.

1.12 Gross, L. (1978). A study of the relationship between selected oral readings in sex-role oriented children's literature and the personal and social adjustment of the self-concept of children in grades one and three. (Doctoral dissertation, Rutgers University). *Dissertation Abstracts International, 38,* 6668A.

This researcher explored the effect of gender in picture books on the self-concept level of first and third graders. The subjects were divided into three groups who were read one book a day for three weeks. Group one was read male-oriented books, group two was read female-oriented books, and group three was read books which were both male and female oriented. Pre- and post-test scores on the California Test of Personality showed that combination picture books were most positive for improving self-concept.

1.13 Hoffstaedter, P. (1987). Poetic text processing and its empirical investigation. *Poetics, 16,* 75–91.

This study examined the degree to which "poeticity" is a property of learned text-processing strategies rather than a property of text elements. Forty adults rated 29 texts (poems, passages from novels, and articles) according to the degree to which the texts were "poetic," noted the words that contributed to their ratings, and reformulated the text to make them less "poetic." Certain text properties—syntactical deviations and recurrences or parallelisms—consistently contributed to a sense of "poeticity." When the same 24 poems were presented to readers as selections in a poetry anthology or as passages from newspaper articles, there were significant differences between the two contexts for "poeticity" ratings for 10 of the 24 poems, a mixed result. Case-study analyses of the think-alouds of a native and nonnative reader indicated that the nonnative reader perceived text difficulty as contributing to a sense of "poeticity."

1.14 Holland, N. (1973). *Poems in persons.* New York: W. W. Norton.

This book explores the mind of the poet H. D. to reveal the relation between her poetic style and her total identity. The author then compares the personalities and experiences of two people reading a selected poem by H. D. The book explores the ways in which personal experiences can be shared and private readings become communal.

1.15 Holland, N. (1975). *Five readers reading.* New Haven: Yale.

This study used psychological tests and extensive interviews to explore the ways in which five readers responded to classic short stories. Results support a transactional theory of literary response, in which readers apprehend literary texts through their own personality styles, defenses, fantasies, adaptive structures, and identities.

1.16 Hunt, R. & Vipond, D. *The reader, the text, the situation: Blocks and affordances in literary reading.* Unpublished report, Department of Psychology, St. Thomas University, New Brunswick, Canada. (ERIC Document Reproduction Service No. ED 284 298)

Analysis of college students' responses to John Updike's "A & P" indicated that the majority of the responses were negative. Content analysis of responses indicated that the negative evaluations were due to students' confusion over the use of descriptive details and disapproval of the characters' behavior and the story's resolution. These students may have read the story in terms of a "story-driven" orientation rather than a "point-driven" orientation. Those students who adopted a point-driven orientation were more likely to define the intentional use of descriptive details or the characters' actions as contributing to understanding the point of the story.

1.17 Hunt, R., & Vipond, D. (1985). Crash-testing a transactional model of literary learning. *Reader, 14,* 23–39.

This report of three studies dealing with readers' orientations was based on analyses of one-hour interviews employing "think-alouds" and retrospective questions.

In the first study, 12 undergraduates' and 12 faculty members' ratings of response statements indicate that undergraduates were significantly more likely to prefer a "story-driven" orientation (focusing on the enjoyment of the story) as compared to a "point-driven" orientation (reading in terms of the point).

The purpose of the second study was to determine students' ability to attend to "evaluations" signaling "tellability" or the point of a story (Labov, 1972). College students responded to two different versions of a story—the original with "evaluations" and a version with the evaluations replaced. After each page, students were asked to list phrases that were most likely to "catch their eye." Students were most likely to list the evaluations. (For "tellability," see: Labov, W., [1972] *The language of the inner city.* Philadelphia: University of Pennsylvania Press.)

The third study determined the effects of reading stories from three different perspectives. Seventy college students were assigned to one of three different treatments involving responses to three stories—"information-driven" (short-answer responses about details in the stories); "story-driven" (short summary of the main events); and "point-driven" (short summary of the main events and purpose of the story). Students responded to open-ended questions and response probes. Students in the information-driven group had significantly slower reading times than students in the other groups. Students in the point-driven group were most likely to slow down in the final pages and were more likely to interpret than students in the other groups.

1.18 Jacobsen, M. (1982). Looking for literary space: The willing suspension of disbelief revisited. *Research in the Teaching of English, 16,* 21–38.

This study compared the orientations of 26 college students in terms of their willingness to enter into the "world" or "potential space" of two short stories. Students were asked to describe their physical experiences of their "place" or "space" by visualizing their responses in diagrams and discussing those diagrams. Students varied in their willingness to suspend their disbelief or to apply their own experience, their lack of interest in the text, their difficulty with language, their lack of trust in the speaker, and their critical reaction to the attitudes implied by the text.

1.19 Kintgen, E. (1986). Expectations and processes in reading poetic narratives. *Empirical Studies of the Arts, 4,*(1), 79–95.

This study analyzed two adult readers' oral taped responses to an experimental poem in terms of the influence of their expectations on their responses. Readers expected that poetry is unified, each part contributing to a coherent whole; that certain poetic devices are employed; and that a serious tone is employed. The degree to which readers' expectations were or were not satisfied shaped their evaluations and responses.

1.20 Kintgen, E., & Holland, N. (1984). Carlos reads a poem. *College English, 44,* 459–86.

This study focuses on the response and interpretation processes of one graduate student reader. The focal informant was given an "I-test" based on Kelly's personal construct theory and asked to respond to a poem. Results indicated that reading combines both communal and personal aspects, and that readers use communal resources to fulfill personal aims, choosing only those interpretive approaches to texts that serve their own needs, goals, and values.

1.21 Lee, S. (1985). Comparative responses to literature by Korean and American college students. (Doctoral dissertation, University of Pittsburgh). *Dissertation Abstracts International, 47,* 1635A.

Sixty Korean and 41 American college freshmen were asked to write responses to two stories, one from each culture. Analysis of responses using the Purves (1968) categories indicated that each group's response patterns remained the same whether the story was from their own culture or the second culture. Both groups responded most strongly in the category of perception. Koreans responded more frequently in the category of engagement and Americans in the category of evaluation; the differences reflecting differences in cultural values. (For Purves categories, see Purves, A., & Rippere, V. [1968]. *Elements of writing about a literary work: A study of response to literature.* Urbana, Ill.: National Council of Teachers of English).

1.22 Mauro, L. (1983). Personal constructs and response to literature: Case studies of adolescents reading about death. (Doctoral dissertation, Rutgers University). *Dissertation Abstracts International, 44,* 2072A.

This study examines the influence of five adolescent subjects' personal constructs regarding death in their responses to selected literature about death and dying. Oral responses were analyzed according to implied personal constructs; Applebee's (1978) response modes (see 2.3); and use of evaluative response. The results revealed that each student's response was highly complex and personal. The diversity of readers' perceptions of death and dying, their expectations about the texts, and their assumptions about the response process were all reflected in their response to the texts. Evaluations of texts were related to the confirmation and disconfirmation of content, form, and readers' processing.

1.23 McConnell, M. (1983). The effect of literature exposure and writing practice on the original narrative writing of second-grade children. (Doctoral dissertation, Ohio State University). *Dissertation Abstracts International, 43,* 2619A.

The effect of experience with literature and writing practice on original narrative writing of second graders was explored. The results revealed that those students with high literature exposure and frequent writing practice were correlated with high holistic ratings on their creative writing.

1.24 McCormick, K. (1987). Task representation in writing about literature. *Poetics, 16,* 131–54.

This study discussed examples of "response statements" representing different cognitive and cultural representations of the response task. Students varied in their conception of strategies and goals appropriate for certain tasks. They also developed an awareness of the influence of cultural attitudes on their responses.

1.25 Meutsch, D. (1987). Cognitive processes in reading literary texts: The influence of context, goals, and situations. *Empirical Studies of the Arts, 5,* 115–35.

The purpose of this study was to determine the influence of stance and goals on readers' responses. Seventy-two college students were assigned to one of four groups in a 2 (stance: literary versus nonliterary) x 2 (goal: summary versus interpretation) design. Students responded in a free-response mode to a report. Students adopting a literary stance made more literary elaborations, while students with a non-literary stance made more non-literary elaborations.

1.26 Noda, L. A. (1981). Literature and culture: Japanese and American reader responses to modern Japanese short stories. (Doctoral dissertation, New York University). *Dissertation Abstracts International, 41,* 4894A.

The differences in responses of adult Japanese readers to adult American readers were investigated in this case study. Modern Japanese short stories were read by both groups, and their responses were recorded in an interview. The results indicated that culture is an important factor in reader-response.

1.27 Petrosky, A. (1976). The effects of reality perceptions and fantasy on response to literature: Two case studies. *Research in the Teaching of English, 10,* 239–58.

This study examined the influence of two 9th-grade students' personality orientations on their responses as determined by analysis of patterns in the responses to the Thematic Apperception Test and to various texts. One student's need to control was manifested in her reluctance to express her thoughts and feelings. In contrast, the other student's need to share and desire to explore were manifested in a willingness to express her thoughts and feelings.

1.28 Purves, A., Foshay, A., & Hansson, G. (1973). *Literature education in ten countries.* New York: John Wiley.

The purpose of this international assessment was to determine the degree to which 14- and 17-year-old students' response preferences, as determined by selecting 5 most preferred response options from 20 options representing different response types, varied across 10 different countries and across different short stories. Students' responses varied across countries, with 17-year-olds being more consistent than 12-year-olds. Despite some consistencies across the different countries, student preferences varied across countries according to two basic continuums: emphasis on "content" versus "form," and an "impersonal" versus "personal" orientation, differences that reflected the particular response emphasis of the literature curriculums of each of those countries.

1.29 Ross, C. (1978). A comparative study of the responses made by grade eleven Vancouver students to Canadian and New Zealand poems. *Research in the Teaching of English, 12,* 297–306.

This study examined the influence of knowing the geographical setting of poetry on students' responses. Four hundred seventy-seven 11th-grade Canadian students listened to tapes of pairs of poems, one poem from Canada and the other from New Zealand. Half of the poems were labeled and half were unlabeled regarding their setting. Students' written responses were categorized according to response types. Students' responses did not differ between Canadian and New Zealand poems.

1.30 Salvatori, M. (1983). Reading and writing a text. *College English,* 45(7), 657–66.

This case-study analysis of a female college student's written responses sought to determine the relationship of that student's self-concept as a "writer" to her responses. Analysis of the student's writing over the period of a course indicated that the student shifted from an impersonal stance of "distancing" herself from a text to a stance of active engagement and reflection on the relationship between a text and her own life.

1.31 Shedd, P. (1976). The relationship between attitude of the reader towards women's changing role and response to literature which illuminates women's role. (ERIC Document Reproduction Service No. ED 142 956)

The effects of the attitude of the reader toward women's changing role on the reader's response to literature that illuminated women's changing role was explored. Six male and six female high school seniors with I.Q.'s of 120 or above were selected because half favored women's changing role and half did not. Students read and responded to four short stories: two short stories illuminated women's role and two short stories had no bearing on that issue. Results were obtained from quantitative data and a qualitative analysis of individual interviews. Results revealed that readers who favored women's changing role made a significantly higher proportion of affective responses to the stories which dealt with that subject than did their peers, while the two groups did not differ in response to the neutral stories.

1.32 Somers, A. B. (1973). Responses of advanced and average readers in grades seven, nine, and eleven to two dissimilar short stories. (Doctoral dissertation, Florida State University). *Dissertation Abstracts International, 33,* 4252A.

This study analyzed the responses of 7th-, 9th-, and 11th-grade students who were advanced and average readers. Students read short stories and produced written free responses to their readings. Purves (1968) categories were used to analyze responses. Results indicated that students primarily preferred the evaluative mode, but also were concerned with perception and interpretation of content, especially characters and events. Excepting plot, students rarely responded to form or technique. Seventh-grade students were more involved in the stories, and advanced readers made significantly more interpretations to theme oriented stories.

1.33 Svensson, C. (1985). *The construction of poetic meaning: A cultural-developmental study of symbolic and nonsymbolic strategies in the interpretation of contemporary poetry.* Lund, Sweden: Liber Forlag.

The purpose of these two studies was to determine the relationship between readers' background knowledge of literature and their ability to interpret literature. In the first study, 72 subjects at ages 11, 14, and 18 completed questionnaires regarding their literary background (amount of story-telling in the home, amount of reading, and orientation in reading). Students also responded to four poems and were interviewed about their inferences about the point of the poems and reasons for their inferences. Interview answers were categorized as "literal descriptive," "literal interpretive," "mixed literal/thematic," "thematic," "mixed literal/symbolic," and "symbolic." There was a significant relationship between background knowledge of literature and level of interpretation across age levels. Age level was also significantly related to level of interpretation (see Svensson, 1987; 2.42).

The second study was designed to determine the influence of the typographical arrangement of poems on students' inferences about figurative and symbolic meanings. One hundred forty-four students at ages 11, 14, and 18 responded in writing to the original versions of poems and to poems rearranged into "prose." Differences in graphic arrangements affected the number of figurative and symbolic inferences, particularly in the older groups. The fact that graphic arrangement was significantly related for the 14-year-old group, but not for the 11-year-old group suggests an increasing knowledge of literary form.

1.34 Viehoff, R. (1986). How to construct a literary poem? *Poetics, 15,* 287–306.

This study deals with the ways in which readers manage their understanding of textual material. Sixteen subjects were tested individually while thinking aloud about unknown textual material. Results indicated that readers shifted their focus of attention from nonliterary ("common") strategies to literary ones if and only if they felt free to refer to their past experience with literature. Results further underscore the idea that literary understanding is governed by established literary conventions.

1.35 Vipond, D., & Hunt, R. (1984). Point-driven understanding: Pragmatic and cognitive dimensions of literary reading. *Poetics, 13,* 261–77.

Using a modern short story, these authors illustrate the cognitive strategies associated with a point-driven orientation toward literary texts. These cognitive operations include coherence, narrative surface, and transactional strategies. The authors suggest a number of testable hypotheses about literary reading and suggest possible methods for testing them.

1.36 Werner, C. (1987). Responses of college readers with different cultural backgrounds to a short story. (Doctoral dissertation, Georgia State University, 1988). *Dissertation Abstracts International, 48,* 2266-A.

College students in three ESL and three developmental reading classes wrote responses to a story. The majority of the responses were descriptive in nature rather than interpretative or evaluative. There were no differences in response-types between students' responses in the ESL and developmental reading classes.

1.37 Wheeler, V. (1983). Field orientation as a predictor of reader-response to literature. (Doctoral dissertation, Illinois State University). *Dissertation Abstracts International, 44,* 2756A.

This study analyzed the relationship between the field orientation of community college students as measured by the Group Embedded-Figures Test and their response to a short story. Subjects wrote essays in response to a short story; responses were categorized using the Purves (1968) categories. Subjects who were field independent and older tended to employ interpretation/evaluation responses. Subjects who were field dependent and younger tended to employ engagement-involvement/perception responses.

1.38 Wilson, R. R. (1976). In-depth book discussions of selected sixth graders: Response to literature. (Doctoral dissertation, Ohio State University). *Dissertation Abstracts International, 36,* 7195A.

This study explored the responses of eight 6th-grade students to books. Students participated in discussion groups. Their responses were gathered using a repertory grid and categorized using the Squire (1964) categories. Results indicated that discussions centered on recurrent themes of friendship, author's purpose, meaning of certain symbols, fantasy situations in realistic works, illustrations in one book, and unique characteristics of the character. The researcher also found that in-depth discussions seemed to generate interest in reading. (For Squire categories see: Squire, J. (1964) *Study of Adolescents' Response to Short Stories.* National Council of Teachers of English.)

1.39 Wilson, J. R. (1965). *Responses of college freshmen to three novels.* (NCTE Research Report No. 7). Urbana, IL: National Council of Teachers of English.

This study was conducted to explore student responses to literature and the influence of classroom experiences on those responses. Each of 54 freshman English students read one of three novels, took notes while reading, and wrote their immediate reactions in class. After three discussion periods, they wrote follow-up reactions. This procedure was repeated with the other novels, resulting in 280 written reports. Responses were coded in seven categories: literary judgment, interpretational, narrational, associational, self-involvement, prescriptive, and miscellaneous. Case studies of 9 students suggested that the students' ways of responding to literature were changed—both statistically and individually—by the study of that literature. Students made fewer literary judgments, more interpretations, fewer retellings, and fewer self-involvement responses. The study concluded by making a number of instructional suggestions.

*See also: 2.9, 2.26, 3.4, 3.6, 3.9, 4.3, 4.14, 4.17, 5.4, 6.2, 7.5, 8.10

2. Development

2.1 Amigone, G. (1983). Apprehending a literary work of art: A comparative study of interventions into a poem by experienced and inexperienced readers. (Doctoral dissertation, State University of New York at Buffalo). *Dissertation Abstracts International, 44,* 486A.

This study compared responses to Robert Lowell's "Skunk Hour" of 10 inexperienced readers—students enrolled in a freshman literature class—with responses of 5 experienced readers with extensive backgrounds in literature. Readers gave holistic responses as well as reactions to preformulated responses in terms of whether the responses were "new" versus "familiar" or "works in my reading" versus "doesn't work."
    Experienced readers were more likely to apply knowledge of scientific and biographical information and poetic devices and to conceive of the poem as a gestalt than were the inexperienced readers. The preformulated responses were helpful in stimulating response for the inexperienced readers.

2.2 Applebee, A. (1978). Children's construal of stories and related genres as measured with repertory grid techniques. *Research in the Teaching of English, 10,* 226–38.

The researcher studied 6-, 9-, and 16-year-olds' thinking about a variety of genres: short stories, television, comics, and film. Using a repertory grid technique, he found no differences due to genre, but did find developmental differences. Six-year-olds think a story really happened and tend to look at events rather than at the story as a whole plot sequence. Nine-year-olds perceive a story as "made-up" but want to see all endings as happy. Sixteen-year-olds become more tolerant of works which challenge the reader's views, move from concerns of readability to concerns with the complexity of adult books, and become more aware of the distance which they perceive between themselves and the work.

2.3 Applebee, A. (1978). *A child's concept of story.* Chicago: University of Chicago Press.

Based on a Piagetian model of development, analysis was conducted of 9-, 13-, and 17-year-olds' use of retelling, synopsis, summary, analysis, generalization, and evaluation in discussing stories. The 9- and 13-year-olds were more likely to employ retelling and synopsis, while 17-year-olds were more likely to employ analysis and generalization.

Analysis of the predominant method employed in evaluating the quality of a text indicated that 9-year-olds were significantly more likely to employ a "categoric" method; 13-year-olds were more likely than 9-year-olds to employ an "analytic" method; and 17-year-olds were more likely than 13-year-olds to employ a "generalizing" method.

Relative to different Piagetian stages, preoperational-stage readers characteristically responded in a narrative, retelling mode; concrete operational, a summarization, categorization mode; early formal operational, an analytic/identification mode; and late formal operational, a generalization/interpretation mode.

2.4 Beach, R. & Brunetti, G. (1976). Differences between high school and university students in their conceptions of literary characters. *Research in the Teaching of English, 10,* 259–68.

This research probed developmental differences between 10th graders and college students in how they conceptualized literary characters. An adjective checklist was used. Results revealed a significant difference due to age of student in conception of character. Younger students were more likely to project their self-concept onto the characters.

2.5 Beach, R., & Wendler, L. (1987). Developmental differences in response to a story. *Research in the Teaching of English, 21,* 286–97.

The purpose of this study was to determine the developmental differences between high school and college students' inferences about short story characters' acts, beliefs, and goals. Eighth-graders, 11th graders, college freshmen, juniors, and seniors responded to specific acts in a story. Students' act, belief, and goal inferences were clustered according to similarity of content, resulting in composite categories for each answer. Ratings of these composite categories indicated that the college students were significantly more likely than the high school students to conceive of the action categories according to degree of focus on social or psychological beliefs as opposed to feelings, and to conceive of the goal categories according to long-term as opposed to short-term goals.

2.6 Bennett, S. (1979). The relationship between adolescents' levels of moral development and their responses to short stories. (Doctoral dissertation, University of California, Berkeley). *Dissertation Abstracts International, 40,* 34A.

The relationship between levels of moral development and preferred modes of response to literature was investigated. Subjects were 74 white, middle-class adolescent boys from a suburban high school in the San Francisco Bay Area. Students were classified for moral development using James Rest's Determining Issues Test. High or low moral reading had a significant effect on the mode of response. Principled-level thinkers more often chose interpretive responses than did conventional thinkers.

2.7 Bunbury, R. (1985). Levels of response to literature. *Australian Journal of Reading, 8,* 220–28.

Sixty Australian 7-, 9-, and 11-year-old students were interviewed about responses to three different modes: poems, folk tales, and stories. The percentages of literal versus inferential responses were as follows: 7-year-olds: 73% and 19%; 9-year-olds: 61% and 29%; and 11-year-olds: 35% and 54%. While differences in literary mode had no effect on level of inference, the nature of the interviewer/student interaction did have an influence.

2.8 Crowhurst, M., & Kooy, M. (1986). The use of response journals in teaching the novel. *Reading-Canada-Lecture, 3,* 256–66.

Thirty-two 9th-grade and fourteen 12th-grade students responded in daily journal entries to novels. Journals were analyzed according to comments about structure, hypotheses, personal responses, and style. Ninth graders were more likely to respond to structure and less likely to respond to style than 12th graders. There were no grade-level differences for hypotheses and personal responses.

2.9 Cullinan, R., Galda, L., & Harwood, K. (1983). The readers and the story: Comprehension and response. *Journal of Research and Development in Education, 16,*(3) 29–38. See 1.6.

2.10 Fisher, R. (1985). A comparison of tenth-grade students' discussion to adults' small group discussions in response to literature. (Doctoral dissertation, Virginia Polytechnic Institute). *Dissertation Abstracts International, 47,* 2062A.

This study compared how the responses of a tenth-grade student discussion group compared with an adult discussion group. Groups were divided by treatments: a reflective reading group which used highly structured, teacher-directed questions; the question group, which had no adult leader but chose questions from the list used by the reflective group; and a free discussion group, which participated in free discussions with no direction and no adult guide. Tape recordings were made of the discussion sessions and transcribed. Categories analyzed were: comprehensiveness of discussion, length of responses, nature of inappropriateness, breadth of participation, and change of mind of a discussant. Responses were also categorized as factual, inferential, experiential, judgmental, miscellaneous, and appropriate or inappropriate. No clear patterns of change were found as a result of treatment, but students in free response groups offered responses that were categorically more like the responses of adults in their final free response.

2.11 Fusco, E. (1983). The relationship between children's level of cognitive development and their response to literature. (Doctoral dissertation, Hofstra University). *Dissertation Abstracts International, 45,* 05A.

This study explored the relationship between students' cognitive level of development and their response to literature.

Middle school students' oral and written responses in a group discussion about a book were recorded and their scores were analyzed using the SOLO response taxonomy. Three cognitive ability tests were gathered and compared to students' performances in the discussion group. Major findings indicated: (1) analyzing student responses to questions provided a developmental sequence of the characteristics of different cognitive levels; (2) students respond to questions that are matched to their cognitive level of development; (3) the students' cognitive level and not their age are related to the mean cognitive level of response; (4) in predicting a student's mean cognitive level, the most significant variables will be the mean cognitive level of the questions and the student's reading achievement.

2.12 Golden, J. (1978). A schema for analyzing response to literature applied to the responses of fifth and eighth graders to realistic and fantasy short stories. (Doctoral dissertation, Ohio State University). *Dissertation Abstracts International, 39,* 5996A. (ERIC Document ED 192 306)

This study compared fifth and eighth graders' responses to two different genres of story: fantasy and realistic. Ten students at each level listened to the stories as they read along, and then gave answers to questions designed to elicit retelling, evaluation, and interpretation responses. Responses were analyzed by discourse level, cognitive operation, and reference pattern. Fifth graders were more likely to make expressive responses, while eighth graders made more interpretive responses. The realistic story evoked more identification responses, especially for fifth graders, while the fantasy story prompted eighth graders to connect their responses to other fantasy stories.

2.13 Hansson, G. (1973). Some types of research on response to literature. *Research in the Teaching of English, 7,* 260–84.

This study compared responses of readers with extensive versus little background knowledge of literature. "Experts" (scholars and literature teachers), university literature majors, and skilled workers completed 25 seven-point bipolar scales at each of 12 points in a poem. The across-group ratings were highly similar, suggesting that, despite differences in background, respondents shared similar evaluative orientations. The one area of difference was that more educated readers made more diversified judgments about formal qualities than did the less educated readers.

2.14 Hansson, G. (1974). *Litteraturlasning i symasiet* [Reading literature in the gymnasium]. Stockholm: Utbildnings-forlajet.

Secondary and college students applied 14 unipolar seven-point semantic-differential scales and written responses to six points in each of four poems commonly studied in Swedish schools. Despite variation in prior knowledge and age, students' ratings were highly similar, while written responses reflected sharper differences in the amount and content of interpretation. Older students were more likely to produce interpretations consistent with the "expected" interpretation than younger students, whose written responses varied more than those of older students. The investigator cautions that, in using written responses in developmental research, writing ability may be a confounding factor, a factor eliminated by the use of scales.

2.15 Hickman, J. (1980). Children's response to literature: What happens in the classroom. *Language Arts, 57,* 524–27.

This ethnographic study analyzed children's response to literature at various developmental stages and in a variety of natural classroom contexts. Ninety children aged 5 to 11 were observed during a four-month period. Data were collected on log sheets and then categorized into the following: listening behaviors, contact with books, acting on the impulse to share, oral responses, actions and drama, making things, and writing. Students' responses were compared according to age-level differences. Teacher strategies for influencing the classroom were also categorized. Accessibility of a book was of primary importance in children's willingness to express their responses. Teacher manipulation of the classroom had a strong influence on student response.

2.16 Hickman, J. (1983). Everything considered: Response to literature in an elementary school setting. *Journal of Research and Development in Education, 16,* 8–13.

This ethnographic study investigated the responses of elementary students, kindergarten through grade six, to two children's books. Spontaneous as well as solicited verbal responses were analyzed. Children in kindergarten and first grade were most likely to employ non-verbal modes, facial expressions and pantomimes. Second and third graders were most likely to share and demonstrate their oral reading skills. Fourth and fifth graders were most likely to make references to art work, and to write about the books. Solicited responses were acquired by giving students a tape recorder and asking them to talk about their responses freely. All ages made evaluative statements and referred to illustrations. Younger students were most likely to employ partial retelling and summarizing than older readers.

2.17 Hynds, S. (1983). Interpersonal cognitive complexity as related to the character perceptions, literary response preferences, story comprehension, and literary attitudes of adolescent readers. (Doctoral dissertation, George Peabody College of Vanderbilt University). *Dissertation Abstracts International, 43,* 07.

This study investigated relationships between adolescents' levels of cognitive complexity and their levels of literary response. Eleventh graders completed a written response in reference to two peers and two characters in a short story. These written responses were analyzed to determine students' character complexity and cognitive complexity. Students also completed measures of story comprehension, interpretation, response preference, literary interest, and literary transfer used in the IEA study. The analysis showed that cognitive complexity is related to inferential comprehension but not literary comprehension. No significant differences on response preference appeared for any Purves category. Peer complexity and literary interest were predictors of character complexity. High complexity readers preferred responses dealing with character motivation and comparison of literary works rather than engagement/involvement. There was a significant relationship between literary interest and cognitive complexity.

2.18 Hynds, S. (1985). Interpersonal cognitive complexity and the literary response processes of adolescent readers. *Research in the Teaching of English, 19,* 386–402.

This study examined the relationships between interpersonal cognitive complexity and adolescents' character impressions, story comprehension, response preferences, and literary attitudes. Eighty-three 11th-grade students completed a cognitive complexity measure: a two-character role category questionnaire about a liked and a disliked peer. After reading a story, students completed a response preference measure and a comprehension test, as well as a reading interests/literary transfer inventory. Cognitive complexity was positively related to perceptions of character complexity. High complexity was related to higher inferential comprehension, interest in actions and motivations of characters and people, and relating the story to other stories.

2.19 Hynds, S. (1989). Bringing life to literature and literature to life: Social constructs and contexts of four adolescent readers. *Research in the Teaching of English, 23,* 30–61.

The purpose of this study was to examine social influences on the reading processes of four adolescent readers, as well as the relationship between factors of social cognition and these readers' responses to short stories. Four case-study participants, all seniors in high school, were chosen from a group of 56 students in a suburban school. Results underscored the need for more varied and systematic assessments of reading competence, as well as an understanding of the interplay of competence, pragmatics, and volition in the likelihood that readers will bring social-cognitive processes to bear on reading.

2.20 Ice, M. (1984). A child's sense of story: A two-year study. (Doctoral dissertation, University of Missouri–Columbia, 1984). *Dissertation Abstracts International, 44,* 3001A.

This study examined children's emerging sense of story as it related to age and teacher's theoretical orientation. Seven children's oral stories were analyzed at the beginning of first grade and at the end of second grade according to sources of story, narrative form, use of formal elements, number and kinds of characters, number of connectors between clauses, and number of T-units. Developmental changes were evidenced in source of story, stage of narrative form, formal elements, number and kinds of characters, and connections between clauses and T-units. Children's conceptions of story form varied considerably; children also varied in the pace of their development of story-concept formation.

2.21 Jose, P., & Brewer, W. (1984). Development of story liking: Character identification, suspense, and outcome resolution. *Developmental Psychology, 20,* 911–24.

This study analyzed by age of reader the story factors that contribute to story liking. Forty-four 2nd-, sixty-four 4th-, and sixty-four 6th-grade students rated four three-page suspense stories on ten affective scales. Similarity to character enhanced identification, which, in turn, was related to enhanced suspense. Younger readers preferred positive outcomes regardless of the character attributes, good or bad. Older children liked positive endings for good characters and negative endings for bad characters. Path analysis indicated that character identification, suspense, and liking of outcome all independently contributed to story liking.

2.22 Lehr, S. (1988). The child's developing sense of theme as a response to literature. *Reading Research Quarterly, 23,* 337–57.

This study examined developmental differences in children's thematic inferences based on their awareness of intertextual similarities in the portrayal of themes in folktales and realistic books. Based on scores on a literature exposure inventory, 10 lowest- and 10 highest-scoring kindergarten, second-, and fourth-grade students listened to oral readings of three folktales and three realistic books, noted similarities in the portrayal of themes, and in inferred themes. Analysis of interview transcripts indicated that kindergarten children were able to identify thematic similarities for 80% of the realistic books and 35% of the folktales. There was a high correlation between age and ability to generate thematic statements: kindergarten children were more likely to summarize stories and to consider reactions to characters, while second- and fourth-grade children were more likely to analyze and make generalizations. Children's high level of inferences relative to previous research was attributed to the use of interviewing.

2.23 Liebman-Kleine, J. (1987). Reading Thomas Hardy's *The Mayor of Casterbridge:* Toward a problem-solving theory of reading literature. *Reader, 17,* 13–28.

This report demonstrated the application of a problem-solving model of response to the author's own responses to a Hardy novel. In this model, "problems" are defined in terms of a violation of expectation, while "solutions" are derived from application of relevant prior knowledge.

2.24 Maloney, B. (1980). An examination of response to literature in relation to reading maturity. (Doctoral dissertation, Washington State University). *Dissertation Abstracts International, 41,* 2034A.

This research explored the differences between mature and less mature tenth-grade readers' responses to short stories as analyzed using the Purves categories, as well as degree of transfer as determined by the Purves "transfer" inventory. Significant differences were found in response categories of mature compared to less mature readers. Mature readers were more likely to apply literature to everyday life situations.

2.25 Meek, M. (1983). *Achieving literacy: Longitudinal case studies of adolescents learning to read.* London: Routledge and Kegan Paul.

Case study analyses of British adolescents' responses indicated that students' knowledge of narrative conventions as implied by their storytelling ability was related to their understanding of stories. Prior "reading instruction" with basal readers had not prepared students to infer points of view, engage in perspective-taking, make predictions, or link episodes.

2.26 Mertz, M. P. (1973). Responses to literature among adolescents, English teachers, and college students: A comparative study. (Doctoral dissertation, University of Minnesota). *Dissertation Abstracts International, 33,* 6066A.

This study compared the responses of 10th-grade students, English teachers, and college students to short stories. A response form was used to gather responses, and Purves categories were used as a basis of analysis. A significant difference in responses was seen between adults and adolescents. Economic status also affected response in that low-SES readers used perception more often, while high-SES readers used interpretation and evaluation.

2.27 Mikkelson, N. (1983, May). *Patterns of story development in children's responses to literature.* Paper presented at the Annual Meeting of the Canadian Council of Teachers of English, Montreal, Canada. (ERIC Document Reproduction Service No. ED 234 399)

This descriptive study analyzed how children aged 7 to 10 created stories after hearing a selection of folk tales. Students heard folk tales and then wrote and told their own stories. The analysis of the children's stories showed developmental differences in that younger children relied more on borrowing and re-creating, while older children produced more blendings and transformations. However, all children found ways to fuse traditional literary elements with material from their own experience.

2.28 Otto, B. (1984). Evidence of emergent reading behaviors in young children's interactions with favorite storybooks. (Doctoral dissertation, Northwestern University). *Dissertation Abstracts International, 45,* 08A.

The purpose of this study was to examine children's emergent reading abilities by contrasting assisted and independent storybook interactions prior to conventional reading. The subjects were children between the ages of two-and-a-half and five years, enrolled in a day care center. Twenty-four children were interviewed in one study, and 17 in a second, two months later. For each study, six storybooks were introduced and used in the classroom for two weeks, following which each child's storybook interactions with a familiar adult examiner were audio- and videotaped. Analysis of the assisted storybook interactions indicated that children's responses fell into five categories: (1) nonverbal response; (2) conversational response; (3) echo-like response; (4) semantically equivalent response; (5) verbatim-like response. In nearly all assisted-independent combinations, children's responses gave evidence of higher levels of emergent reading ability when receiving assistance than when interacting independently. Children's responses during assisted and independent storybook interactions did not appear to occur randomly, but were based on the child's developing knowledge about written language and reading.

2.29 Parnell, G. (1984). Levels of aesthetic experience with literature. (Doctoral dissertation, Brigham Young University). *Dissertation Abstracts International, 45,* 06A.

This research project investigated the possibility of cognitive developmental structures underlying the aesthetic responses of children and adults to poetic literature. Children in Grades 3, 6, 9, 12, and college were interviewed as they discussed four well-known poems. The data indicated that, based on relevance to the content and context of the poems and differing ability to see the poem from perspectives of others, it would be possible to discriminate several levels of response to the poems. These levels are suggestive of the developmental stages of Piaget and Kohlberg.

2.30 Perine, M. (1978). The response of sixth-grade readers to selected children's literature with special reference to moral judgment. (Doctoral dissertation, Columbia University). *Dissertation Abstracts International, 39,* 2729A.

The relationship between the literary responses and the moral responses of 11-year-old children to selected literary works was explored. The responses to the literary works which contained moral dilemmas were given in peer-group interactions. The Purves categories and Kohlberg moral stages were used to categorize responses. Results indicated that correlations between engagement/involvement, perception, and interpretation and stage three of moral judgments existed. Personal involvement in literature and reasoning also stimulated moral judgment.

2.31 Petrosky, A. (1975). Individual and group responses of fourteen- and fifteen-year-olds to short stories, novels, poems, and Thematic Apperception Tests: Case studies based on Piagetian genetic epistemology and Freudian psychoanalytic ego psychology. (Doctoral dissertation, State University of New York at Buffalo). *Dissertation Abstracts International, 36,* 852A.

Based on both Piaget's developmental stage model and Holland's model of "identity style" as reflecting personality needs and orientation, this study analyzed 14- and 15-year-olds' individual and group responses. Readers operating at an initial formal operations stage respond to surface, concrete aspects of texts, while those at the later stage are better able to interpret. The degree to which students have the freedom to share and interact often shapes the quality of students' group responses.

2.32 Pillar, A. (1983). Aspects of moral judgment in response to fables. *Journal of Research and Development in Education, 16,*(3) 39–46.

This study examined the developmental differences of 2nd-, 4th-, and 6th-grade students' judgments and reasons in response to questions about intentionality, relativism, and punishment as related to moral dilemmas in fables. Responses were scored as "immature" (constraint-oriented), "mixed," or "mature" (cooperation-oriented). There was a significant relationship between grade level and level of maturity of the responses, with the most significant occurring for responses to questions about punishment. Sixth graders responded at a more conventional level than did younger readers.

2.33 Pollock, J. C. (1973). A study of responses to short stories by selected groups of ninth graders, eleventh graders, and college freshmen. (Doctoral dissertation, University of Colorado at Boulder). *Dissertation Abstracts International, 33,* 4224A.

This study compared 9th and 11th graders' and college-age students' written responses to short stories. Analysis of responses using the Purves categories indicated that the 9th graders produced the largest percentages of perception and evaluation, while 11th graders produced more engagement responses. A positive correlation was found between total responses and interpretation; total responses and evaluation were negatively correlated.

2.34 Purves, A. (1975). Research in the teaching of literature. *Elementary English, 52,* 463–66.

The developmental differences in the responses of elementary school children to short stories and poems are presented. Students in Grades 3 through 12 read the works and then participated in taped oral interviews. Results revealed developmental differences in that 3rd-grade students were concerned with the literal aspects of the work. Their evaluation was based on whether they liked or disliked a work. Fourth-grade students put themselves into the roles of the characters and did more elaboration on their evaluations. Fifth-grade students produced more thought units, more evaluations and personal reactions, and some evaluations dealing with formal aspects of the works. However, 3rd-, 4th-, and 5th-grade students all dealt primarily with literal aspects of the works in their reactions and evaluations. In 6th grade, students offered some interpretation in the form of questions about characters. In grades 7 and 8, students gave an increased number of interpretations and their evaluations were concerned with meaning and understanding. Grades 8 and up began to look for hidden meaning. By Grade 12 students responded primarily with interpretation, and evaluation was related to meaning rather than with engagement or evaluation of the works' evocative power.

2.35 Purves, A. (1981). *Achievement reading and literature: The United States in international perspective.* Urbana, IL: National Council of Teachers of English.

This book presents the results from an international study of achievement and discusses responses of 14- and 17-year-old students in the United States. Results indicated the 14-year-olds made more diverse responses, and high achieving high school students use a moralistic interpretive pattern, but both are concerned with interpreting the text and giving an emotional response to the text. A sex difference was discovered in that girls were more concerned with hidden meaning, theme, organization, the relation of form and content, and the work's success in involving them. They were not concerned with part-whole relationships, personal interpretation, identification, or moral lesson to be learned. Boys were more subjective in their responses than girls. Overall student achievement is correlated with patterns of response that look at the significance of the work and which deal with the emotion and the particular implications of the work. Students with high scores on transfer revealed a pattern of response of relating the characters to the reader's world, responding to the emotional impact of the work, and noting the work's success in involving the reader. Also, thematic and moralistic patterns were learned and correspond with academically oriented teachers.

2.36 Rubin, S., & Gardner, H. (1985). Once upon a time: The development of sensitivity to story structure. In C. Cooper (Ed.), *Researching response to literature and the teaching of literature.* Norwood, NJ: Ablex.

This study compared children's ability to explain characters' actions and solve problems posed by the text across different age levels. Students in first, third, and sixth grade were read two different versions of a fairy tale: the complete version and a version in which the motivation was deleted. Students were asked to provide an ending, retell the story, and then, three days later, to give a delayed retelling. In contrast to younger children, sixth graders who were exposed to the original version were better able to supply more information about motivation on a delayed retelling than an immediate retelling. This reflected the sixth graders' superior knowledge of the fairytale schema. Older children were better able to solve the more complex, thematic problems posed by the stories and were better able to integrate endings with the stories than younger children.

2.37 Schlager, N. (1975). Developmental factors influencing children's responses to literature. (Doctoral dissertation, Claremont Graduate School). *Dissertation Abstracts International, 35,* 5136A.

The purpose of this study was to investigate characteristics other than literary ones which make a book acceptable or unacceptable to a child. Key concepts of child development from the works of Piaget, Erikson, and Anna Freud were examined in relation to the 7- to 12-year-old child. Results indicated that the deciding factor monitoring children's selection of books seemed to be the biological, cognitive, and affective developmental characteristics to which all human beings are subject, regardless of ethnicity or nationality.

2.38 Somers, A. B. (1973). Responses of advanced and average readers in grades seven, nine, and eleven to two dissimilar short stories. (Doctoral dissertation, Florida State University). *Dissertation Abstracts International, 33,* 4252A. See 1.32.

2.39 Sulzby, E. (1985). Children's emergent reading of favorite storybooks: A developmental study. *Reading Research Quarterly, 20,* 458–81.

This research, consisting of two studies, examined children's early reading attempts when asked to read to an adult in the context of the adult-child interaction. In the first study, transcripts of the interactions between 24 kindergarten children and an interviewer at the beginning and the end of the year were content-analyzed according to the degree that the reading attempts were governed by print, by pictures with formed stories, by pictures without formed stories, and by refusals. The children demonstrated a significant increase over the period of a year.

The second study, comparing age-differences in reading attempts of two-, three-, and four-year-olds using the same content analysis system employed in the first study, found some increase in the degree to which children responded to print and responded with formed stories.

2.40 Sulzby, E., & Teale, W. (1987). *Young children's storybook reading: Longitudinal study of parent-child interaction and children's independent functioning.* Final Report to the Spencer Foundation. Ann Arbor: The University of Michigan.

This report summarizes research on young children's storybook reading. Two separate studies analyzed: (1) eight families in San Antonio representing different classes and ethnic groups and (2) large groups of preschool and kindergarten children in Chicago.

Analysis of voice-tone patterns indicated that parent and child interact with similar tones during storybook reading. Listening to stories was related to learned ability to reproduce connected discourse.

The investigators posit the following generalizations: storybook reading was integral to family life and is a socially constructed activity; storybook reading interaction becomes internalized; language variation occurs in storybook reading; and children engage spontaneously in storybook reenactments.

2.41 Svensson, C. (1985). *The construction of poetic meaning: A cultural-developmental study of symbolic and non-symbolic strategies in the interpretation of contemporary poetry.* Lund, Sweden: Liber Forlag. See 1.33.

2.42 Svensson, C. (1987). The construction of poetic meaning: A developmental study of symbolic and non-symbolic strategies in the interpretation of contemporary poetry. *Poetics, 16,* 471–503.

Based on a social-constructivist model as opposed to a cognitive-stage model of aesthetic development, this study compared levels of responses to poetry. Seventy-two subjects at ages 11, 14, and 18 were interviewed regarding their inferences about the point of four poems and the reasons for their inferences. Interview answers were categorized as "literal descriptive," "literal interpretive," "mixed literal/thematic," "thematic," "mixed literal/symbolic," and "symbolic." Forty-nine percent of the 18-year-olds, 22% of the 14-year-olds, and 14% of the 11-year-olds were classified as "thematic," "mixed literal/symbolic," and "symbolic." There was a significant chi-square relationship between age level and level of interpretation.

2.43 Thomson, J. (1987). *Understanding teenagers' reading.* New York: Nichols.

This book reports on a research project devised to investigate what secondary students read, why they read or don't read, and how they go about reading. The research data consisted of the written questionnaires completed by a total of 1,007 students in year eight (13- and 14-year-olds) and year ten (15- to 16-year-olds) attending two state high schools in Bathurst, NSW in 1978 and 1984. Transcripts of individual interviews with five percent of these students and written questionnaires completed by their English teachers revealed that "a colossal" amount of time was spent watching television or videos and considerably less time was spent reading literature. The questionnaires completed by the English teachers revealed three main difficulties experienced in teaching fiction: (1) distraction of television; (2) pupils' negative attitudes to reading; (3) pupils' reading abilities. The author devised a hierarchical and developmental model of reading based on student interviews and the theory of D. W. Harding. The process stages are: (1) unreflective interest in action; (2) empathizing; (3) analogizing; (4) reflecting on the significance of events (theme) and behavior (distanced evaluation of characters); (5) reviewing the whole work as the author's creation; (6) consciously considered relationship with the author, recognition of textual ideology, and understanding of self (identity theme) and of one's own reading processes. Process strategies correspond to process stages and are: (1a) rudimentary mental images (stereotypes from film and television); (1b) predicting what might happen next in the short term; (2c) mental images of affect; (2d) expectations about characters; (3e) drawing on the repertoire of personal experiences, making connections between characters and one's own life; (4f) generating expectations about alternative possible long-term outcomes; (4g) interrogating the text, filling in gaps; (4h) formulating puzzles, enigmas, accepting hermeneutic challenges; (5i) drawing on literary and cultural repertoires; (5j) interrogating the text to match the author's representation with one's own; (5k) recognition of implied author; (6l) recognition of implied reader in the text; (6m) reflexiveness, leading to understanding of textual ideology, personal identity, and one's own reading processes.

2.44 Trimble, C. (1988). The relationship among fairy tales, ego development, grade level, and sex. (Doctoral dissertation, University of Alabama). *Dissertation Abstracts International, 45,* 935A.

This study examined the effects of an instructional strategy for teaching fairy tales on the ego levels of children in Grades 1, 3, 5, and 7. The experimental groups were exposed to an instructional strategy on fairy tales designed to enhance ego development. Pre- and post-interviews and pre- and posttest scores on the Loevinger Sentence Completing Test Protocols were analyzed to determine changes in ego development. No significant differences were found between the experimental and control groups. However, a significant relationship between levels of ego development and sex was observed for Grades 3, 5, and 7, with girls scoring as more psychologically mature than boys. Significant relationships between the ego levels of students and their grade level were also indicated. A relationship also existed between specific responses of students and degrees of psychological maturity for grade and sex.

2.45 Weiger, M. L. (1978). Moral judgment in children: Their responses to children's literature examined against Piaget's stages of moral development. (Doctoral dissertation, Rutgers University). *Dissertation Abstracts International, 38,* 4065A.

This study compared second-, fourth-, and sixth-grade students' responses to issues in children's literature as reflecting differences in their level of moral development. Three stories that were recommended for each particular grade were presented through audiovisual media; students responded through individual interviews and focused questions. Analysis of the data revealed that the stages of students' responses corresponded to Piaget's stages of moral judgment.

*See also: 1.28, 1.32, 1.33, 2.1, 5.10, 8.9, 8.16, 8.18

3. Gender

3.1 Ash, B. (1970). The construction of an instrument to measure some aspects of literary judgment and its use as a tool to investigate student responses to literature. (Doctoral dissertation, Syracuse University). *Dissertation Abstracts International, 30,* 5332A.

The investigator developed an instrument for measuring literary responses and judgment. One hundred 11th-graders were interviewed. The results showed that girls scored higher than boys. Eleven categories of response were found: guess, misreading, unsupported judgment, supported judgment, poetic preconception, isolated element, narrational, technical, irrelevant association, interpretation, and self-involvement.

3.2 Beaven, M. (1972). Responses of adolescents to feminine characters in literature. *Research in the Teaching of English, 6,* 48–68.

This study used a questionnaire to study how high school students responded to male and female literary characters. The results indicated that while girls identified with both sex roles, boys only identified with masculine sex roles.

3.3 Bleich, D. (1986). Gender interests in reading and language. In E. Flynn & P. Schweickart (Eds.), *Gender and Reading.* 213–38. Baltimore: Johns Hopkins Press.

This study analyzed the responses of four adult males and four adult females to Charlotte Brontë, Emily Dickinson, Herman Melville, and William Wordsworth. Readers did not differ according to the gender of the author or in their responses to poetry, but did differ in their responses to fiction. Males were more likely to focus on the narrative voice as rhetorically acting to affect the reader, while women focused more on entering and experiencing the world of the narrative.

In a second study, analysis of 50 male and 50 female college freshman students' retellings of Faulkner's "Barn Burning" indicated the males were more likely to recount the text objectively in order to "get the facts straight," while females were more likely to reflect on the experience with a story, focusing on understanding the character relationships.

3.4 Flynn, E. (1983). Gender and reading. *College English, 45,* 236–53.

This study considered the degree to which college students' adoption of a "submissive" versus "dominant" orientation varied according to gender differences. Analysis of 26 male and 26 female college students' written responses to stories by James Joyce, Ernest Hemingway, and Virginia Woolf indicated that most students adopted a submissive orientation as reflected in uncertainty, frustration, use of summary retelling, and lack of critical distance. Male students, particularly in response to the Joyce and Hemingway stories, were more likely than females to adopt a dominant orientation, as reflected in their imposition of their own attitudes and beliefs onto the stories.

3.5 Holland, N. (1977). Transactive teaching: Cordelia's death. *College English, 39,* 276–85.

Based on a psychoanalytical theory of response as reflecting fantasy/identity themes, this study compared the responses of five women and four men to *King Lear.* Male readers focused on the theme of the need to be in control. Women focused on the theme of conflict with a patriarchal culture.

3.6 Radway, J. (1984). *Reading the romance: Women, patriarchy, and popular literature.* Chapel Hill: University of North Carolina Press.

The purpose of this study was to determine reasons for the emotional and cultural appeal of romance novels to women. Sixteen avid female readers were interviewed, and 42 readers completed questionnaires about their responses to romance novels. Readers preferred heroine types who were intelligent, attractive, moral, nurturing, and emotional; they disliked portrayals of violence and rape. They responded positively to instances in which the heroine transforms the male hero from an impersonal to a more personal character. From these responses, Radway explains the appeal of the romance novel as reflecting a cultural need for reinforcement of the women's own nurturing role within the context of a traditional, patriarchal society.

3.7 Shurden, K. (1976). An analysis of adolescent responses to female characters in literature widely read by students in secondary schools. (Doctoral dissertation, University of Tennessee). *Dissertation Abstracts International, 36,* 6589A.

High school students' perceptions of female characters were analyzed. Students produced written ratings of characters they had read about. Results demonstrated that students' sex did not affect perception of character, and that characters had more unstereotypical than stereotypical qualities.

3.8 Tanner, L. (1977). Sex bias in children's response to literature. *Language Arts, 54,* 48–50.

This study examined the degree to which elementary students' evaluation of stories varied according to the author's gender. Fifty-six male and 41 female elementary students evaluated stories with male and female authors. Females gave more positive evaluations to male-authored stories than for female-authored stories. Their positive evaluations were higher than male evaluations of stories by either gender.

3.9 Willinsky, J., & Hunniford, R. M. (1986). Reading the romance younger: The mirrors and fears of a preparatory literature. *Reading-Canada-Lecture, 4,* 16–31.

This study applied Radway's methods (see Radway, 1984; 3.6) to analysis of adolescent females' responses to romance novels. The adolescents, like the older women in Radway's study, identified with the female heroines in terms of reinforcing the role model of the nurturing female.

*See also: 1.12, 4.11, 6.3, 6.4

Text Variables

These studies explore the effects of literary selections, genres, and other text characteristics on readers' responses.

4. Studies on the Influence of Text Response Processes

4.1   Angelotti, M. (1972). A comparison of elements in the written free responses of eighth graders to a junior novel and an adult novel. (Doctoral dissertation, Florida State University). *Dissertation Abstracts International, 33,* 2603A.

This study examined the influence of textual difficulty on the written responses of 66 eighth graders to an adult novel (*A Separate Peace*) and a young adult novel (*Tuned Out*). Responses to the adult novel included more descriptions of the content, while responses to the young adult novel included more interpretative responses. Analysis of responses across four divisions of the novels (exposition, development, climax, and conclusion) indicated a steady increase in involvement, while evaluation decreased. Interpretation was more likely to increase in the young adult than in the adult novel.

4.2   Bazelak, L. (1974). A content analysis of tenth-grade students' responses to black literature. (Doctoral dissertation, Syracuse University). *Dissertation Abstracts International, 34,* 6246A.

This study investigated the differences in the written free responses of tenth graders to short stories written by black authors. The research found responses to fall into seven categories: literary judgment, literary interpretation, literary narrative, association, self-involvement, prescriptive judgment, and miscellaneous.

4.3   Bruner, J. (1986). *Actual minds, possible worlds.* Cambridge: Harvard University Press.

Based on Todorov's theory of the transformation of verb tense in narrative from time-past to time unfolding, the study analyzed adult readers' retelling of James Joyce's story, "Clay," which contains extensive use of such transformations. Analysis of the retellings indicated a similar use of transformations (defined as the reader's "subjunctivizing" of language) and reflects the readers' adoption of the narrator's perspective.

4.4 Cornaby, B. (1974). A study of the influences of form on responses of twelfth-grade students in college preparatory classes to dissimilar novels, a short story, and a poem. (Doctoral dissertation, University of Washington). *Dissertation Abstracts International, 35*, 4856A.

This study examined the influence of literary form and level of dogmatism on high school students' responses to two novels, a story, and a poem. Responses to a more traditional novel (*Crime and Punishment*) were more content-oriented, while responses to a more modern novel (*A Passage to India*) were more form-oriented. There was no relationship between response and dogmatism as measured by the Rokeach Dogmatism Scale.

4.5 Cornaby, B. (1978). *Literature for gifted young adults and their response to that literature.* (ERIC Document ED 185 550)

This study discusses variations in response by gifted high school seniors to four dissimilar literary selections: two structurally different novels, a free-verse poem, and a short story. Results showed that the form of literary selection influenced students' responses. When responding to dissimilar literary selections, approximately three-fourths of the students were inconsistent in their choices or response modes. The traditional novel elicited a structurally oriented response mode, while the nontraditional novel elicited responses that were neither structure- nor content-oriented.

4.6 Ericson, B. O. (1984). A descriptive study of the individual and group responses of three 10th-grade readers to two short stories and two textbook selections. (Doctoral dissertation, Syracuse University). *Dissertation Abstracts International, 46*, 388A.

A case-study approach was used to describe and compare the oral responses of three 10th-grade girls to two short stories and two textbook selections. They were interviewed to gain information about their family lives, interests, preferences for (and experiences with) reading, general expectations for fiction and exposition, and experiences with whole-class and small-group discussions. Tape recordings of individual- and small-group discussions following the readings provided data for analysis. The study indicated that (1) each girl had a preferred pattern of response to both short stories and textbook readings; (2) the purpose for reading informed all other general expectations for the text; (3) establishment of text-specific expectations was central to responses to short stories but not to textbook readings; (4) both types were evaluated according to expectations and knowledge of text form and content; (5) all three girls exhibited metaresponse awareness and monitoring of their responses, and were sensitive to the response patterns of the other group members; (6) group discussions were beneficial.

4.7   Johnston, D. (1983). Gifted fifth and sixth graders' references and responses regarding contemporary or classic literature. (Doctoral dissertation, University of Washington). *Dissertation Abstracts International, 44,* 126A.

Twenty gifted fifth- and sixth-grade students read contemporary and classic books paired for similarity over a 10-week period and wrote responses which were analyzed using the Purves categories. There was a higher percentage of perception responses for contemporary books. Males made more perception responses, while females made more engagement responses.

4.8   Jose, P. (1984). *Story interestingness: Goal importance or goal attainment difficulty.* (ERIC Document Reproduction Service No. ED 243 080)

This study tested the structural-affect theory that goal importance and the difficulty of attaining that goal are linked to story liking. First-grade, third-grade, and college students read narratives that varied in terms of the importance of the goal to be attained by the protagonist and the difficulty encountered in attaining that goal. Data from all age groups confirmed the theory. Adults also expected that the more important the goal, the harder it would be to attain.

4.9   McNamara, S. (1981). Responses of fourth- and seventh-grade students to satire as reflected in selected contemporary picture books. (Doctoral dissertation, Michigan State University). *Dissertation Abstracts International, 41,* 2978A-2979A.

This descriptive study looked at the responses of 12 fourth-grade students and 12 seventh-grade students to picture books containing satire. The books were read aloud, and questionnaires were used to collect student responses. The results indicated that students do accept satire in the works they enjoy and respond to works of satire that they find humorous. Students also demonstrated that they were capable of responding in a critical in-depth manner beyond the literal level.

4.10 McNamara, S. (1984). Children respond to satire in picture books. *Reading Improvement, 21*,(4), 303–23.

Twenty-four 4th- and 7th-grade students responded to a questionnaire about genre characteristics and preferences in response to oral readings of satiric picture books published after 1970. While students enjoyed the texts, they did not relate them to their own lives. They did not comprehend sarcasm, ridicule, or social criticism. Seventh graders demonstrated more critical understanding of satiric techniques than did fourth graders.

4.11 Morrongiello, D. (1976). *The effect of point of view upon attitude in response to literature.* (ERIC Document ED 126 530)

This study examined the influence of point of view on readers' attitudinal response. Based on differences in attitudes towards mental illness, tenth-grade students were divided into positive, neutral, and negative groups. Analysis of written responses to a first-person, a neutrally-narrated, and an editorially-narrated version of the same text portraying mental illness revealed that students with neutral attitudes responded most positively to the first-person and least positively to the neutrally-narrated versions. Students with negative attitudes responded negatively to the first-person and positively to the neutrally-narrated versions.

4.12 Nicol, E. (1973). Student response to narrative technique in fiction. (Doctoral dissertation, Stanford University). *Dissertation Abstracts International, 33,* 6737A.

This study examined the degree to which high school students appreciate authors' use of literary techniques. One hundred sixty-five high school students read two short stories and evaluated the use of techniques by selecting from a list of comments. Students' selections were compared with professionals' critiques of the stories. Students preferred the simpler story, but their responses coincided with the critics' responses more with the difficult story. Students responded more to the immediately significant story aspects than to the more formal aspects.

4.13 Purves, A. (1981). *Reading and literature: American achievement in international perspective.* Urbana, IL: National Council of Teachers of English.

This reanalysis of the American response-preference data from the IEA assessment (Purves, 1973; see 1.28) indicated that 13- and 17-year-olds' response preferences varied according to story differences, with older students being more consistent across stories. Across different stories, responses involving hidden meaning, inferring a lesson, thematic importance, organization, and emotions were consistently chosen—an orientation possibly reflecting the literary critical analysis orientation of American high school teachers. Females and higher SES students tended to adopt a more critical stance than males and lower SES students. Higher scorers on the literature achievement test tended to focus more on critical understanding and the significance of a text. Students scoring high on transfer preferred to relate the text to their own world and to respond emotionally. The more students liked a text, the more they preferred to interpret that text.

4.14 Ross, C. (1978). A comparative study of the responses made by grade eleven Vancouver students to Canadian and New Zealand poems. *Research in the Teaching of English, 12,* 297–306. See 1.29.

4.15 Short, K. (1986). Literacy as a collaborative experience: The role of intertextuality. In Niles, J., & Lalik, R. (Eds.), *Issues in literacy: A research perspective.* 35th Yearbook of the National Reading Conference (227–332). Rochester, New York: National Reading Conference.

This ethnographic study explored first-grade students' use of intertextuality in response to literature. Results indicated that the self-generation of hypotheses and intertextual ties is important to critical thinking and that learning should be a process of authorship; of constructing one's own stories by making connections with past stories.

4.16 Smith, L. (1984). Rereading: A response to literature. (Doctoral dissertation, University of Minnesota, 1985). *Dissertation Abstracts International, 45,* 2382A.

The extent and nature of rereading activity among children was described. Six hundred-nineteen students completed survey forms which indicated the nature of their reading activity. Twenty-four students were chosen at random from those who indicated that they reread books. These were then interviewed. Of books reread, realistic fiction was reread most often (52.1%), followed by fantasy and science fiction (24.9%), and nonfiction (11.1%). The most reread books were mentioned 74.7% of the time by female students. Rereaders were more likely to have first heard about their favorite books from a friend than from a teacher, a parent, a sibling, or a film. Answers to open-ended interview questions were categorized according to the Purves categories, with perception as the most common response. Students appeared reluctant to discuss a book beyond a quick answer and often that answer was a retelling of an event or events.

4.17 Studier, C. (1978). A comparison of the responses of fifth-grade students to modern fantasy and realistic fiction. (Doctoral dissertation, University of Georgia). *Dissertation Abstracts International, 39,* 7201A-7202A.

This study examined the differences between responses to fantasy and realistic literature as they varied with reading ability. Eighty-nine 5th-graders wrote free responses to two fantasy and two realistic books of fiction. Analysis of response types indicated that there was more retelling with the fantasy and more engagement and interpretation with the realistic fiction. Better readers made more evaluative responses to both forms than did poorer readers.

4.18 True, E. A. (1981). Responses of children to two sports stories, one recommended by adults and one non-recommended by adults. (Doctoral dissertation, University of Minnesota). *Dissertation Abstracts International, 42,* 2545A.

This research explored the responses of fifth-grade students to sports fiction books, one of which was recommended by adult reviewers. Students produced written responses to structured and unstructured questions. Data were analyzed using the

Purves categories. Results indicated that most student responses were in the perception category and that few were in the interpretive category.

4.19 Uffman, B. (1981). Responses of young children and adults to books with a lesson. (Doctoral dissertation, University of Minnesota). *Dissertation Abstracts International, 42,* 119A.

This study examined the influence on elementary students' responses to books previously determined to contain a moral lesson. Analysis of students' responses indicated that, relative to other story elements, students do not consider the lesson to be an important influence on their responses.

4.20 White, V. (1973). An analysis of the responses of fifth-grade children to the characteristics of the heroes in four short stories. (Doctoral dissertation, Boston University). *Dissertation Abstracts International, 34,* 1781A.

This study examined fifth-grade students' responses to hero characteristics in four short stories. Data were collected in individual interviews and placed into three categories: literal, inferential, and evaluative. Most responses were literal. Students responded more to heroes in physical danger than to those not in physical danger.

4.21 Zaharias, J. (1986). The effects of genre and tone on undergraduate students' preferred patterns of response to two short stories and two poems. *Research in the Teaching of English, 20,* 56–68.

In order to determine the degree to which response preference varied by genre (story versus poetry) and tone (serious versus light-hearted), 166 college students applied the Response Preference Measure (Purves, 1981) to two poems and two stories. Both genre and tone had significant main effects on response preferences for engagement, description, interpretation, and evaluation, but there were also significant interaction effects. Students preferred descriptive responses in reaction to light-hearted texts and to poetry, while preferring engagement, interpretation, and evaluation responses in reaction to more serious texts. Stories were more likely to elicit engagement responses than poetry. (For Response Preference Measure see:

Purves, A. [1981]. *Reading and literature: American achievement in international perspective.* Urbana, IL: National Council of Teachers of English.)

4.22 Zipperer, F. J. (1985). A descriptive study of selected fifth- and eighth-grade students' involvement with futuristic science fiction. (Doctoral dissertation, University of Georgia). *Dissertation Abstracts International, 47,* 111A.

This study examined the involvement of 12 fifth- and eighth-grade readers with futuristic science fiction. Readers at both grade levels chose science fiction because of its predictive nature, its images of the future, its wide imaginative scope, and its scientific and technological content. Most readers preferred characters of their own age and sex, although sex of the character was mentioned less often by male readers. Settings preferred by eighth-grade readers covered a wider range of possibilities that those of fifth-grade readers. Some readers perceived the authors as playful storymakers, while others perceived them to be using their writing to predict impending danger.

*See also: 1.13, 2.13, 8.1, 8.36

Response Processes

The following studies focus on readers' responses. For purposes of this review, these studies are categorized as:

5. *Response Processes: General.* These studies focus on a variety of different response categories.

6. *Response Processes: Engagement.* These studies focus on the emotional, affective, and subjective experience with the text.

7. *Response Processes: Interpretation.* These studies focus on the reader's conceptual, interpretive, and analytic response to the text.

5. Response Processes: General

5.1 Cullinan, R., Harwood, K., & Galda, L. (1983). The reader and the story: Comprehension and response. *Journal of Research and Development in Education, 16,* 29–38. See 1.6.

5.2   de Beaugrande, R. (1985). Poetry and the ordinary reader: A study of immediate responses. *Empirical Studies of the Arts, 3*(1), 1–21.

This study examines the open-ended written responses of college students to a series of poems. The responses are discussed in terms of demonstrating a range of response strategies unique to responding to poetry: staging, hedging, citing, keyword associations, paraphrasing, normalizing, and generalizing. Examples of each of these strategies are provided.

5.3   de Beaugrande, R. (1987). The naive reader: Anarchy or self-reliance? *Empirical Studies of the Arts, 5,* 145–70.

Following classroom experiences in selecting and responding to poems without instruction in technical analysis, 42 college students responded in writing to three poems. Analysis of students' responses by amalgamating direct quotes into composite types demonstrated that, contrary to expectations that their responses would be chaotic and uninformed, the students were able to make systematic and coherent inferences about the poems.

5.4   Dias, P. (1987). *Making sense of poetry: Patterns in the process.* Ottawa, Canada: Canadian Council of Teachers of English.

This study sets out to discover the ways in which adolescent readers respond to, and make sense of, their readings of poetry. The study's patterns of process are broken into three basic sections: approach, findings, and implications for classroom practice. The use of the responding-aloud protocol is considered essential to the research and understanding of student reading patterns.

5.5   Galda, L. (1982). Assuming the spectator stance: An examination of the responses of three young readers. *Research in the Teaching of English, 16,* 1–20.

The researcher performed a case-study investigation of three 5th-grade girls in their individual and group responses to two novels. Nine categories of response were recorded: (1) personal statements about the reader; (2) personal statements about the work; (3) descriptive statements of the plot; (4) descriptive statements about aspects of the work; (5) interpretive statements about parts of the work; (6) interpretive statements about the whole of the work; (7) evaluative statements about the evocativeness of the work; (8) evaluative statements about the construction of the work; (9) evaluative statements about the meaningfulness of the work. Findings indicated that, although each girl had her own style of response, the primary response mode was evaluation. Perspective and concept of story affected their ability to maintain the spectator stance which is required for mature literary judgment.

5.6 Kintgen, E. (1985). Studying the perception of poetry. In C. Cooper (Ed.), *Researching response to literature and the teaching of literature.* Norwood, NJ: Ablex.

Analysis of 18 graduate students' and 8 faculty members' oral taped responses to a poem generated a range of different processes involved in responding to poetry: comment/narrate; read/select/locate; focus on word/phonology/syntax/form; deduce/generalize/connect to poem/nature/history or literature; test/justify/qualify/specify/; and interpret.

5.7 Martinez, M. F. (1983). Young children's verbal responses to literature in parent-child storytime interactions. (Doctoral dissertation, University of Texas at Austin). *Dissertation Abstracts International, 44,* 1044A.

Case studies of four preschool children examined parent-child storytime interactions using the following categories: utter-ance, episode, topic, and nonstory talk. While responses were primarily narrational, children's responses varied when listening to unfamiliar short stories. Children's response profiles were similar to response profiles of their parents.

5.8 Miall, D. (1985). The structure of response: A repertory grid study of a poem. *Research in the Teaching of English, 19,* 254–68.

This study examined clustering of readers' personal constructs as related to positive and negative evaluations of eight segments of a poem. Twenty-one college students responded to the Samuel Taylor Coleridge poem, "Frost at Midnight," by using repertory grid rating scales based on bipolar adjectives. Students rated the poem's segments positively and negatively in an expected manner. Students responded more frequently to the negative aspects of the poem.

5.9   Miall, D. (1986). Authorizing the reader. *English Quarterly, 19*, 186–
       95.

       Based on Kelly's theory of personal constructs as shaping
       emotional responses, this study examined one student's written
       responses in terms of quotations, emotions, constructs, and
       superordinate constructs. For each of three stages of response,
       the student began with emotions and moved towards personal
       constructs; i.e., moved from an intuitive to a more cognitive
       orientation.

5.10   National Assessment of Educational Progress. (1981). *Reading,
       thinking and writing: Report of the National Assessment of Education
       Progress: Reading/Literature Assessment, 1979/80.* Denver, CO:
       Educational Commission of the States. (For summaries, see also
       Petrosky, A. Reading achievement; and Galda, L. Assessment:
       Responses to literature. In A. Berger and H. A. Robinson (Eds.),
       Secondary school reading. (1985). Urbana, IL: National Conference
       on Research in English. For descriptions of the measures and
       criteria see W. Fagan, J. Jensen, & C. Cooper (Eds.), *Measures for
       Research and Evaluation in the English Language Arts, Vol. 2.* (1985).
       Urbana, IL: National Council of Teachers of English.)

       The purpose of the 1979/80 NAEP assessment of reading and
       literature was to determine 9-, 13-, and 17-year-old students'
       reading interests and attitudes; differences in the ability to
       explain their engagement, interpretation, and evaluation
       responses; and their preferred response mode in essay responses
       as compared to similar tasks in the 1969/70 assessment.

       Students' engagement, interpretation, and evaluation
       responses to poems and stories were analyzed using separate
       primary trait scoring systems. While 81% of 9-year-olds enjoy
       reading "very much," only 42% of 17-year-olds do. Fifty-three
       percent of 9-year-olds and 33% of 17-year-olds read something
       daily. Few 17-year-olds read more than an hour daily; in contrast,
       61% watch more than an hour of television a day. Most would
       prefer to go to a movie rather than read a book.

       Seventeen-year-olds were much better able to explain
       assertions about novels and characters on a multiple-choice test
       than in their essay responses. In evaluating poems and stories,
       most students listed vague assertions with little supporting

evidence from the text. In their ability to cite support from their counterparts, 17-year-olds declined from the 1969/70 assessment. The investigators attributed students' lack of problem-solving and critical thinking to an instructional focus on reading skills during the 1970s.

Students' overall essay-response preferences in reaction to four poems and one story were analyzed in terms of primary response types represented according to the following categories: egocentric; retelling; emotional; personal/global; personal/analytic; evaluation; general reference to other works; specific reference to other works; superficial analysis; elaborated analysis; inferencing; and generalization. Students' primary response focus varied according to text; one poem evoked 71% inferencing, while another story, 67% personal-analytic responses. Retellings, evaluations, emotions, and inferencing were common across essays; there were few instances of egocentric, personal/global references to other works, and analysis responses.

5.11 Newkirk, T. (1984). Looking for trouble: A way to unmask our readings. *College English, 46,* 756–66.

This study examined the types of difficulties college students experienced in understanding poems, and their use of problem-solving strategies to cope with these difficulties. Analysis of college freshmen writing about aspects of poems that gave them difficulty yielded four types of difficulties: an unwillingness to explore meanings resulting in a premature cessation of inquiry, a difficulty comprehending word meanings, a resistance to the poem's implied attitudes, and an inability to connect the poem's images. Students who could cope with these difficulties demonstrated effective problem-solving strategies.

5.12 Nissel, M. (1987). The oral responses of three 4th-graders to realistic fiction and fantasy. (Doctoral dissertation, Fordham University). *Dissertation Abstracts International, 48,* 04A.

This case-study analysis of three 4th-grade females' oral responses to realistic and fantasy short stories generated a category system organized according to responses to: (1) characters (empathetic and text-centered evaluations versus supported and unsupported inferences); (2) events (evaluations versus inferences); and (3) themes (isolated versus integrated). The majority of the students' responses referred to character. Of those responses, evaluations of characters were more frequent than inferences. Response types varied across student and story.

5.13 Rogers, T. (1988). *Students as literary critics: The interpretive theories, processes, and experiences of ninth grade students.* (Doctoral dissertation, University of Illinois).

This research analyzed eight 9th-grade students' think-aloud responses to short stories and critical paragraphs written about the stories according to the following categories: retelling, elaborating, engaging, questioning, hypothesizing, analyzing, drawing conclusions, generalizing, evaluating, monitoring, and miscellaneous. The sources of response were also categorized as: textual-structural, character, extratextual, authorial, comparative, and personal. Results indicated that interpretations were primarily related to textual factors of structure and character. Students preferred critical paragraphs written from a personal viewpoint, but this did not surface in their own protocols. The majority of responses were in the analysis category followed by retelling and drawing conclusions. Students' think-aloud responses did not resemble their classroom responses because students believed they should "stick to the text" in the classroom.

5.14 Taylor, E. A. (1986). Young children's verbal responses to literature: An analysis of group and individual differences. (Doctoral dissertation, University of Texas at Austin). *Dissertation Abstracts International, 47,* 1599A.

Four- and five-year-olds' individual and group oral responses during story reading were analyzed according to the following categories: contributing participant (teacher, child); form of talk (question, comment, answer); type of verbalizations (narrative, interpretive, evaluative, associative, predictive, informative, or elaborative); and focus of response (title, setting, character, detail, event, language, or story). Children's type of focus of story talk differed according to whether students responded in a group setting or as individuals. Teachers' responses also differed significantly in type and focus. Both the situation in which a story was read and the teacher presenting the story influenced children's verbal responses.

5.15 Tsruta, D. (1978). Community college students' responses to selected ethnic poetry and mode of presentation. (Doctoral dissertation, Stanford University). *Dissertation Abstracts International, 39,* 09A.

This study examined written responses of students of various ethnic groups after they had read selected poems written by members of their own ethnic groups as well as poems written by members of ethnic groups other than their own. The results suggest that students did not reveal racial stereotyping in their responses to the three ethnic literatures, nor did the students reveal personal racial biases of their own.

5.16 Tutton, B. (1979). Response to short stories as related to interest among community college students. (Doctoral dissertation, University of Minnesota). *Dissertation Abstracts International, 40,* 3003A.

This study examined the relationship between college students' interest in short stories and the types and amount of responses. Correlations between interest ratings and analyses of type and amount of response indicated that degree of interest was positively correlated with amount and level of interpretation.

5.17 Wade-Maltais, J. (1981). Responses of community college readers to a short story when audience interpretations are not known. (Doctoral dissertation, University of California, Riverside). *Dissertation Abstracts International, 43,* 01A.

This study examined whether, when no audience expectations were provided, responses of four groups of community college students to a short story would converge towards the text, regardless of the instructional approach—or whether students' public responses would converge towards instruction while their private responses converged towards the text. Results indicated that instructional treatment groups showed a trend toward effects of teaching, while noninstructional treatment groups mainly responded with interpretation and evaluation.

*See also: 1.19, 1.22, 1.25, 1.28, 1.34, 2.41, 2.43, 4.5, 4.21, 6.7, 8.3, 8.14, 8.21, 8.33, 8.39, 9.3, 9.9

6. *Response Processes: Engagement*

6.1 Chasser, C. (1977). How adolescents' affective responses to four short stories relate to the factors of age, sex, and intelligence. (Doctoral dissertation, University of Connecticut). *Dissertation Abstracts International, 38,* 717A-718A.

This study examined the differences in the engagement responses of fifty 7th-, 9th-, and 12th-grade students to four stories. Four types of responses were analyzed: judgment, sympathy, empathy/identification, and degree of involvement. Response types did not differ according to grade level or intelligence. Males expressed significantly less engagement than did females.

6.2 Golden, J., & Guthrie, J. (1986). Convergence and divergence in reader-response to literature. *Reading Research Quarterly, 21,* 408–21.

This study examined the degree of convergence and divergence in high school students' empathy with texts. Sixty-three 9th-grade students responded to preformulated responses representing readers' beliefs, empathy, events, and conflict. Students' ratings agreed more on ratings of beliefs and events, and varied more on empathy and conflict. Students who empathized with a certain character were more likely to identify the story conflict as pertaining to that character than were students who did not empathize with the character. Students' attitudes regarding mother-daughter relationships were related to the nature of their belief inferences.

6.3 Hansson, G. (1986). *Emotional processes engendered by poetry and prose reading.* Stockholm: Almqvist & Wiksell.

The purpose of this series of studies was to determine the relationship between specific textual aspects of poetry and emotional reactions, in some cases in terms of gender differences. In one study, 28 female adult students rated a poem according to mood, activation, perception/appraisal, and stimulus-specific emotional reactions. There was a high significant correlation between perception/appraisal and stimulus-specific ratings.

In another study, 149 male and female adult readers responded to three different versions of the same poem: the original poem, a positive-tone version, and a negative-tone version. There were significant gender differences in ratings of specific feelings, but not in evaluations. Females were more affected by the poems. Females who were unhappy before reading the negative-tone poems were even more unhappy after reading the poems than were males.

6.4 Kuehn, W. (1974). Self-actualization and engagement-involvement responses to literature among adolescents. (Doctoral dissertation, University of Minnesota). *Dissertation Abstracts International, 34,* 6947A.

This study analyzed the relationship between self-actualization and engagement/involvement with a literary work. Eleventh-grade students read three short stories and wrote responses categorized under the Purves categories. Results indicated that there was a correlation between engagement/involvement responses to a short story and self-actualization. This correlation was stronger with boys than with girls.

6.5 Monseau, V. (1986). Young adult literature and reader-responses: A descriptive study. (Doctoral dissertation, University of Michigan). *Dissertation Abstracts International, 47,* 404A.

This study compares the reading logs of high school students with English teachers' responses to four works of young adult fiction. Participants kept reading logs of their responses; group discussions were recorded and transcribed. Readers' degree of engagement with literature strongly influenced evaluations of literary quality. Although student readers employed a more indirect approach and less sophisticated language than did their teachers, they responded to the same literary elements.

6.6 Nell, V. (1988). The psychology of reading for pleasure: Needs and gratifications. *Reading Research Quarterly, 23,* 6–40.

As one of five studies on characteristics of readers who read extensively for pleasure, this study examined the fantasy processes involved in pleasurable reading, particularly the degree to which reading involves visual imagery. Thirty-three adult readers were administered two personality inventories as well as rating scales about mood responses. Vividness of imagery ratings correlated positively (.47) with degree of involvement. Most of the readers were introverts.

6.7 Purves, A. (1978). Using the IEA data bank for research in reading and response to literature. *Research in the Teaching of English, 12,* 289–96.

This report demonstrates possible uses for further analysis of computer data-bank results from the IEA reading/literature assessment. For example, the degree of liking of each of four stories correlated positively but moderately with understanding and judging of those stories. Students who liked the stories were more likely to select involvement, organization, and thematic/ aesthetic aspects from the Response Preference Measure. Those who disliked the text were more likely to distance themselves by placing the text in the context of a genre or historical period.

6.8 Sadoski, M., & Goetz, E. (1985). Relationships between affect, imagery, and importance ratings for segments of a story. In J. Niles & R. Lalik (Eds.), *Issues in literacy: A research perspective.* 35th Yearbook of the National Reading Conference, (180–85). Rochester, NY: National Reading Conference.

The study examined the relationships between emotional reactions and the relative importance of story segments and imagery. Three groups of 15 college students each read a story. One group rated story segments for importance; a second group, for visualness and memorability of imagery; a third group, for degree of emotional reactions. Significant partial correlations controlling for paragraph length were found between imagery and affect (.37) and importance and affect (.75).

6.9 Sadoski, M., Goetz, E., & Kangiser, S. (1988). Imagination in story response: Relationships between imagery, affect, and structural importance. *Reading Research Quarterly, 23,* 320–36.

The purpose of this study was to examine the convergence and divergence in readers' imagery and emotional response as related to their perceptions of story episodes' importance in plot structure. Thirty-nine college students read three similar stories, rating paragraphs according to degree of mental imagery, evoked emotions, and importance to the overall story. They were also asked to explain reasons for their ratings of certain paragraphs in a free-response format. Imagery, affect, and importance ratings were moderately correlated. There was considerable agreement in the nature of imagery, feelings, and importance, while the most divergence occurred with imagery.

*See also: 1.8, 2.22, 2.39, 4.1, 4.8, 8.28, 8.46, 8.47

7. Response Processes: Interpretation

7.1   Beach, R. (in press). The creative development of literary response: Readers' use of autobiographical responses to interpret stories. In S. Straw and D. Bogdan, (Eds.), *Beyond communication: Reading comprehension and criticism.* Portsmouth, NH: Boynton/ Cook.

This study examined the relationship between college students' autobiographical journal responses and their level of interpretation of short stories. Journal entries about five short stories were analyzed according to the following categories: engaging, autobiographical, describing, interpreting, judging, and metacognitive. The level of interpretation of each entry and the degree of elaboration of autobiographical responses were determined using rating scales. The amount and the degree of elaboration of autobiographical responses were positively related to amount and level of interpretation, respectively.

7.2   Blake, R., & Lumm, A. (1986). Responding to poetry: High school students read poetry. *English Journal, 75*(2), 68–73.

This study analyzed five untrained high school students' responses to a poem. The students were asked to read a poem aloud and to tape-record their interpretation. The taped responses were analyzed to determine differences in readers' approaches to problematic parts of the poem. Results indicated that individual readers respond differently to the same poem and that rereading is essential to poetry understanding.

7.3   Harste, J. (1986). *What it means to be strategic: Good readers as informants.* Paper presented at the National Reading Conference. Austin, TX. (ERIC Document Reproduction No. ED 278 980)

This descriptive study analyzed the content of graduate students' responses to a novel. The responses were made in journal entries written after reading each chapter of a novel. The results of analysis revealed that the majority of readers' time is spent off the page making connections, recasting what they already know, criticizing themselves and the author's performance, or applying what they have read to see what it says about life. The analysis also supports the view that the context of the reading situation affects the process of interpreting the content.

7.4   Hillocks, G., & Ludlow, L. (1984). A taxonomy of skills in reading and interpreting fiction. *American Educational Research Journal, 21,* 7–24.

The skills in the interpretation of fiction proposed in this paper are defined by seven item-types. Four sets of questions, based on four different texts, were administered to between 77 and 127 students each. Results confirm experimentally the hierarchical and taxonomic nature of the item-types.

7.5   Petrosky, A. (1981). From story to essay: Reading and writing. *College Composition and Communication, 33*(1), 19–36.

Based on a theory of interpretation as driven by the verification of personal needs and concerns, this study compared differences in the quality of college students' autobiographical written responses as related to their interpretation of novels. Students who were able to elaborate on the details of their autobiographical responses were more effective in applying their experience to interpret novels than were students who did not elaborate.

*See also: 1.3, 1.16, 1.35, 2.3, 2.5, 2.14, 2.18, 2.22, 2.36, 2.42, 4.1, 8.2

Instruction

These studies focus on the effects of the instructional context on readers' responses.

8. Studies on the Influence of Instruction

8.1   Ambrulevich, A. K. (1986). An analysis of the levels of thinking required by questions in selected literature anthologies for grades eight, nine, and ten. (Doctoral dissertation, University of Bridgeport). *Dissertation Abstracts International, 47,* 769A.

This study analyzed the level of complexity of questions in selected literature textbooks for 8th, 9th, and 10th grades. Fifteen literature anthologies from five publishing houses provided a stratified random sample of short stories from which 180 questions were classified according to six major cognitive categories of Bloom's taxonomy. The study found that while some questions fall within the higher half of the taxonomy (application and synthesis), most of the sample questions fall within the lowest categories of thinking (comprehension and knowledge).

8.2 Appleman, D. (1986). The effects of heuristically-based assignments on adolescents' responses to literature. (Doctoral dissertation, University of Minnesota). *Dissertation Abstracts International, 47,* 11A.

The purpose of this study was to determine the effects of adding prewriting activities to the response assignment prompts employed in the 1979/80 NAEP literature assessment on students' level of interpretation. Two hundred-thirteen 11th- and 12th-grade students were assigned to write essays in response to two poems and two stories using either the NAEP prompts alone or the NAEP prompts with additional prewriting. The essays were rated according to quality of interpretation. Differences in assignment prompt had a significant effect, favoring the modified version for only one of the four essays. Across treatments, students' ratings were significantly higher for writing about short stories than for writing about poems.

8.3 Beach, R. (1972). The literary response process of college students while reading and discussing three poems. (Doctoral dissertation, University of Illinois). *Dissertation Abstracts International, 34,* 656A.

This study compared the effects of three different pre-discussion activities on 36 junior and senior English majors' group-discussion responses to poems. Following the reading of a poem, students either taped a free-association response, wrote a free-association response, or had no assignment. Discussion groups in which students employed free association used more interpretations and less digressions than did discussion groups with students who did not prepare for the discussion. Free-association responses resulted in more engagement and autobiographical responses, while written responses resulted in more interpretive responses.

8.4 Calder, J. (1984). The effects of story structure instruction on third-graders' concept of story, reading comprehension, response to literature, and written composition. (Doctoral dissertation, University of Washington). *Dissertation Abstracts International, 46,* 387A.

This study examined the quality of third graders' responses to stories by comparing the influence of instruction using activities based on concrete incidents from the stories to instruction using activities based on abstract themes derived from the stories. Concrete activities resulted in greater gains in students' concept of story, response to literature, and quality of narrative writing.

8.5 Casey, J. (1978). The affective responses of adolescents to a poem read in three different classroom situations of reading: Teacher-directed class discussion, self-directed small group discussion, and private reading. (Doctoral dissertation, Rutgers University). *Dissertation Abstracts International, 39,* 6491A.

This study compared secondary students' response-types in response to a poem in three different contexts: teacher-directed class discussion, self-directed small group discussion, and private reading. Response-types differed significantly across contexts. There were more divergent responses in group discussions and in private reading than in teacher-directed discussions.

8.6 Colvin-Murphy, C. (1987). Eleventh graders' critical comprehension of poetry through written response. (Doctoral dissertation, University of Nebraska at Lincoln, 1988). *Dissertation Abstracts International, 48,* 1718A.

The purpose of this study was to determine the influence of extended writing on response. Eighty-five 11th graders responded to two poems within one of three treatment groups: extended writing involving guided responses to poems, restricted writing involving short answer responses, and discussion. Pre- and post-test written responses to poems were holistically rated for quality and degree of engagement. Treatment had a significant effect for both ratings favoring the extended writing group, particularly for degree of engagement.

8.7 Coss, D. (1983). The responses of selected groups to social, objective, and affective theories of literature. (Doctoral dissertation, Southern Illinois University.) *Dissertation Abstracts International, 43,* 2318A.

Freshmen/sophomores, juniors/seniors, masters' and doctoral students responded to a poem, to statements about the poem, and to statements that represented social, objective, and affective theories of literature. The preferred response statements about the poem were objective, while the preferred statements about critical theory were affective. There was a significant positive correlation between the affective and the social statement ratings. The higher the grade level, the more the objective theory was preferred.

8.8 Doerr, D. (1980). A study of two teaching methods emphasizing the responses to literature of junior college students. (Doctoral dissertation, University of Pittsburgh). *Dissertation Abstracts International, 40,* 4451A.

The influence of two teaching methods on college students' written responses to short stories was studied. One group was instructed in subjective responses based on David Bleich's (1978) method of literary understanding and one group received training in the Purves categories. Results revealed that the affective group improved significantly more on a personal orientation inventory and also preferred that teaching method more than did students in the Purves group. (See: Bleich, D. (1978). *Subjective Criticism.* Baltimore: Johns Hopkins University Press.)

8.9 Fisher, R. (1985). A comparison of tenth-grade students' small group discussions to adults' small group discussions in response to literature. (Doctoral dissertation, Virginia Polytechnic Institute, 1986). *Dissertation Abstracts International, 47,* 2062A. See 2.10.

8.10 Folta, B. (1981). Effects of three approaches to teaching poetry to sixth-grade students. *Research in the Teaching of English, 15,* 149–61.

This study compared the effects of three instructional treatments for cuing sixth graders' attention to metaphor in poetry: teachers modeling their own verbal cuing, use of slides to focus on poetic images plus teacher modeling, and use of poets providing instruction. These treatments were compared with a control receiving no instruction in poetry. Three intact classes were randomly assigned to each of the treatments and the control. Students received instruction with 24 poems over an eight-day period. Pre- and posttest measures consisted of Form A and Form B respectively of the ETS "A Look at Literature" test. The results favored instruction involving media and/or poets over the teacher-only or the control group.

8.11 Graup, L. (1985). Response to literature: Student-generated questions and collaborative learning as related to comprehension. (Doctoral dissertation, Hofstra University). *Dissertation Abstracts International, 47,* 482A.

This study examined the effects of collaborative learning and student-generated questions on sixth graders' understanding and interpretation of literature. Thirty-two 6th-grade students were placed into four groups: discussion with instruction in inferential question generation; discussion without question instruction; individual response with inferential question instruction; and individual response without question instruction. Students read literary texts, generated questions, and wrote essays. The findings indicated that discussion groups resulted in better comprehension than did the individual response groups. Students who received instruction produced significantly more inferential questions and fewer literal and total questions. Students who received instruction in question generation produced a greater number of interpretive responses in their essays.

8.12 Grimme, D. (1970). The responses of college freshmen to lyric poetry. (Doctoral dissertation, University of Northern Colorado, 1971). *Dissertation Abstracts International, 31,* 4004A-4005A.

This study compared the effects on college freshman students' responses of three methods of poetry instruction: structural analysis; an experiential, reflective approach; and a limited instructional approach. The structural analysis approach resulted in more use of a combination of perception and interpretation responses. The experiential approach resulted in more use of interpretation supported by personal references. Students in the experiential approach had significantly more positive attitudes towards literature than did students in the other two groups.

8.13 Harris, L. (1982). A description of the extent to which affective engagement with literature takes place using three different classroom strategies: Teacher-directed lecture-discussion, self-directed small group, and creative drama exercises. (Doctoral dissertation, Rutgers University, 1983). *Dissertation Abstracts International, 44,* 411A.

This study questioned the effects of three different classroom strategies (teacher-directed lecture/discussion, self-directed small group discussion, and creative drama exercises) on 60 tenth graders' responses to three different texts. Analysis of the data revealed that while there was a significant treatment effect on students' cognitive responses, there was no significant treatment effect on affective responses.

8.14 Haug, F. (1975). Young children's responses to literature. (Doctoral dissertation, University of Minnesota). *Dissertation Abstracts International, 35,* 4859A.

This research examined how an introduction before presenting a story to first graders affects their response to a realistic and a make-believe story. The introduction was designed to emphasize different categories of response to literature. The students' responses were collected in individual oral interviews and analysed according to the following categories: engagement-involvement, perception, interpretation, evaluation, retelling, and other. The findings indicated that there were few differences due to treatment. There were no differences in response due to gender or to type of story.

8.15 Heil, C. (1974). A description and analysis of the role of the teacher's response while teaching a short story. (Doctoral dissertation, University of Pittsburgh, 1975). *Dissertation Abstracts International, 35,* 7771A.

The purpose of this study was to determine certain consistent patterns of response-types in teachers' and students' classroom responses. Analysis of eight secondary school teachers teaching a short story yielded two distinct, different patterns. Teachers focused either on engagement/involvement responses, resulting in a wide variety of student response; or they focused on perception/interpretation responses, resulting in a more focused student response.

8.16 Hickman, J. (1980). Children's response to literature: What happens in the classroom. *Language Arts, 57,* 524–29.

This ethnographic study analyzed children's response to literature at various developmental stages and in a variety of natural classroom contexts. Ninety children aged 5 to 11 were observed during a four-month period. Data were collected on log sheets and then categorized according to: (1) listening behaviors; (2) contact with books; (3) acting on the impulse to share; (4) oral responses; (5) actions and drama; (6) making things; (7) writing. Examples of students' responses were compared according to age-level differences. Teacher strategies of manipulating contextual settings were also categorized. Major findings indicated that the accessibility of a book was of primary importance in children's willingness to express any response to it at all, and that the most powerful feature of the classroom context was the teacher's manipulation of the text.

8.17 Hickman, J. (1981). A new perspective on response to literature: Research in an elementary school setting. *Research in the Teaching of English, 15,* 343–54.

This ethnographic analysis of three elementary school classes over a four-month period examined various response events involving listening, contact with books, sharing, oral responses, drama, artwork, and writing. The degree to which these events occurred varied according to the students' language and cognitive development, the social conventions operating in the classroom, and the teacher's influence.

8.18 Hickman, J. (1983). Everything considered: Response to literature in an elementary school setting. *Journal of Research and Development in Education, 16*(3), 8–13.

This researcher investigated the responses of elementary students in grades K–6 to two children's books. The participant-observer presented reading material to the children and studied their reactions. Students' spontaneous responses as well as solicited verbal responses were analyzed. Developmental differences emerged in spontaneous responses. Children in kindergarten and first grade used nonverbal modes, facial expressions, and pantomimes. Second and third graders would share and demonstrate their skill in reading. Students in fourth and fifth grades would read aloud, make casual references to art work, and write about the books. Solicited responses were acquired by giving students a tape recorder and asking them to talk about their responses freely. All ages made evaluative statements and referred to illustrations. Partial retelling and summarizing were common, but students in fourth and fifth grades did not do as much of that kind of response as did younger children.

8.19 Hill, S. (1985). Children's individual responses and literary conferences in the elementary school. *The Reading Teacher, 38,* 382–86.

This study examined students' responses in the context of a literature-based reading program for a one-year period. Student-teacher book conferences for four students in a fifth/sixth grade classroom were analyzed. Analysis of transcripts indicated four major categories: recall of story content, literary analysis, personal response, and guidance/miscellaneous. The three better readers focused more on analysis and response, while the poorer readers focused on recall of content.

8.20 Hillocks, G. (1989). Literary texts in classrooms. In P. W. Jackson & S. Haroutunian-Gordon (Eds.). *From Socrates to software: The teacher as text and the text as teacher.* 88th Yearbook of the National Society for the Study of Education.

Contrastive case studies of two highly experienced expert teachers indicate that they have radically different assumptions about their students and about effective teaching. The case studies show remarkably different levels of engagement, response, and understanding on the part of the students.

8.21 Jackson, J. (1980). Reading poetry in high school: An experimental study of response. (Doctoral dissertation, Indiana University). *Dissertation Abstracts International, 41,* 139A.

This study examined the effects of teacher and peer interaction on response. One hundred ninety-two 10th-grade students were randomly assigned to respond to two poems in one of three conditions: teacher-led discussion, peer-discussion groups, or individually. After participating in the groups, students were interviewed. Of the four Purves categories employed in the interview analysis, the groups differed only on perception and evaluation responses for one poem. Low-, middle-, and high-ability groups differed significantly in levels of engagement, perception, and interpretation.

8.22 Lennox, W., Small, J., & Keeling, B. (1978). An experiment in teaching poetry to high school boys. *Research in the Teaching of English, 12,* 307–20.

This study analyzed the effects of experiential/informal poetry instruction versus more conventional instruction on written responses to poetry. One class of 11th-grade males received the former, while another class received the latter. Analysis of pre- and posttest essay responses to poetry according to fluency and overall quality favored the experiential group over the control group for both fluency and quality.

8.23 Lucking, R. (1976). A study of the effects of a hierarchically-ordered questioning technique on adolescents' responses to short stories. *Research in the Teaching of English, 10,* 269–74.

The effect of questioning techniques on 10th-grade students' responses was analyzed using the Purves categories. The type of questions asked had a significant effect on response. Hierarchically ordered questions led to significantly broader, more interpretational responses and produced a more positive attitude toward reading than did nonhierarchical questions.

8.24 Major, A. (1975). The relationship of a teacher characteristic to student written response to literature. (Doctoral dissertation, University of Kentucky). *Dissertation Abstracts International, 36,* 3548A.

This study questioned the relationship between college students' written responses to literature and the teachers' intellectual disposition. I. A. Richards' categories of response were used to analyze student responses. Results suggested that teachers with a high preference for complexity and a tolerance for ambiguity made a positive contribution to students' ability to interpret literature.

8.25 Marlow, D. (1983). How directed discussions and nondirected discussions affect tenth-grade students' responses to four selected short stories. (Doctoral dissertation, Georgia State University). *Dissertation Abstracts International, 44* 2433A.

This study compared 69 tenth-grade male students' and 60 tenth-grade female students' discussion responses to four short stories. Teachers alternated between directed and nondirected discussions in presenting the stories. Sex differences did not significantly affect the overall patterns of responses of males or females.

8.26 Marshall, J. (1987). The effects of writing on students' understanding of literary texts. *Research in the Teaching of English, 21*, 30–63.

This study examined the long-range effects of different approaches to writing about texts on students' ability to interpret. Observation of students in three 11th-grade classes for three-and-a-half months indicated that their teacher employed a relatively academic, analytic approach with less attention to personal aesthetic responses. Students in these classes were then assigned to one of four treatments: restricted (short answer responses); extended (personal-analytic or formal-analytic responses); or no writing. Students employed these approaches in writing about a series of stories. Composing-aloud protocols elicited before and during writing were also analyzed.

Posttest answers and essays were analyzed in terms of length, response type, and rated level of interpretation. Students in the extended treatments wrote more, were more likely to employ analytic operations, and had a significantly higher level of interpretation than did students in the restricted treatment. Students in the formal-analytic treatment had a significantly higher level of generalization than did students in other groups. Students in the no-writing group did as well as students in the restricted group.

8.27 Martinez, M. (1983). Young children's verbal responses to literature in parent-child storytime interactions. (Doctoral dissertation, University of Texas at Austin). *Dissertation Abstract International, 44*, 1044A.

This case study of four preschool children explored the verbal responses of children during parent-child storytime interactions. The categories: (1) utterance; (2) episode; (3) topic; and (4) nonstory talk were used to measure the children's responses to the stories. The findings revealed that there was a quantitative difference in story talk across subjects. Responses were primarily narrational, but also demonstrated a broad range that was similar across children. Children's form and focus of responses were varied when children listened to unfamiliar short stories. While children primarily talked to share reactions and seek information, their response profiles were similar to those of their parents.

8.28 McClure, A. (1985). Children's responses to poetry in a supportive literary context. (Doctoral dissertation, Ohio State University, 1986). *Dissertation Abstracts International, 46*, 2603A.

This ethnographic study focused on children's responses to, and writing of, poetry in an intermediate elementary school classroom. Due to positive teacher strategies, students evinced a wide range of relatively complex responses. Over time, students developed more varied preferences and an understanding of various elements of poetry.

8.29 McCurdy, S. H. (1976). A study of relationships between goals for the teaching of literature and teachers' attitudes towards the major categories of written student responses to literature. (Doctoral dissertation, Florida State University). *Dissertation Abstracts International, 36,* 4995A.

This study investigated English teachers' attitudes towards students' written responses to literature. The essay responses were analyzed using the Purves categories, with a survey questionnaire being used to identify the preferences of teachers toward the four categories. The findings indicated that, overall, teachers preferred interpretation as a response. Evaluation was the least desired response.

8.30 McGreal, S. (1976). Teacher questioning behavior during classroom discussion of short stories. (Doctoral dissertation, University of Illinois). *Dissertation Abstracts International, 37,* 2798A-2799A.

This study examined the relationships between teachers' questions posed during instruction, teachers' question preferences, and students' responses. Analysis of the response-types represented by questions and student responses for three teachers each at grades 8, 10, and 12 indicated a positive but moderate correlation between type of questions asked and type of students' responses, particularly at the 8th grade.

8.31 McPhail, I. (1979). A study of response to literature across three social interaction patterns. *Reading Improvement, 16*(2), 55–61.

This study compared differences in responses of five 3rd-grade students in three kinds of discussion groups: adult-dominated, peer-dominated, and adult-student balanced. The structure of the social interaction pattern was related to the degree of participation, with students participating more in peer-dominated groups.

8.32 Mertz, M. (1973). Responses to literature among adolescents, English teachers, and college students. (Doctoral dissertation,

University of Minnesota). *Dissertation Abstracts International, 33,* 6066A.

This study compared the types of written responses employed by 52 English teachers, 52 college preservice English teachers, and 160 tenth graders in response to three short stories. There were significant differences among the groups in the types of responses employed, with teachers employing a significantly higher percentage of interpretation responses.

8.33 Michalak, D. (1977). The effect of instruction in literature on high school students' preferred ways of responding. (Doctoral dissertation, State University of New York at Buffalo). *Dissertation Abstracts International, 37,* 4829A.

This study examined the effect of a teacher's preferred response style on high school students' responses to short stories. The IEA response-preference measure was used as a pre- and posttest measure to determine the effects of teacher style on changes in student responses. Students initially preferred interpretation responses. The teacher's style had a significant effect on changes in students' response preferences, with students adopting the teacher's style.

8.34 Morrow, L. (1988). Young children's responses to one-to-one story readings in school settings. *Reading Research Quarterly, 23,* 89–107.

This study examined differences in the effects of repeatedly reading aloud the same versus different books on low-SES preschool students' comments and questions. Seventy-nine students in three urban daycare centers were randomly assigned to one of three treatment groups: (1) reading a different book a week for ten weeks; (2) repeated readings of three different books; and (3) reading-readiness activities. Transcripts of students' oral responses were analyzed according to the following types: number of questions and comments; focus on story structure; meaning; print; and illustration. There were also subcategories within each of these categories. Students in reading-aloud groups showed significant increases in the number and complexity of questions and comments. Students in the repeated-reading group made more interpretative responses and responses focusing on print and story structure than did the students who listened to different books.

8.35 Peters, W., & Blues, A. (1978). Teacher intellectual disposition as it relates to student openness in written response to literature. *Research in the Teaching of English, 12,* 127–36.

This study demonstrated that college students of professors who scored high on the Complexity Scale of the Omnibus Personality Inventory (a test of tolerance for ambiguity and uncertainty) tended to make fewer "misinterpretations" (based on I. A. Richards' four categories) than did students of professors who scored low on the same test. The researchers concluded that different interpretation styles were the result of differences in teaching.

8.36 Purves, A., Foshay, A., & Hansson, G. (1973). *Literature education in ten countries.* New York: John Wiley. See 1.28.

8.37 Rapport, R. (1982). Reader-initiated response to self-selected literature compared with teacher-initiated responses to teacher-selected literature. (Doctoral dissertation, University of Minnesota). *Dissertation Abstracts International, 44,* 413A.

This study explored the differences in student responses to the works of Marguerite Henry as reflected in letters written to the author. One group of letters was written freely by children on their own, and one group of letters was written to fulfill a class assignment. The letters were analyzed according to letter-writing style, degree of requests for facts and information, types of response, and perception of Henry as author or human being. Letters from children writing on their own included more personal information and more questions than did letters from children assigned to write. Assigned letters contained more retellings and evaluations on a literal, simplistic level. Both groups focused primarily on characters, and both related their emotional reactions to Henry's books.

8.38 Reamy, R. (1979). A study of the differential responses to three modes of presentation of poetry as exhibited in the writings of high school juniors. (Doctoral dissertation, University of South Carolina, 1978). *Dissertation Abstracts International, 39,* 6053A.

This study was designed to investigate the effectiveness of three specified modes of teaching poetry (audio-visual, lecture, and socio-psychological) and the kinds of written responses obtained from 11th-grade students for each method of presentation. Responses were categorized according to the scheme developed by Squire (see 1.38). Results indicated significant differences between the types of student responses and teaching method employed.

8.39 Roser, N., & Martinez, M. (1985). Roles adults play in preschoolers' response to literature. *Language Arts, 62,* 485–90.

The purpose of this study was to examine preschool children's responses to stories during storytime at home and in school as influenced by the nature of the adult-child interactions. Four- and five-year-old students listened and responded to 10 stories read three times each by teachers; four child-parent home interactions were also examined over a 10-month period. Transcripts were analyzed according to the types and focus of talk about stories. Children asked more questions in school than in home settings. Children tended to employ those responses modeled by the teacher or parent within a teacher-student group or parent-child pair. Adults functioned in three different roles: co-responders, informers/monitors, and directors.

8.40 Sabo, F. (1980). Students' self-selected reading choices after being exposed to oral reading and a discussion of Purves' four categories of response to literature. (Doctoral dissertation, University of Pittsburgh). *Dissertation Abstracts International, 41,* 2533A.

This study explored the effects of genre (fiction and non-fiction) and question type on third- and fourth-grade students' reading interests and responses. Question-types for discussion were developed using the Purves categories. Certain classes were then exposed to only certain types of questions. Students recorded all the books they read for six weeks and also completed written responses to hearing and discussing books that were read aloud in class. Engagement/involvement and evaluation question-types produced the most amount of reading done by the students at both grade levels. The least amount of reading was produced by those students exposed to literary perception questions at both grade levels. Seventy percent of the questions teachers employed were of a literal level. Older students enjoyed hearing stories read to them more than did younger students. The study concluded that students were motivated to read if they were read to and if discussions focused on engagement/involvement and evaluation.

8.41 Spor, M. (1987). The effect of four methods of response to literature on reading comprehension. (Doctoral dissertation,

University of Pittsburgh). *Dissertation Abstracts International, 48,* 92A.

This study explored the effect of mode of response in instructional study on students' comprehension of literature. Eighth-grade students produced written free responses, written focused responses, oral free responses, and oral focused responses to short stories. Analysis of responses revealed that written response groups had significantly higher comprehension of the stories as indicated by posttest scores. There were no different effects on comprehension, however, between students who gave free and focused responses.

8.42 Story, D. (1978). A study of fifth graders' verbal responses to selected illustrations in children's books before and after a guided study of three styles of art and illustrated fairy tales. (Doctoral dissertation, Michigan State University). *Dissertation Abstracts International, 39,* 660A.

This study examined the effects of training first-grade students in styles of art on their verbal responses to story illustrations. Data were gathered through individual interviews and categorized as stylistic, emotional, or evaluative. Instruction affected responses to art, in that the group that received training had higher gain scores in verbal expression content. Both groups rejected the expressionistic style over cartoon and representational styles, and both groups preferred to discuss content rather than style.

8.43 Sullivan, K. (1974). The effects of response pattern analysis on the content of high school students' written responses to short stories. (Doctoral dissertation, State University of New York at Buffalo). *Dissertation Abstracts International, 35,* 3701A.

This study examined the effects of instruction in the use of the Purves categories on high school students' responses. Analysis of students' written essays after receiving instruction indicated that, after a three-month period, students who received the instruction were employing a wider range of response types than were control group students.

8.44 Sulzby, E., & Teale, W. (1987). *Young children's storybook reading: Longitudinal study of parent-child interaction and children's independent functioning.* Final Report to The Spencer Foundation. Ann Arbor: The University of Michigan. See 2.40.

8.45 Van de Weghe, R. (1988). Making and remaking meaning: Developing literary responses through purposeful, informal writing. *English Quarterly, 20,* 38–51.

This study examined students' uses of informal writing to enhance their understanding of texts. Analysis of 70 college students' informal reading logs indicated that students used logs to generate hypotheses, infer new insights, cope with difficulties of understanding, define analogies, and discover meaningful problems.

8.46 Vipond, D., & Hunt, R. (in press). Literary processing and responses as transactions: Evidence for the contribution of reading, texts, and situations. In D. Meutsch & R. Viehoff (Eds.). *Comprehension of literary discourse: Interdisciplinary approaches.* Berlin: Bruyter.

The purpose of this study was to determine the influence of a framing technique designed to enhance students' engagement by providing them with a purpose for reading and responding. College students in an experimental group were given a letter purported to be written by someone who recommended the story to be read to another reader, noting that it illuminated the writer's own life. Students receiving the framing had a significantly higher degree of engagement than control group students not receiving any framing.

8.47 Vipond, D., Hunt, R., & Wheeler, L. (1987). Social reading and literary engagement. *Reading Research and Instruction, 26,* 151–61.

This study examined the degree to which reading a text aloud in a purposeful, socially meaningful context enhances engagement with the text. Sixty-eight college students were asked to read a story aloud to an audience in a manner that communicated the story's intentions. Students in a nonsocial context read the story aloud to themselves in order to prepare for a comprehension test. After completing the stories, students rated statements regarding their engagement. The reading-aloud was analyzed for instances of miscues. Students in the social reading context were less engaged but made more attempts to convey the point of the story than did students in the nonsocial contexts. There was no relationship between miscues and engagement. The investigators argue that reading aloud—a common school practice—may actually reduce engagement.

8.48 Walker, K. (1979). Variables related to the literary response style preferences of high school English teachers. (Doctoral dissertation, George Peabody College, 1980). *Dissertation Abstracts International, 41,* 213A.

Twelve 9th/10th grade and twelve 11th/12th grade teachers wrote model responses to a short story and led classroom discussions. They also rank-ordered the importance of response categories for writing about literature and discussions. There were no differences in responses according to the teachers' grade level. Across levels, there were significantly higher uses of perception/interpretation responses than engagement/evaluation. Teachers employed more perception responses than indicated by their rankings of response preferences. Inservice instruction in the teachers' use of responses and students' positive attitude towards literature were positively related to use of engagement and negatively related to use of perception responses.

8.49 Webb, A. J. (1980). *Introducing the transactive paradigm for literary response into the high school literature program: A study of the effects on curriculum, teachers, and students.* (ERIC Document Number ED 203 322).

A year-long holistic study was conducted to determine the effects of using a transactive methodology which focused on the students' involvement with the text, and nondirective teaching strategies involving public conversation, private conversation, and free association. Responses of 93 students in four 10th-grade English classes receiving this instruction were compared with responses of 98 tenth graders in four English classes who received traditional literary instruction. There was no significant difference in reading achievement between the two groups; however, transfer was significantly improved in the experimental classes. Attitude toward literature also improved in the experimental classes.

8.50 Wilson, R. R. (1976). In-depth book discussions of selected sixth graders: Response to literature. (Doctoral dissertation, Ohio State University). *Dissertation Abstracts International, 36,* 7195A. See 1.38.

8.51 Yocom, J. (1988). Children's responses to literature read aloud in the classroom. (Doctoral dissertation, The Ohio State University). *Dissertation Abstracts International, 48,* 2300A.

The purpose of this one-year ethnographic study was to analyze second graders' responses to teacher and parent read-alouds in school and in the home. From transcriptions of events and observations, five categories of responses emerged: linking; explaining; responses to characters; responses to the reader's own world; and responses to illustrations. Analysis of parents' questionnaire responses regarding reactions in the home was hampered by parents' difficulty in describing students' responses.

*See also: 1.38, 1.39, 2.10, 2.40, 2.44

Research Methods

These studies validate methods of analyzing literary response.

9. Studies on Research Methodology

9.1   Cooper, C., & Michalak, D. (1981). A note on determining response styles in research on response to literature. *Research in the Teaching of English, 15,* 163–69.

This essay argues that the most valid measure for determining an individual's preferred mode of response is essay analysis. The Response Preference Measure and statement analysis are not viewed as valid measures.

9.2   Dias, P. (1986). Researching response to poetry—Part II: What happens when they read a poem. *English Quarterly, 19,* 9–21.

The report demonstrates the application of a responding-aloud analysis technique involving oral think-aloud responses to rereadings and questions about a text to one 16-year-old student's responses to a poem. Responses are discussed in terms of different rereadings and personal evaluations of the poem.

9.3   Lester, N. (1982). A system for analyzing characters' values in literary texts. *Research in the Teaching of English, 16,* 321–38.

The purpose of this study was to determine the validity of a content-analysis system for analyzing characters' values as implied by specific linguistic cues. Using the system, a judge analyzed characters in seven stories to determine specific value attributes for each character. Responses of four adult readers were consistent with the results of the analysis. However, due to the intensity of readers' emotional reactions to instances in which characters' values conflicted with their own, readers often failed to explore reasons for characters' behaviors.

9.4   MacLean, M. (1986). A framework for analyzing reader-text interactions. *Journal of Research and Development in Education, 19*(1), 17–21.

This researcher conducted a descriptive study which explored the responses of three adult readers to six expository texts. Filmore's levels of envisionment and Galda's categories were used to analyze oral think-alouds in response to a rational cloze exercise completed after reading each text. Three categories of readers were explained. The text-bound reader placed emphasis on the text and related little prior knowledge to the text. The equal reader referred to the text and prior knowledge equally and summarized the text to integrate prior knowledge and the text. The reader-bound reader was led more by prior knowledge than by the text and only loosely connected his/her comments to the text. This study exemplified how readers have different patterns of reader-text interactions.

9.5   Morris, E. (1976). Critique of a short story: An application of the elements of writing about a literary work. *Research in the Teaching of English, 10,* 157–75.

This report discusses the application of the Purves categories to determine variation in secondary students' written responses to a short story. The report also discusses pedagogical implications for use of the Purves categories as a basis for classroom discussion.

9.6   Odell, L., & Cooper, C. (1976). Describing response to works of fiction. *Research in the Teaching of English, 10,* 203–25.

This report demonstrates the application of both the Purves categories and a set of categories for analyzing intellectual strategies as derived from tagmemics: focus; contrast; classification; change; and reference to time sequence, logical sequence, and physical context. The two category systems were applied to one 11th grader's written responses to three novels. Analysis using the Purves categories indicated that the student responded most frequently with descriptive responses, followed by engagement and interpretative responses. Analysis of students' use of intellectual strategies indicated that students only employed a limited set of potential strategies.

9.7 Zaharias, J., & Mertz, M. (1983). Identifying and validating the constituents of literary response through a modification of the response preference measure. *Research in the Teaching of English, 17,* 231–41.

The principal purpose of this study was to determine the low-inference constituents of literary response. Data were obtained from 166 college undergraduates enrolled in nine introductory literature courses. A stimulus condition consisting of six dissimilar short stories and poems was devised. After reading each literary work, subjects were asked to complete a modified version of the International Association for the Evaluation of Educational Achievement's Response Preference Measure. To determine empirically the constituents of literary response, subjects' ratings for each item for all six forms of the Response Preference Measure were jointly subjected to the principal-axis method of common factor analysis. The following four factors were interpreted and labeled: personal statement, descriptive response, interpretive response, and evaluative response.

*See also: 5.8, 5.10, 5.12

Author List

The following alphabetical list of authors cited in this bibliography is provided as a service to readers.

Fusco, E., 2.11
Galda, L., 1.6; 2.9; 5.1; 5.5; 5.10
Gallo, D., 1.2
Gardner, H., 2.36
Gilman, I., 1.11
Goetz, E., 6.8–9
Golden, J., 2.12; 6.2
Graup, L., 8.11
Grimme, D., 8.12
Gross, L., 1.12
Guthrie, J., 6.2
Hansson, G., 1.28; 2.13–14; 6.3; 8.36
Harris, L., 8.13
Harste, J., 7.3
Harwood, K., 1.6; 2.9; 5.1
Haug, F., 8.14
Heil, C., 8.15
Hickman, J., 2.15–16; 8.16–18
Hill, S., 8.19
Hillocks, G., 7.4; 8.20
Hoffstaedter, P., 1.13
Holland, N., 1.14–15; 1.20; 3.5
Hunniford, R. M., 3.9
Hunt, R., 1.16–17; 1.35; 8.46–47
Hynds, S., 2.17–19
Ice, M., 2.20
Jackson, J., 8.21
Jacobsen, M., 1.18
Jensen, J., 5.10
Johnston, D., 4.7
Jose, P., 2.21; 4.8
Kangiser, S., 6.9
Keeling, B., 8.22
Kintgen, E., 1.19–20; 5.6
Kooy, M., 2.8
Kuehn, W., 6.4
Labov, W., 1.17
Lee, S., 1.21
Lehr, S., 2.22
Lennox, W., 8.22
Lester, N., 9.3
Liebman-Kleine, J., 2.23
Lucking, R., 8.23
Ludlow, L., 7.4
Lumm, A., 1.4; 7.2
MacLean, M., 9.4
Major, A., 8.24
Maloney, B., 2.24
Marlow, D., 8.25
Marshall, J., 8.26

Martinez, M., 8.27; 8.39
Martinez, M. F., 5.7
Mauro, L., 1.22
McClure, A., 8.28
McConnell, M., 1.23
McCormick, K., 1.24
McCurdy, S. H., 8.29
McGreal, S., 8.30
McNamara, S., 4.9–10
McPhail, I., 8.31
Meek, M., 2.25
Mertz, M., 8.32; 9.7
Mertz, M. P., 2.26
Meutsch, D., 1.25
Miall, D., 5.8–9
Michalak, D., 8.33; 9.1
Mikkelson, N., 2.27
Monseau, V., 6.5
Morris, E., 9.5
Morrongiello, D., 4.11
Morrow, L., 8.34
National Assessment of
    Educational Progress, 5.10
Nell, V., 6.6
Newkirk, T., 5.11
Nicol, E., 4.12
Nissel, M., 5.12
Noda, L. A., 1.26
Odell, L., 9.6
Otto, B., 2.28
Parnell, G., 2.29
Perine, M., 2.30
Peters, W., 8.35
Petrosky, A., 1.27; 2.31; 5.10; 7.5
Pillar, A., 2.32
Pollock, J. C., 2.33
Purves, A., 1.21; 1.28; 2.34–35; 4.13;
    4.21; 6.7; 8.36
Radway, J., 3.6
Rapport, R., 8.37
Reamy, R., 8.38
Rippere, V., 1.21
Rogers, T., 5.13
Roser, N., 8.39
Ross, C., 1.29; 4.14
Rubin, S., 2.36
Sabo, F., 8.40
Sadoski, M., 6.8–9
Salvatori, M., 1.30
Schlager, N., 2.37

Editors

Edmund J. Farrell has been professor of English education at the University of Texas at Austin since 1978. A former associate executive director for the National Council of Teachers of English, in 1982 he received the NCTE Distinguished Service Award. From 1959 to 1970, he was supervisor of secondary English at the University of California at Berkeley. A past president of both the California Association of Teachers of English and the Texas Joint Council of Teachers of English, Farrell began his teaching in Oroville, California, in 1951, and from 1954 to 1959 was chair of the English department at James Lick High School in San Jose, California. A former chair of the NCTE Commission on Literature, Farrell publishes frequently on the teaching of literature as well as on issues confronting the English profession. Since 1964 he has coauthored twenty anthologies of literature in the *America Reads*, *Gateway*, and *Fountainhead* Series, published by Scott, Foresman and Company. His most recent publication is "Instructional Models for Teachers of English," a chapter in the *Handbook of Research on Teaching the English Language Arts* (Macmillan, in press). Farrell holds a B.A. and an M.A. from Stanford University and a Ph.D. from the University of California at Berkeley.

James R. Squire is executive consultant for Silver Burdett & Ginn and senior vice president (retired) of Ginn and Company. A former executive secretary of the National Council of Teachers of English and chair of NCTE's Committee for a Fund to Support and Advance the Teaching of English, he is also past president of the National Council on Research in English. Squire received his Ph.D. from the University of California, Berkeley, in 1956, and has been lecturer in education, supervisor of the teaching of English, and codirector of teacher education at Berkeley, and professor of English at the University of Illinois. He has also been visiting lecturer at many institutions, including the University of Calgary, the University of New Brunswick, UCLA, and the Harvard Graduate School of Education. He has published more than 100 articles and numerous books; most recently, he is coeditor of the *Handbook of Research on Teaching the English Language Arts* (Macmillan, in press). Squire serves on the advisory boards of The Center for the Study of Reading and *Book Research Quarterly*. In 1988 he was elected to the Hall of Fame in Reading by the International Reading Association.

Contributors

Arthur N. Applebee is a professor in the School of Education, State University of New York at Albany, and director of the Center for the Learning and Teaching of Literature. Applebee specializes in studies of language use and language learning, particularly as these occur in school settings. In addition to articles in the areas of writing, reading, psychology, and literature, Applebee's major works include a developmental study of children's story-telling and story-comprehension skills (*The Child's Concept of Story: Ages Two to Seventeen*, 1978); a national study of the teaching of writing in the major secondary school subject areas (*Writing in the Secondary School: English and the Content Areas*, 1981; *Contexts for Learning to Write: Studies of Secondary School Instruction*, 1984); and a comprehensive history of the teaching of literature in American secondary schools (*Tradition and Reform in the Teaching of English*, 1974). He is coauthor of *How Writing Shapes Thinking: A Study of Teaching and Learning* (1987), and of a series of reports on reading and writing achievement from the National Assessment of Educational Progress (1981, 1985–88). He is coeditor of *Research in the Teaching of English*.

Mary Barr is director of the California Literature Project, the staff development agent to support implementation of the California *English Language Arts Framework*. She received her Ed.D. from New York University in 1982 and was the curriculum consultant for English in the San Diego City Schools for seven years, codirector of the San Diego Area Writing Project for its first four years, and an English teacher, both elementary and secondary, in urban and suburban schools, for many years. As director of the California Literature Project she makes presentations and writes articles on *Framework* implementation throughout California. She is a member of the Executive Planning Committee for the English Language Arts Advisory to the California Assessment Program.

Richard Beach is professor of English education at the University of Minnesota. A former high school English teacher, he earned his doctorate at the University of Minnesota in 1973. He is author of *Writing About Ourselves and Others* (1977); coauthor of *Literature and the Reader* (1972) and *Teaching Literature in the Secondary School* (in press); and coeditor of *New Directions in Composition Research* (1984) and *Becoming Readers and Writers During Adolescence and Adulthood* (1990). His research focuses primarily on response to literature and on various aspects of composition. He is currently treasurer of the National Conference on Research in English and is a trustee of the Research Foundation of the National Council of Teachers of English.

Rudine Sims Bishop is professor of education at Ohio State University where she teaches courses in children's literature in their program in language, literature, and reading. Bishop began her career teaching in elementary classrooms and before moving to Ohio State she taught for several years at the University of Massachusetts. She earned her doctor's degree at Wayne State University where she participated in the Reading Miscue Research studies. She is active in NCTE and IRA and is the author of the NCTE publication, *Shadow and Substance: Afro-American Experience in Contemporary Children's Fiction* (1982), as well as many articles and chapters on reading and literature. Her most recent book, *Presenting Walter Dean Myer* (1990), is a critical examination of Myer's novels for adolescents.

James Bradley will complete his master's degree in English literature at the State University of New York at Albany in 1990. He received his B.S. from Union College, where he served as editor of *The Undergraduate Review* and as both features and arts editor of *The Concordiensis*. He has taught high school English and he is presently a research assistant and an editor at the Center for the Learning and Teaching of Literature.

John Dixon, now retired, spent his formative years teaching in inner city schools before moving to Bretton Hall College, Leeds, to join a creative group of colleagues working in teacher education. During the past twenty-five years he has been involved in international movements to change and broaden written responses to literature. In the course of this work, Louise Rosenblatt's theoretical modeling has become an invaluable resource, and his brief tribute is an attempt to indicate how much he has learned—and is still learning—from her.

Ken Donelson is professor of English at Arizona State University. He has taught high school English for thirteen years in Iowa. In addition to articles and chapters in books, he edited the 1972 edition of *The Students' Right to Read* and collaborated with Alleen Pace Nilsen on *Literature for Today's Young Adults* (Scott, Foresman, 1980, 1985, 1989). He edited the *Arizona English Bulletin* for nine years and with Nilson coedited the *English Journal* for another seven years. He has served the National Council of Teachers of English as chair of CEE and as president of ALAN.

Stephen Dunning lives and writes in Ann Arbor, Michigan. Recent recognitions for his fiction include two PEN Syndicated Fiction awards (1986, 1988) and two MCA (Michigan Council for the Arts) Creative Artist grants (1984, 1989). Dunning began his academic career by teaching high school in three states, and until his retirement in 1987 as professor of English and of education, he directed the University of Michigan's program in English and education. He was president of the National Council of Teachers of English in 1975. Dunning's writings on the teaching of literature include *Teaching Literature to Adolescents: Poetry* (1966) and *Short Stories* (1968). He has written and published five chapbooks of poetry—most recently, *Menominee* (1987)—and expects publication of *"To the Beautiful Women": Eight Stories* in Spring 1990.

Susan Hynds is an associate professor in the Reading and Language Arts Center at Syracuse University where she serves as director of English education and director of the Writing Consultation Center. Her research explores the relationships between social understanding and response to literature, as well as the interpersonal dimensions of writing conferences. Articles have appeared or are forthcoming in *Research in the Teaching of English, The Journal of Teaching Writing, The English Record, The Reading Teacher, Contemporary Psychology,* and *The Review of Education.* She is coeditor of *Developing Discourse Practices in Adolescence and Adulthood* (Beach and Hynds, forthcoming) and *Perspectives on Talk and Learning* (Hynds and Rubin, forthcoming). Hynds is currently chair of the NCTE Assembly on Research and cochair of the AERA Special Interest Group on Literature. In 1989 she was awarded an NCTE Research Foundation Grant for a project involving social aspects of response to literature.

Robert Probst is professor of English education at Georgia State University in Atlanta. Previously he taught English (in both junior and senior high school) in Maryland, and was supervisor of English for the Norfolk, Virginia, public schools. Interested in the teaching of both writing and literature, he has written *Response and Analysis: Teaching Literature in Junior and Senior High School* (Boynton/Cook, 1988) and was part of the team that prepared *New Voices,* a high school English textbook series published by Ginn. He has published articles in *English Journal, Journal of Reading, Educational Leadership, The Clearing House,* and elsewhere. Probst is a member of the National Council of Teachers of English where he has worked on the Committee on Research, the Commission on Reading, and the Board of Directors of the Adolescent Literature Assembly. He is also a colleague and faculty member of the Creative Education Foundation and a member of the National Conference on Research in English.

Alan C. Purves is director of the Center for Writing and Literacy, associate director of the Center for the Learning and Teaching of Literature, and professor of education and humanities at the University of Albany, State University of New York. He received his A.B. from Harvard and his M.A. and Ph.D. in English from Columbia University. Before coming to Albany he taught at Columbia and Barnard Colleges, the University of Illinois and Indiana University. Purves has served in many professional organizations and has been president of the National Council of Teachers of English and is currently chairman of The International Association for the Evaluation of Educational Achievement (IEA). He has written or edited some twenty-five books and seventy articles dealing with literature, written composition, reading and measurement. Two forthcoming publications are *An Essay on the Life and Future of The Scribal Society* and *A More or Less Complete Guide to a Response-Centered Literature Curriculum or How Porcupines Make Love.* An Episcopalian, he has also served on boards of church and mountain-climbing organizations.